COMMUNICATION STRATEGIES FOR MANAGING CONFLICT

COMMUNICATION STRATEGIES FOR MANAGING CONFLICT

A GUIDE FOR ACADEMIC LEADERS

Mary Lou Higgerson

JB JOSSEY-BASS™

A Wiley Brand

Published by Jossey-Bass
A Wiley Brand
One Montgomery Street, Suite 1000, San Francisco, CA 94104-4594—www.josseybass.com

Jossey-Bass books and products are available through most bookstores. To contact Jossey-Bass directly call our Customer Care Department within the U.S. at 800-956-7739, outside the U.S. at 317-572-3986, or fax 317-572-4002.

Wiley publishes in a variety of print and electronic formats and by print-on-demand. Some material included with standard print versions of this book may not be included in e-books or in print-on-demand. If this book refers to media such as a CD or DVD that is not included in the version you purchased, you may download this material at http://booksupport.wiley.com. For more information about Wiley products, visit www.wiley.com.

Library of Congress Cataloging-in-Publication Data

Names: Higgerson, Mary Lou, author.
Title: Communication strategies for managing conflict : a guide for academic
    leaders / Mary Lou Higgerson.
Description: San Francisco, CA : Jossey-Bass, 2016. | Includes
    bibliographical references and index.
Identifiers: LCCN 2015040851 (print) | LCCN 2015043429 (ebook) |
    ISBN 9781118761625 (cloth) | ISBN 9781118761656 (pdf) | ISBN 9781118761663 (epub)
Subjects: LCSH: Universities and colleges—Faculty. | Communication in
    personnel management. | College personnel management.
Classification: LCC LB2331.7 .H54 2016 (print) | LCC LB2331.7 (ebook) | DDC
    378.1/2–dc23
LC record available at http://lccn.loc.gov/2015040851

Cover image: © Maciej Noskowski | iStockphoto
Cover design: Wiley

Printed in the United States of America

FIRST EDITION

HB Printing 10 9 8 7 6 5 4 3 2 1

ABOUT THE AUTHOR

Mary Lou Higgerson is vice president for academic affairs emeritus at Baldwin Wallace University. Since the 1980s she has used her knowledge of organizational communication and more than 30 years of experience in higher education administration to help other college administrators. Dr. Higgerson has been a regular presenter at the American Council on Education Chairing the Academic Department Workshop series and the Kansas State University Academic Chairperson's Conference. She has consulted at numerous institutions and is known for publications and presentations that offer immediately useful insights for practicing administrators. Recipient of eight prestigious teaching awards, including the Distinguished Teacher Award at Southern Illinois University Carbondale and the Bill Cashin Award for outstanding research contributions to the study and practice of higher education administration, Dr. Higgerson brings a helpful clarity to complex issues that pose stressful conditions for chairs, deans, and other academic leaders.

CONTENTS

INTRODUCTION

THE ROLE OF DEPARTMENT chair has become more complex and challenging as institutions of higher education face increased public scrutiny, more competition for students and extramural funding, and tighter fiscal constraints. Institutions depend on effective chair leadership to help develop and implement changes deemed essential to navigating the formidable challenges facing higher education. Chairs are also expected to mobilize and improve faculty performance in support of the institution's response to these changing conditions that, on occasion, threaten institutional welfare. Consequently, many of the tasks on any chair's to-do list fall into the general categories of leading change and enhancing faculty performance—two responsibilities that require chairs to be skilled in managing the conflict that can occur when faculty resist change in the department and/or their performance. This text is designed to serve as a resource for chairs, who find themselves charged with leading change and enhancing faculty performance. In particular, this text will help chairs become more effective in managing the conflict that can occur when leading change and addressing problem faculty performance.

This book has relevance for all practicing administrators who have reason to sharpen their leadership skill in managing conflict when leading change or improving performance because the cases, analyses, and leadership communication strategies presented are generalizable to other leadership positions and situations. However, the cases presented describe scenarios managed by department chairs and the analyses presented discuss specifically the chair's role in managing the case scenarios. To be clear, when referring to the department chair, this text is referring to role responsibilities and leadership communication strategies that are relevant for program, school, division, or department chairs or directors and any frontline leadership position in which the incumbent works directly with faculty or staff in leading change and improving performance.

Why Focus on Chair Leadership?

Having worked at both large, public doctoral granting research and small, private liberal arts institutions and having served at every administrative level of the institution from chair to positions in central administration, I know full well how dependent senior administrators are on effective chair leadership. There is no way a provost or dean can implement changes at the department level without effective chair leadership. The changes deemed necessary in responding to public scrutiny, fiscal constraints, new accreditation standards, and other such conditions and challenges rely heavily on chair leadership for effective implementation.

More institutions are investing in leadership development opportunities for chairs through on-campus programs and through support for chair participation in national meetings and webinars. Individual chairs frequently seek out specific conferences, webinars, and other resources that will enhance their effectiveness in managing chair responsibilities. This text is designed to help support personal leadership development for chairs and be a resource for persons charged with developing chair leadership. This text can be used to facilitate leadership development in other academic leaders because the case scenarios and their leadership communication strategies are generalizable to situations managed by other academic leaders.

Why Focus on Managing Conflict in Leading Change and Improving Faculty Performance?

I have known many bright and talented individuals who elected to leave the chair role after a short tenure in the position because they found the task of managing conflict too time-consuming and stressful. From my work with countless chairs serving at all types of institutions during the past 30 years, I recognize that individuals must be able to manage conflict effectively and comfortably for them to remain in the chair position or accept other administrative positions.

Leadership communication strategies can be taught so that every chair can learn to manage conflict more effectively and, in turn, more comfortably. The demands being placed on chairs today require them to lead change and improve faculty performance—two tasks that frequently involve managing conflict. The focus for this text is the point at which leading change and improving faculty performance intersects with the need to manage conflict. In other words, this text does not include cases or leadership communication strategies for improving faculty performance in those instances where routine mentoring and other support for faculty development are working as intended. Instead, this text focuses on the most difficult situations encountered when leading change and addressing problem faculty performance. At the same time, the text is written to help readers generalize beyond the specific case scenarios presented and use the leadership communication strategies in other situations and in other academic leadership positions.

How to Read and Use This Book

The entire book is designed to help enhance the reader's leadership effectiveness in managing conflict generally and more specifically when leading change and addressing issues of problem performance. For this reason, it is preferable to read this entire book, even though one need not read the chapters sequentially. The text is divided into two parts: Part One focuses on leading change, and Part Two focuses on addressing problem faculty performance. The chapter titles are intentionally descriptive, so it is possible to identify a specific chapter that has relevance for a particular situation.

Part One, "Managing Conflict When Addressing Changing Conditions and Leading Change," includes chapters on communication with today's students and their parents, leading curriculum revision, revising organizational structures, developing a new program without faculty support, and managing resistance when you were hired to lead change. Part Two, "Managing Conflict When Addressing Problem Faculty Performance," includes chapters on managing an unsuccessful promotion application, mentoring a seasoned professional hired into an untenured faculty position, managing the dismissal of a first-year tenure track faculty member, managing inappropriate behaviors of tenured faculty, and managing the dismissal of a tenured faculty member. The issues addressed in these 10 chapters provide the reader with risk-free leadership development experience in managing conflict among faculty, between faculty and the chair, between the department and the administration, between faculty and students, and between department faculty and other constituencies on- and off-campus.

Special Features

Relevant Leadership Communication Strategies

For each administrative task, relevant leadership communication strategies are presented in the form of practical guidelines for chairs. Special care is taken to present these strategies in a way that is meaningful for practicing chairs who may not possess formal training in communication theory. The objective is to equip department chairs with practical strategies that can be immediately useful in carrying out assigned leadership responsibilities.

Putting Theory into Practice

Short case studies follow the sections on relevant leadership communication strategies. The case study method allows the reader to observe how communication functions in the context of real-life situations and, in particular, to witness how effective leadership communication can enhance leadership effectiveness when leading change and improving faculty performance. Cases are not presented all at once but are given in episodes that help the reader see how it develops and allows the other features listed below to be used to enhance the reader's engagement with the case scenario and the reader's ability to apply it to their own situations.

The case study method provides readers with an opportunity to learn from the experience of others in a risk-free environment. The use of case studies accelerates the type of learning that typically accompanies professional experience making it true that one does not need to live it to learn it. For this benefit to be fully realized, the reader must remain an active participant and not slip into the more comfortable role of third-person observer. Chairs will benefit most from this text by placing themselves in the case situations, analyzing the available alternatives, and developing strategies for managing the leadership challenges presented in each case study.

Let's Analyze the Case

This text does not supply the answers because no simple answer transcends all institutional and personality types. Effective chairs seldom start with all the information necessary to address a specific problem, but they must be able to recognize and articulate the important questions that need to be answered. This text helps the reader identify and analyze the key issues, variables, and options for effective leadership by presenting a brief analysis that delineates the major components of each case situation. These insights and analyses are designed to equip chairs with ways of thinking and methodologies that help them identify early warning signs of problems and know how to address them effectively.

It's Your Turn

Each case is followed with a series of questions. These queries invite the reader to participate in the case scenario. They offer the reader an opportunity to consider alternatives and make decisions from the role of the chair in the case. The questions guide the reader in practicing the leadership communication strategies. Analyzing cases in this directed format will improve the reader's ability to think critically about how to effectively use the leadership communication strategies in the case and in his or her own conflict situations.

Please Consider

Sometimes new case information and other considerations are presented that alter how the reader might approach the case situation. These case addendums are intended to prevent the reader from truncating the analysis of the problem before gaining a compete understanding of all variables. Solutions are workable only if they accurately account for the dynamic interrelationship of all relevant components of the problematic situation. This section will help the reader comprehend the true complexity of each case.

Let's Recap

This section completes the loop, moving the reader from the specific case back to the leadership communication strategies that were described earlier in the chapter. It presents the reader with a checklist for assessing the merit of his or her proposed strategy for managing the case scenario. It also serves to reinforce the leadership communication strategies that can be generalized beyond the immediate case study.

Hindsight

Hindsight is 20/20. This section addresses actions that the chair in the case might have taken to avert or ease the immediate problem. When chairs learn when and how to intervene before a conflict situation escalates, the task of managing conflict becomes easier and less stressful.

PART ONE

MANAGING CONFLICT WHEN ADDRESSING CHANGING CONDITIONS AND LEADING CHANGE

THIS SECTION OF THE text discusses leadership communication strategies that can be helpful in managing the conflict often encountered when responding to changing conditions and leading change. To be effective leaders, department chairs must help department faculty, staff, and students understand and embrace changes needed to assure departmental and institutional viability. Each of the following chapters addresses a specific change scenario in which departmental and institutional success depends on effective chair leadership.

Chapter 1: Communicating with Today's Students and Their Parents

Chapter 2: Leading Curriculum Revision

Chapter 3: Revising Organizational Structures

Chapter 4: Developing a New Program without Faculty Support

Chapter 5: Managing Resistance When Hired to Lead Change

COMMUNICATING WITH TODAY'S STUDENTS AND THEIR PARENTS

MANY OF TODAY'S TRADITIONAL-AGE students enter college with an unrealistic assessment of their preparation for doing college-level work. Moreover, doing academic work is seldom the only or even a top priority for many of today's traditional-age students, who find it essential to work to help afford college and a lifestyle that includes perceived essentials such as cell phones and vehicles. Some traditional-age students need time for personal commitments such as girlfriends or boyfriends or ill family members that detract from studying. Many traditional-age freshmen are accustomed to, and reliant on, parents who help them make decisions and manage daily activities. Some traditional-age students are accustomed to relying on parents to help with such routine tasks as getting up on time for school, doing daily homework assignments, and completing projects by the assigned deadline. When parental support is insufficient to earn the desired grade in high school, students may have relied on extra credit work to rescue a final grade. Consequently, many high school graduates boast transcripts that are not always a true reflection of their academic ability or their preparedness to do college work.

Nonetheless, today's traditional-age students are typically experienced at being successful. They grew up in a time when even losing athletic teams were recognized for their efforts and when parents and educators alike were conscious of providing feedback that bolstered their self-esteems. Consequently, faculty members find themselves teaching traditional-age students who are accustomed to receiving good grades despite not being well prepared to do college work and being insufficiently experienced to independently manage academic work and life. At times, department chairs must manage parents who are poised and ready to intervene to help their child succeed and avoid the discomfort that sometimes accompanies a hard-learned lesson. For more about the societal influences that shape the attitudes and behaviors of today's students, see Levine (2005) and Twenge (2006).

The goal of this chapter is to help department chairs deal more effectively with today's traditional-age students and their parents. A second goal of this chapter is to suggest strategies that department chairs may use in the professional development of all faculty members to enhance their communication with today's students and, when appropriate and necessary, their parents. Although the case scenarios presented in this chapter focus on traditional-age students, the same leadership communication strategies can be used to enhance department chair and faculty communication with all students.

Defining the Task

Communicating effectively with today's traditional-age students and their parents requires an understanding of their perceptions of, and expectations for, college work. Many of today's traditional-age students possess a confidence level that exceeds their personal experience and skill development. Many have not experienced or learned from the actual consequences that derive from making poor decisions or taking imprudent action. The learning that comes from trial and error was stifled for many of today's traditional-age students by well-meaning parents and, in some instances, educators who worry too much about damaging students' self-esteem to permit them to experience and learn from making mistakes or enduring the natural consequences of doing inadequate work. Moreover, many traditional-age students are not experienced at getting themselves up in time for class or managing their discretionary time on a day-to-day basis. Consequently, many of today's traditional-age students enter college expecting to be successful without working any harder or differently than they did in high school.

Many parents are simultaneously apprehensive and relieved about sending their children off to college. Most parents recognize that their children will need sufficient guidance and support to successfully transition to college life, and many parents hope, and sometimes expect, faculty and staff to pick up where they left off in nurturing and caring for their children. Parental expectations may vary with the type of institution. For example, parents are more likely to hold higher expectations for individual attention for their children when paying to send them to a private residential campus than when their children continue to live at home and commute to a nearby college. Still, the fact that more and more institutions of higher education plan for parents to attend new student orientation programs affirms that parents of traditional-age students are becoming more involved in the lives of today's college students.

Like it or not, parents are a constituency that institutions of higher education cannot afford to ignore. Ironically, the more dependent a student is on his or her parents, the more influence the parent has over his or her student's decision to enroll or remain at a particular institution. The fact that many institutions of higher education employ recruitment strategies and messages that are designed to persuade parents that the institution is a good fit for their children affirms the importance of parents as a constituency. Savvy institutions take a proactive posture with involved parents by structuring the nature of their involvement. Some institutions, for example, have instituted parent councils or send newsletters to parents updating them on opportunities that are available for their students. When dealing with parents, department chairs will find it useful to reference the existence of newsletters or other things in place that are intended to keep parents informed about available educational opportunities and demonstrate the institution's commitment to the welfare of its students.

Relevant Leadership Communication Strategies

Department chairs can use the following leadership communication strategies to be more effective in communicating with today's students and their parents while protecting instructional quality and academic integrity.

Discern the Real Issue

With today's traditional-age students focused on grades and finding employment after graduation, the real issue of concern may be something other than what is being articulated by the student or his or her parent. A student, for example, may complain that a teacher refuses to offer work for extra credit or grades too harshly when the real issue is that the student has not learned how to study effectively to do college work successfully. Similarly, parents may be focused on what a particular instructor is or is not doing for their child when they should instead be focused on how they might help their student adapt to college work and life.

Adapt Communication to the Student's Perspective and Expectations

Sadly, many individuals communicate with the belief that it is the listener's responsibility to understand what is being said. This practice seldom leads to effective communication. Moreover, this practice can alienate the individual who is articulating a concern. For example, should a student be concerned about graduating on time, it will do little good to suggest that the student enroll in an elective course that would deepen his or her understanding of the discipline. The suggestion to enroll in an elective course would appear more reasoned if the department chair explains how taking the course would not slow progress to degree completion and would aid in seeking employment after graduation. Similarly, if a student is stressed about taking a night class, which will interfere with the student's part-time job, it does little good to assert that the course is more important than his or her part-time job. Even reminding the student that the course is a requirement will not address the student's concern about disrupting a work schedule. To more effectively address the student's concern about missing work, the department chair needs to first learn more about the work conflict. It is possible that understanding the situation more fully will enable the department chair to suggest how the student might revise the work schedule (e.g., trading work schedules with someone else, asking the boss for permission to start work an hour later on one night a week) that the student has not considered.

Only when department chairs fully understand the student's perspective and expectations can they structure their message in a way that will be meaningful to the student. Exercising this leadership communication strategy can save time and prevent conflict that can result when students believe the department chair is refusing to hear and respond constructively to their concerns. If, for example, the department chair can help a student brainstorm ways to approach a schedule conflict with work, the department chair is more likely to secure the student's cooperation to enroll in the recommended course. Only when department chairs take the time to understand the student's perspective and expectations can they realistically model for the student how to manage college work and life. Student concerns left unaddressed will likely build and fester in ways that present more challenging conflicts for the department chair in the form of involved parents, complaints to the administration, or enrollment decline.

Please note that understanding a student's perspective and expectations does not mean that department chairs should grant every student request. At times, the best and only option is for department chairs to deny a student's request. Especially in these instances, it is important for department chairs to first understand the student's perspective and expectations and to use this information in explaining the basis for the negative decision or outcome. Assume, for example, a student requests to take a course without first completing the prerequisite for that course. A department chair would be right to deny this request without discussion or debate because department chairs know the educational purpose for course prerequisites. The student, however, likely perceives the request as reasonable because the student does not understand the role or value of course prerequisites. It is more likely that the denied request will incent the student to involve his or her parents or pursue the matter with others on the campus when the student perceives the denial of his request as unreasonable. The minute others get involved, the department chair will spend more time on the matter even though denying the student's request is the right decision. If, however, the department chair learns that the request is motivated by the student's desire to take courses that meet around a busy work schedule, the chair can address the real issue of concern by suggesting alternatives for managing the student's problem that eliminate the need for the student's request for an exception to policy.

Employ Three-Way Communication

Parents seldom have all the information when they call on behalf of their student. Department chairs can save a lot of time if they focus on listening to the parents to determine what they know and do not know. It is also important to remember that parents will inherently have a biased perspective. Family Educational Rights and Privacy Act (FERPA) regulations influence what faculty and staff can tell parents about their child's academic performance, so it is important to know how your institution views and operationalizes FERPA regulations. Contrary to what some believe, FERPA does not preclude a conversation between faculty and parents or between the department chair and parents. FERPA regulations can be waived when students give permission for their parents to be informed of their academic progress, and many institutions ask each student to stipulate his or her preference in writing during freshman orientation. When a student grants permission, three-way conversations involving parents, the student, and the chair can help to clarify existing misunderstandings and to establish mutual goals and reasonable expectations. Sometimes, three-way conversations make sense when a student has not granted permission to share information with his or her parents. A three-way conversation gives the department chair an opportunity to describe the parents' concern in front of the student. This will quickly sort out misunderstandings between parents and student and give the student ample opportunity to correct the parent's impression about what has or has not happened. It also affords the department chair an opportunity to clarify campus and department policies, academic requirements, resources available to students, and expectations for student performance.

Provide Professional Development for Faculty

Many institutions still employ tenured faculty members who earned their doctorates in the 1970s. These more senior faculty members can sometimes find it difficult to communicate with today's traditional-age students. These struggles are evidenced in faculty complaints about students using cell phones during class, spending more time arguing about a grade than learning the material, and expecting success without investing sufficient effort in the class. Today's students are different from previous generations of students, and faculty more experienced and comfortable with previous generations of students could benefit from professional development that coaches them on how best to communicate to, and work with, today's traditional-age students. Department chairs might organize briefings for faculty during which they hear the perspectives and suggestions of others on the campus who are expert in understanding today's students. For example, colleagues in student affairs are trained to understand the phases of student development. Staff members on campus who have responsibility for assisting students with learning disabilities can be a great resource for faculty. Typically, these individuals are very willing to share their expertise and to partner with faculty to create the best possible classroom environment and experience for today's students.

Putting Theory into Practice

Although these leadership communication strategies may appear to expand the role responsibilities assigned to department chairs, they can minimize the time spent by department chairs to manage conflict when addressing student concerns. In Case 1.1, the department chair must manage an upset parent. Put yourself in the role of the department chair as you read.

Case 1.1: A Call from a Concerned Parent

Michael Hughes, chair of the English department, is busy grading student papers in his office when the department secretary interrupts to tell him that a stressed-out mother is demanding to speak with him. This is not a new circumstance. Having chaired the department for several years, Michael is well aware of the active interest that more and more parents take in their children's education. Resigned that he needs to talk with this mother, Michael picks up the phone.

Department chair: This is Dr. Hughes. How can I help you?

Mother: Are you the department chair?

Department chair: Yes.

Mother: I wish to file a complaint against one of your instructors. My son took English 100 with Mrs. Stevens, and it was a complete waste of his time and the money we spent on tuition for this course.

Department chair: Ms. Stevens is one of our more experienced instructors, and students typically praise her teaching. Who is your son, and what was his issue with Ms. Stevens?

Mother: My son is Patrick Bukowski, and Mrs. Stevens *is* the problem.

Department chair: Can you tell me if your son talked with Ms. Stevens about his concerns?

Mother: Countless times, and every conversation was a complete waste of his time.

Department chair: How so?

Mother: Mrs. Stevens doesn't listen to Patrick. Instead, she is intent on making false accusations about Patrick and his work in the English course. All of Patrick's efforts to improve his grade have been met with hostility from Mrs. Stevens.

Department chair: I must say that your description of Ms. Stevens does not match my experience in working with her for more than 20 years.

Mother: I'm not surprised that Mrs. Stevens would behave differently with you. Perhaps you are too biased to address my concerns. I am prepared to take this matter to the president of the university. Anyone who cares about the welfare of students will want to hear what I have to say.

Department chair: I would like to talk with Patrick to learn of his experience in English 100 with Ms. Stevens. Would you encourage your son to call me so we can set up a time to talk?

Mother: No, my son has been through enough. This experience has devastated him. He wants to transfer to a different institution because he believes that Mrs. Stevens has ruined his reputation on this campus.

Department chair: How could she do that? Can you describe the nature of your son's difficulty with Ms. Stevens?

Mother: My son was sorely mistreated, even bullied by Mrs. Stevens. When Mrs. Stevens dismissed Patrick's concerns. I called her and was treated to the same condescending and rude behavior that my son experienced all semester. That's why I am calling you. When can my husband and I meet with you so we can share the full story with you?

Department chair: Let me suggest that Ms. Stevens and your son join us for the meeting.

Mother: Patrick will come, but I doubt that Mrs. Stevens will show up because there is no way she can explain or defend her actions.

Department chair: Let's plan to meet next Friday morning. I will call to confirm the time after I talk with Ms. Stevens about her schedule.

Mother: Thank you. I will look forward to your call.

Let's Analyze the Case

It is obvious that Patrick Bukowski's mother is upset. She believes Patrick has been mistreated and even bullied by his English 100 instructor, Ms. Stevens. Department chair Michael Hughes is not able to discern the basis for Patrick's mother's accusations about Ms. Stevens. Only by agreeing to meet with Patrick and his parents is the department chair able to keep Patrick's mother from calling the university president. Moreover, the accusations being made by Patrick's mother are not consistent with the department chair's personal assessment of Ms. Stevens's teaching.

The conversation, however, provides the department chair with some understanding of Patrick's mother and her involvement in his education. Patrick's mother appears confident in her assessment of the problem and the necessary remedy. Please notice how Patrick's mother persists in referring to the English 100 instructor as *Mrs.* Stevens, even though the department chair continues to refer to the instructor as *Ms.* Stevens. Although Patrick's mother is intent on having her concerns heard and addressed, she seems unable or unwilling to hear perspectives that differ from her own. When the department chair mentions that other students praise Ms. Stevens's teaching, Patrick's mother accuses him of being biased.

The department chair wisely suggests that Ms. Stevens join the meeting. Having her there will limit the opportunity for Patrick or his parents to make inaccurate statements about what Ms. Stevens said or did. It will also allow Ms. Stevens an opportunity to share her perspective on Patrick's work in the class and to describe her interactions with Patrick.

The department chair needs to structure the meeting with Patrick and his parents and Ms. Stevens in a way that allows everyone to present his or her perspective and, at the same time, encourages all to hear and understand what each other is saying. Failure to manage the communication dynamic in the meeting will inevitably prevent Patrick and his parents from understanding the basis for Patrick's grade and from persuading them that Ms. Stevens has not bullied or mistreated Patrick.

It's Your Turn

Assume the position of the department chair in this case scenario, and think through how you would prepare for the meeting with Ms. Stevens, Patrick Bukowski, and his parents.

1. What, if anything, would you share with Ms. Stevens about the comments made by Patrick's mother? Is it likely that Ms. Stevens will be agreeable to meeting with Patrick and his parents? How important is it that Ms. Stevens join you in talking with Patrick and his parents?

2. What might you do to discern the true nature of the issue of disagreement before meeting with Patrick and his parents? What information might you request from Ms. Stevens, the registrar, Patrick's academic advisor, and other offices on campus?

3. What, if any, campus or department policies you would review prior to the meeting with Patrick and his parents?

4. Give thought to how you might structure the meeting such that the true issue can be uncovered and addressed in a constructive manner. Does your approach take into account the individual perspectives and expectations of Patrick, his parents, and Ms. Stevens? Does your approach incorporate relevant department and campus policy? Does your approach uphold academic quality and integrity?

Please Consider

Based on the phone conversation presented in Case 1.1, it seems that Patrick's mother is intent on righting wrongs done to Patrick by Ms. Stevens in English 100. The department chair needs to deescalate the anger evidenced during his phone conversation with Patrick's mother, or the next conversation could deteriorate quickly without constructive outcome. How the department chair structures the meeting can help to establish a positive tone for the discussion. For example, the department chair might lead the group in some initial small talk that allows for more familiarity among the parties involved. Small talk often sheds light on the individuals in a way that can help with the management of the immediate conflict. For example, informal conversation that reveals Patrick is an only child or that English is Patrick's most difficult subject might be used by the department chair or Ms. Stevens when discussing Patrick's preparation to do good work in English 100. Taking a few minutes for casual conversation to ask Patrick about his high school English curriculum and other such matters can demonstrate the department chair's interest in Patrick and can provide insight that is helpful in managing conflict.

Similarly, the department chair can ease a contentious conversation by ensuring that everyone's perspective is heard and understood and by using language that does not incite more anger. For example, consider the following two statements that the department chair might make to Patrick at the upcoming meeting:

Statement A: "Every student deserves to understand the basis for the grade assigned, and I am committed to helping you learn the basis for your grade English 100."

Statement B: "Given all of the instructor's notations on your papers, you had to know that you were not doing well in the course."

Both statements address the basis for the grade. Statement A affirms the department chair's commitment to helping Patrick learn and understand the basis for his grade English 100. Statement A acknowledges the student's right to understand the basis for the grade without implying Patrick's work was unfairly graded. Statement B would likely make Patrick and his parents more defensive because it implies that Patrick should have known that he was doing poor work. Parents who are convinced that their son was mistreated can be expected to react negatively to statement B. Department chairs can greatly influence and improve the tone of potentially contentious meetings by using language that allows for a discussion of the issue in a way that is respectful of all perspectives.

Again, put yourself in the department chair's role as you answer the following questions:

1. How would you handle introductions at the meeting? What casual questions might you pose to break the tension and demonstrate your genuine interest in Patrick's success at the institution?
2. What is your goal for the meeting? Give some thought to what needs to happen during the meeting for the discussion to be productive?

3. How would you structure the meeting to manage the intensity exhibited by Patrick's mother in the phone conversation with the department chair? When and how would you introduce the issue of conflict?

4. How would you use Ms. Stevens' presence to address the concerns articulated by Patrick's mother? Would you coach Ms. Stevens in advance of the meeting? If so, what advice would you give Ms. Stevens?

Let's Recap

Take a moment to finalize your plan for the meeting with Patrick, his parents, and Ms. Stevens. Review your primary objectives for the meeting, and assess the confidence you have in your plan for achieving these objectives. Does your approach:

○ Discern the real issue?
○ Adapt to the student's perspective and expectations?
○ Adapt to the parents' perspective and expectations?
○ Make optimal use of three-way communication?

Putting Theory into Practice

In Case 1.2, the department chair must manage the faculty member's reaction to the parent's complaint. Continue to assume the role of the department chair as you read.

Case 1.2: The Reluctant Instructor

Michael Hughes isn't looking forward to the meeting with Patrick Bukowski and his parents, but he understands that his intervention is needed to help them obtain a more constructive view of whatever transpired in English 100. Michael has noticed that parents become anxious and quickly involved in issues that can typically be resolved without a formal grievance being filed if all parties are able to sit and talk through the issue of disagreement.

Ms. Stevens is an experienced adjunct professor who has taught successfully in the department for more than 2 decades. Michael has full confidence that Ms. Stevens would never intentionally bully, intimidate, or falsely accuse a student. Convinced that some misunderstanding is the source of the problem, Michael calls Ms. Stevens to brief her on his conversation with Patrick's mother and to learn her preference for meeting times on Friday morning.

Ms. Stevens: This is Sheila Stevens. How may I help you?

Department chair: Hi Sheila. This is Michael Hughes. I hope I'm calling a convenient time.

Ms. Stevens: I have a few minutes before a scheduled meeting with a student.

Department chair: This shouldn't take long. I just had a phone conversation with Patrick Bukowski's mother.

Ms. Stevens: That woman is something else. She called me this morning and would not accept the fact that FERPA regulations prevent me from discussing Patrick's academic performance with her.

Department chair: Yes, I can imagine that she can be very persistent.

Ms. Stevens: I'm grateful that FERPA spares us from ever having to talk with parents.

Department chair: FERPA addresses what we can and cannot say to parents about their children's academic performance, but it does not license us to ignore parents.

Ms. Stevens: Well, I fully intend to leave the parents to you.

Department chair: Patrick's mother contends that her son does not understand the basis for his grade.

Ms. Stevens: That may be true. Nonetheless, I have spent considerable time trying to help Patrick do better work in English 100. He would rather argue about a grade than learn what he needs to know to improve his grade. He became very defensive when I pointed out that the improper referencing of sources used in writing is plagiarism. Even then, he persisted in arguing his grade rather than meeting with me to learn how to cite sourced material appropriately.

Department chair: It sounds like Patrick's mother is unaware of your efforts to help Patrick.

Ms. Stevens: She may be. However, I doubt she wants to hear anything other than that Patrick will get a good grade in the course.

Department chair: How is Patrick doing in the course?

Ms. Stevens: I haven't graded his final essay, but it looks like he will fail the course.

Department chair: I trust you submitted the required midterm warning on Patrick.

Ms. Stevens: No, I didn't. Patrick lacks confidence so instead of filing the midterm warning report, I sent him an email inviting him to meet with me individually to review the problems with his writing. I also suggested that he take full advantage of the support offered through the campus writing lab.

Department chair: Did he follow up on your recommendations?

Ms. Stevens: Not really, He met with me once much later in the semester, but only to argue about the grade on another paper. He never went to the writing lab or allowed me to work with him individually to correct the problems with his writing.

Department chair: So he met with you only one time?

Ms. Stevens: Yes, even though I continued to write, "Please see me" on every essay I returned. In our one meeting about 3 weeks ago, Patrick was very defensive and, at the same time, apologetic for doing poor work. He kept repeating that he never failed a course before and asked for extra credit work to improve his grade. I explained that college work is different from high school and that many students experience difficulty during their first semester. I emphasized that his current grade is a reflection only of what he has not yet learned. When I suggested that we review the problems with his writing, he asked again if he might do work for extra credit. When I asked why he had not acted on my suggestions that he talk with me sooner and seek help from the writing lab, he responded that he thought he was doing okay. He even said he thought he had a B or B+ in the course. Candidly, I don't know how he could have thought that with the margin notes I made on his paper and the numeric value assigned to each essay. I reminded him that the grading scale is in his syllabus. I also told him about the freshman forgiveness policy, which enables him to retake the course to improve the grade that is recorded on his transcript.

Department chair: How did Patrick respond?

Ms. Stevens: Nothing I said seemed to register with him. He just continued to plead for extra credit work so he could bring up his grade. I could tell he was upset when he left, but there was nothing else I could tell him. Then this morning, his mother called me. She said that she had learned from Patrick that he is failing English 100 and that she and her "attorney husband" wanted to talk with me "immediately" about his grade.

Department chair: What did you say?

Ms. Stevens: I told her that campus policy precluded me from discussing Patrick's academic performance with either she or her husband.

Department chair: How did she respond?

Ms. Stevens: She became very upset and told me that she was paying for Patrick's education and therefore had "the right to direct it." I told her I would be happy to talk with Patrick and help him understand the basis for his grade. She offered to come with Patrick to my office, and I told her that I would not talk with Patrick in front of her.

Department chair: This is helpful background information for me. I have agreed to meet with Patrick and his parents this Friday morning. The meeting is an opportunity to set the record straight about your efforts to help Patrick, and I would like you to join me in the meeting.

Ms. Stevens: No thank you!

Department chair: I believe the meeting is an opportunity to explain how you tried to help Patrick improve his writing and grade in English 100.

Ms. Stevens: There is no way I will meet with that woman, and I hope never to meet her "attorney husband."

Department chair: I will run the meeting and promise that you will not treated rudely by Patrick or his parents.

Ms. Stevens: Again, no thank you. As an adjunct professor at this institution, meeting with irate, unreasonable parents is not part of my job description.

Department chair: Please give it more consideration. I hope you will change your mind and join me in the meeting. I fear that your absence will be interpreted by the parents as support for Patrick's claim that you were not helpful to him.

Ms. Stevens: I'm sorry if this leaves you in a difficult position. I would meet with Patrick or you and Patrick, but I refuse to meet with his parents.

Let's Analyze the Case

Talking with Ms. Stevens shed more light on the situation. It seems that Patrick refused to heed the instructor's counsel. This is not the first time the department chair encountered a student who resisted an instructor's offer to help while arguing the grade and seeking opportunities to earn extra credit. Ms. Stevens believes she acted appropriately both in working with Patrick and in talking with his mother. She explains that she chose not to file the required midterm warning as a kindness to Patrick, who impresses her as lacking confidence. Ms. Stevens's refusal to participate in a meeting with Patrick and his parents, however, leaves the department chair in a more difficult position. Instead of mediating a misunderstanding, the department chair now needs to present Ms. Stevens's perspective. Not handled well, this could give the Bukowskis the impression that the department chair is taking sides before hearing Patrick and his parents. Moreover, the fact that Ms. Stevens failed to submit the required midterm warning on Patrick's work in English 100 leaves the chair vulnerable in demonstrating that Patrick received sufficient notice that he was not doing passing work.

Ms. Stevens is obviously uncomfortable meeting with parents. She admits being grateful for FERPA regulations, which she believes free her from talking with a student's parents. When the department chair clarifies that FERPA regulations only direct what can and cannot be said to parents, Ms. Stevens quickly announces that she will leave meeting with parents to the department chair. She adds that as an adjunct professor, meeting with "irate and unreasonable parents" is not in her job description. Whether or not this is the case would depend on Ms. Stevens's contract with university. If there is a job description for adjunct professors, it should be used to clarify the scope of Ms. Stevens's responsibilities. Some institutions do not have a formal job description for adjunct faculty. In such instances, the department chair may wish to devise a job description for adjunct faculty hired to staff department courses. Given the needs and expectations of today's students and their parents, the position description for adjunct faculty might stipulate department expectations for their availability for working with students outside of class, filing midterm grade warnings, and participating in the discussion of student concerns.

It's Your Turn

Continue to assume the department chair's role as you wrestle with the following questions:

1. Would you accept Ms. Stevens's refusal to meet with Patrick and his parents? If not, please describe how you would persuade Ms. Stevens to participate in the upcoming meeting with Patrick and his parents if doing so is not stipulated in her employment contract.

2. How would the conversation with Ms. Stevens alter your preparation for the meeting with Patrick and his parents? Would you, for example, request a copy of Ms. Stevens's email notes to Patrick? What other information would you ask her to supply? Would you, for example, want a copy of the course syllabus and a copy

of Patrick's final paper? Does the conversation with Ms. Stevens prompt you to review any specific departmental or institutional policies? For example, would you review the instructions for submitting midterm grade warnings, the policy on a student's academic responsibility, or FERPA regulations?

3. How would Ms. Stevens's refusal to meet with Patrick's parents alter your plan for structuring and conducting the meeting with Patrick and his parents? For example, how would you explain Ms. Stevens's absence to Patrick and his parents? Please be specific.

Please Consider

Patrick's mother predicted that Ms. Stevens would not attend the meeting because Patrick's mother believes that Ms. Stevens cannot explain or defend her treatment of Patrick. It is therefore critical that the department chair explain Ms. Stevens's absence in a way that does not give further credence to the assertion made by Patrick's mother. This should influence when and how the department chair explains Ms. Stevens's absence. Consider the following possible statements of explanation:

Statement A: Ms. Stevens did not wish to join us.

Statement B: Having already talked with Patrick, Ms. Stevens believes her presence in this meeting would not be helpful. She remains available to Patrick should he want her help in improving his writing skills.

Statement C: I could not persuade Ms. Stevens to join us today.

Of the three statements, statement B is the most prudent. Statements A and C leave room for Patrick's parents to conclude that Ms. Stevens could not face them or defend her treatment of Patrick. Statement C acknowledges the department chair's failure to "persuade" Ms. Stevens to attend, thereby suggesting that the department chair is powerless in supervising Ms. Stevens. This statement could cause Patrick's parents to conclude that the department chair will be unable to help them. Statement B acknowledges Ms. Stevens's previous conversations with Patrick while affirming her continuing interest to support Patrick's learning.

Putting Theory into Practice

In Case 1.3, department chair Michael Hughes does his best to respond to the family's concerns. As you read, consider when and how your approach might vary from his.

Case 1.3: The Meeting with Patrick and His Parents

On Friday morning, Michael Hughes spent almost 2 hours with Patrick and his parents. The essence of his lengthy meeting is captured in the following file note that he wrote to document his conversation with the Bukowskis. Michael hopes that the conversation sufficiently answered the Bukowski's concerns and that Patrick will remain enrolled at the university. However, the incident raises another sticky issue that the department chair needs to address.

File Note

Meeting with Patrick Bukowski and his parents

I met with Patrick Bukowski and his parents for almost 2 hours on Friday, May XX, 20XX. It was a civil, but serious, and sometimes intense conversation.

After some pleasantries and informal conversation, I moved us to the purpose for the meeting and suggested that the best way to proceed would be for me to hear Patrick describe his concerns. Before Patrick could utter a syllable, Mrs. Bukowski asked Patrick if he would like for her to start. Patrick nodded in agreement. For about 10 minutes, Patrick's mother listed their concerns, including Ms. Stevens's dismissal of Patrick's request for help to improve his grade and her "false accusation" about Patrick's work. Their greatest concern, however, is Ms. Stevens's recent refusal to meet with Patrick and his parents to review his "grade." I reminded them that Patrick had met with Ms. Stevens and added that Ms. Stevens believes it is most constructive to work only with the student. I asked Patrick why he preferred to have his parents present when he met with Ms. Stevens to review his work. Patrick said that he would count on his parents to help hear what he needed to learn. The parents asked why any faculty member would reject an opportunity to illustrate the value of his or her instruction by letting parents hear the discussion of the student's work. I explained that often faculty believe more learning takes place when errors are not discussed in front of others.

We spent considerable time reviewing Patrick's essays because he wanted to show me the questions he had about Ms. Stevens's notations. In particular, Patrick showed me several places where a grading notation made on the first draft was not repeated on a subsequent draft. Patrick therefore reasoned that his writing improved. I pointed out that subsequent drafts and the final paper still contained copious margin notes made by Ms. Stevens. Patrick did not bring the grading code that contains the full description for the abbreviated notations and numerical values used by Ms. Stevens in grading, so we discussed only the more obvious instructor notations. Patrick acknowledged that he has things to learn to write better. As we were reviewing Patrick's work, his mother pointed out twice that the process would be easier if Ms. Stevens was in the room because she could explain the abbreviated notations and numeric values used in grading so that Patrick, his parents, and I would understand what she was trying to teach and what is lacking in Patrick's work.

The second significant issue of contention for the Bukowskis is the fact that Patrick, an entering freshman, was not provided the midterm warning notice promised for freshmen who are not doing passing work in a class. I explained that instead Ms. Stevens sent Patrick a personal email in which she stated that she was available to work with him individually and suggested that he use the support offered through the writing lab. I added that based on her teaching experience, Ms. Stevens was convinced that Patrick would pass the course if he accepted her offer to work with him individually. This was not terribly comforting because the Bukowskis are convinced that had Patrick received the midterm warning they would have known that Patrick needed to seek additional help from Ms. Stevens or to take some other action to improve his writing. Without the midterm warning, Ms. Stevens's email was interpreted by Patrick as a kind offer, but one that was not essential to his passing the course.

I asked Patrick to tell me about the "false accusations" that his mother said had been made by Ms. Stevens. Patrick disclosed that Ms. Stevens falsely accused him of plagiarism because he did not know to reference his sources for some of the points he made in a paper. Patrick's mother interjected that the charge of plagiarism is especially "outrageous" because, as a result of Ms. Stevens's poor teaching, Patrick now would be viewed as a cheater by all other instructors. I explained that the term *plagiarism* correctly labels any error in citing a reference improperly and assured Patrick that Ms. Stevens had not filed a formal charge of plagiarism. Patrick quickly explained that it was never his intent to plagiarize, and his parents again expressed their concern about having Patrick labeled in this way. It became clear that they feared this negative attribute would follow Patrick to other courses. I assured them that once Patrick learned to cite references appropriately, no instructor would be able to say he plagiarized.

During the 2-hour meeting, Patrick and his parents often circled back to these two issues: (1) Ms. Stevens's refusal to meet with them; and (2) Ms. Stevens's failure to issue a midterm grade warning. Patrick's mother asserted that, as department chair, I have the "power and responsibility" to force Ms. Stevens to attend a meeting with Patrick and his parents. I asked what she thought might be accomplished with a "forced" meeting, but I never got a clear answer. Patrick's mother said it was not her wish, but Patrick's desire to have Ms. Stevens meet with him and his parents. Patrick said he wanted Ms. Stevens to answer his questions in front of his parents and me. I explained that I could request a faculty member to meet with the student to review academic work and explain the basis for the grade assigned but that I could not force Ms. Stevens to meet with the parents of a student who is of legal age.

Patrick's father asked if there was any way that Patrick could redo his work to earn a passing grade. Patrick asked if he might have his money refunded for the course. I explained why both requests were not possible and described how the Freshman Forgiveness policy would enable Patrick to retake the course with a different instructor to improve his overall GPA. Patrick's parents worry that this would slow Patrick's progress toward graduation. They also believe that it would be unfair for Patrick to retake the course when Ms. Stevens failed to properly notify Patrick that he was doing failing work.

After hearing (again) how Patrick was disadvantaged by not receiving a midterm warning, I advised Patrick of his right to file a formal grievance if he believes he was wronged or that his grade for the course is unfair. I explained that his grievance would be reviewed by a committee of faculty who would show Patrick's formal letter of complaint to Ms. Stevens and permit her an opportunity to respond in writing. I added that the committee would want to see copies of all of his essays to determine whether or not Ms. Stevens graded his work fairly. I offered that, in my opinion, his essays suggest that Ms. Stevens had been conscientious in grading Patrick's work, as evidenced by the number of comments and notations made on every paper. I reviewed for Patrick and his parents the resources that are available for students at the university when they need additional help. In this instance, Patrick could have secured unlimited help from the writing lab as Ms. Stevens suggested.

Toward the end of our meeting, I summarized for Patrick the decision he will need to make. More specifically, Patrick will need to decide whether he is prepared to drop this issue or wishes to pursue a formal grievance. After 2 full hours of conversation, Patrick announced that he plans to drop the issue and not file a grievance. Patrick added that some might conclude he is "giving up," but he believes it is not worth his time and anguish because it is impossible to "fight City Hall." I told

Patrick I admired his ability to converse with me about his concerns in a professional way and offered to be an ever-ready resource for him should he ever have concerns about a future course.

I wish to add information about Patrick's family that I learned during the meeting with them. Patrick's father closed his law practice and retired early due to a disability. His mother holds a part-time office position. Both are very proud of providing a college education to their eldest son. They're especially proud of being able to send Patrick to a private institution where they believe the higher tuition will result in his receiving a better education and more individualized attention. Patrick is working hard to be a good son, and he does not wish to disappoint his parents. Patrick wants to take full advantage of the educational opportunity that his parents are providing. More than once, Patrick commented on how much he appreciates the sacrifice his parents are making in sending him to a private university. At the same time, Patrick does not always know how to put his intentions into constructive action. We spent some time discussing the advantages of keeping current with assignments and making good use of all the available resource support provided at the institution. I gently suggested that Patrick would be better served to focus on daily assignments rather than letting anxiety over one low grade consume his focus and time.

One afterthought: With the increased level of parental involvement we are experiencing, I'm not certain that faculty can or should be able to refuse to meet with parents when students give written consent for their parents to be present in a discussion regarding their academic work. This is not to suggest that faculty should subject themselves to rude treatment from parents. However, faculty members should be prepared to explain their grading in a way that is clear for students and their parents. At least in this instance, the issues of concern would have been managed more easily if the parents could observe an experienced faculty member describe the writing issues in Patrick's work.

Let's Analyze the Case

The file note suggests that closure was reached regarding Patrick's grade in English 100. Near the close of a lengthy meeting, the department chair helps Patrick understand that his options are to accept the grade or file a formal grievance. After learning the process for filing and investigating a formal grievance, Patrick announces that he will not file a formal grievance. Patrick could change his mind, but the department chair hopes that understanding the grievance process will enable Patrick to realize that he does not have a strong case for filing a grade complaint. Hopefully, learning of Patrick's right to file a grievance helps Patrick and his parents understand that taking their concern to the university president is not the next step.

Although the meeting may end the conversation about Patrick's grade in English 100, it may not restore Patrick's parents' regard for the institution. Despite limited income, the Bukowskis enrolled Patrick at a private institution believing he would receive a superior education and more individual support. And even though both Ms. Stevens and the department chair referenced the academic support that Patrick could have used when enrolled in English 100, Patrick did not experience or benefit from the academic support and individual attention that his parents expect Patrick to receive at the private institution. Unless Patrick begins to successfully use available academic support, the family is likely to conclude that Patrick is not getting what his parents believe should be provided given the tuition charged at a private institution. Should Patrick be struggling with more than English 100, it is more likely that he will not continue at the institution. There is no evidence that this department chair considered the larger context from Patrick's perspective. Information about how Patrick is doing in his other first semester courses could be very helpful to talking with Patrick and his parents.

At the end of the file note, the department chair raises the issue of whether faculty members should have the prerogative to refuse to meet with parents. This is a double-edged sword. At times it might be helpful to have the faculty member in a meeting with parents, but many faculty are not prepared for conversations like the one that the department chair in the case scenario had with Bukowskis. It is important that faculty are trained and prepared to carry out performance expectations assigned to them. Should the department chair pursue the implementation of policy that requires faculty to meet with parents when appropriate, the chair will need to ensure professional development training for faculty on how to discuss student issues constructively with upset parents.

It's Your Turn

Review the file note presented as Case 1.3 in answering the following questions:

1. What, if anything, would you do as department chair to improve the chances that the institution retains Patrick Bukowski? If this scenario played out on your campus, whom else might you involve

to enhance the likelihood that Patrick remains enrolled at the institution and advances successfully to graduation? Would you, for example, involve Patrick's academic advisor, professionals in student affairs, or other faculty? Be specific in thinking through what you would ask of each person that you would involve.

2. What, if any, information would you share with Ms. Stevens to debrief her on the meeting with Patrick and his parents? Would you share a copy of the file presented in Case 1.3 with Ms. Stevens? Could you convert this experience into a professional development exercise for the department faculty without embarrassing Ms. Stevens?

3. Would you advise the department chair in this case scenario to develop a departmental policy about how and when faculty members should converse with parents? If yes, what provisions would you recommend? What provisions would you make for faculty development that would prepare them to meet the new performance expectations? What other expertise on the campus might be tapped for this purpose? Would you, for example, involve legal counsel, human resources, or staff from the counseling center?

Let's Recap

Before leaving Case 1.3, assess the effectiveness of the department chair. In particular, did the department chair successfully

- Discern the real issue?
- Adapt his communication to the student's perspective and expectations?
- Adapt his communication to the parents' perspective expectations?
- Make effective use of three-way communication?

Putting Theory into Practice

In Case 1.4, the department chair is once again defending degree requirements to a student. Please put yourself in the role of department chair as you read.

Case 1.4: Why Do I Need English?

Dr. Anthony Lauri is once again trying to defend the merit of a particular course to the student sitting in front of him. Before becoming the chair of the Department of Computer Science, Dr. Lauri could never have imagined how much time would be spent listening to student concerns. A long-time tenured faculty member, Dr. Lauri enjoys teaching and embraces every opportunity to turn students on to his subject matter. Now, he finds himself drained by the challenge of defending course and program requirements to students.

Student: I'm a computer science major, so why do I have to take English composition?

Department chair: English is a component of the core curriculum. All students are required to complete the core curriculum, including English composition.

Student: That makes no sense. It is just a way to have me pay tuition for courses I do not need.

Department chair: You are enrolled in a 4-year degree program, and your tuition covers all of the requirements for the baccalaureate degree.

Student: What does English composition have to do with computer science? I enrolled in computer science, not English.

Department chair: Being able to write well will help you succeed in computer science.

Student: I write well enough. I always got B's and C's in high school English.

Department chair: Those grades suggest that there is room for improvement in your writing.

Student: But English composition takes a lot of time that could be spent learning computer science.

Department chair: If English composition is taking a lot of your time, it suggests that writing may not come easily for you. Again, this suggests that the English composition course is important, and one you should take seriously.

Student: My parents are counting on me to get a good job after graduation. They don't want me to waste time on classes outside my major.

Department chair: Surely, your parents want you to be able to write well.

Student: My parents believe my writing is fine, and they want me to graduate as soon as possible.

Department chair: That does not change the fact that English composition and the entire core curriculum are requirements for all 4-year degrees at this institution.

Student: There must be some schools where I would be expected to study only computer science?

Department chair: There are 2-year degree programs that focus on specific technical aspects of computer science, but earning a 4-year baccalaureate degree will give you a great advantage as you search for employment after graduation.

Student: You mean there are schools where I can graduate and be working after 2 years?

Department chair: Yes, but not at the same starting salary and with little room for professional advancement.

Student: Seriously, I could be earning a paycheck in just 2 years?

Department chair: I don't believe you are hearing me. Your employment opportunities and earning potential for the long term will be significantly better with a 4-year baccalaureate degree.

By this point in the conversation, Dr. Lauri is trying to figure out how his defense of English composition as a core requirement has this student thinking about the benefits of a 2-year degree. The department recruits prospective students into the bachelor's program by documenting the benefit of earning a 4-year degree when seeking employment. How can it be that this student now seems both surprised and pleased to discover the availability of 2-year degree programs?

Let's Analyze the Case

By this point in the conversation, Dr. Lauri must feel as if he is stuck in an infinite loop. Dr. Lauri recognizes that the student does not want to take English composition and does not perceive value in this course or the core curriculum. Although many of us may join Dr. Lauri in wishing that students would accept the requirements as important and necessary for their education, today's students sometimes challenge requirements. Today's students tend to very practically focused. They are investing in higher education on the promise that it will provide gainful employment and a brighter future. They are motivated to attend college to earn a degree and not necessarily for the learning associated with earning that degree. Consequently, degree requirements that do not make sense to students are often perceived as unnecessary obstacles to earning a degree as quickly as possible. Department chairs often find themselves defending the value of instruction or the importance of specific degree requirements.

In Case 1.4, the student is concerned about wasting time and tuition dollars. When Dr. Lauri makes the point that there is a long-term professional advantage to earning a baccalaureate degree in computer science, the student misses the point entirely. Instead, the student fixates on the possibility that he could earn a degree and be gainfully employed after only 2 years if he went to a different college. The department chair understands the issue being raised by the student but is not on the same page as the student in discussing the issue. Dr. Lauri is speaking truths that are understood by faculty employed in higher education. The student, however, will perceive the department chair's words as truth only if the student can comprehend and accept what the chair is saying. This particular student challenges the purpose for the English composition requirement. Because the department chair is not successful in making sense of the English requirement to this student, it is also likely that the student will not be receptive to the chair's contention that having a 4-year degree will be worth extra tuition and time in school. Because the chair is not making sense to the student when defending the English composition requirement, his credibility is generally suspect with this student.

The department chair's challenge is twofold. First, the chair must accurately comprehend the student's issue. Second, the chair must take the student's perceptive into account when responding to the student's query. Department chairs who quickly dismiss student concerns as unfounded or illogical often discover themselves involved in prolonged conversations. In this case scenario, Dr. Lauri expands his response to the student by linking the course requirement to core and degree requirements for a 4-year baccalaureate degree. To do this before the student is persuaded of the merit of taking English composition opens Pandora's box. The student pounces on Dr. Lauri's mention of 2-year degree programs because the student's focus is on removing a course requirement that the student perceives as an unnecessary obstacle to degree completion. Dr. Lauri's defense of 4-year baccalaureate programs is as abstract to this student as his defense of English composition. The student is selectively hearing what the student wishes to hear because Dr. Lauri's response to the initial student concern does not take into account the student's perspective which is a desire to skip requirements that appear to the student as unnecessary.

It's Your Turn

Assume the position of department chair in this scenario as you review the conversation.

1. At what point in the conversation would you change what the chair says to the student?

2. How would you script the chair's remarks from this point forward? Be specific in deciding what language you would use and how you would frame the points you would make.

3. What, if any, support would you offer for your comments? For example, would you provide salary data or give the student an article to read that espouses the benefits of a baccalaureate degree in computer science?

4. Take a moment to anticipate how this particular student might react to each of your comments, and consider how you would manage the student's response.

Please Consider

When department chairs find that they have hit a brick wall in trying to persuade a student of a particular view, it is helpful to reflect on how the argument being made might be better framed to improve student comprehension. Especially with today's traditional-age students, effective communication requires that department chairs understand the student's perspective and expectations so they can frame issues and use language that will help students better comprehend and accept the substance of what the department chair is saying. What seems intuitive to a department chair may not be logical to a student. For example, most students are unmoved to hear how carefully faculty consider degree requirements. Because students may view degree requirements as obstacles to degree completion, they see nothing wrong with challenging the basis for them. Students expect department chairs to defend degree requirements and therefore are skeptical of the department chair's explanation about the value of a particular course or degree requirement. This poses a problem for department chairs who believe it should be sufficient to explain that the course or requirement in question is necessary for degree completion.

Department chairs will find it easier to communicate with today's students when they take the time to first understand and then demonstrate their understanding of the student's perspective and expectations. This involves actively listening to the student's request. For example, in this case scenario, the student seeks permission to bypass English composition. The student's request appears simple and easy to comprehend. Less obvious is the student's motivation for making the request. There exists a range of possibilities. The student may worry that the English grade will negatively impact the overall GPA. The student may believe the course material is not relevant to the major. It is possible that the student has a strong command of English composition and finds the course content repetitive. Perhaps the student finds the instructor difficult or boring. In reality, there are countless reasons that a student might seek to bypass a specific course or degree requirement. When department chairs take the time to learn the basis for the specific student request, they have an advantage in knowing how best to communicate with that student. For example, if fear of a poor grade is the basis for the request, the department chair can inform the student of additional support available through the writing lab on campus. If the request derives from difficulties the student may have with a particular instructor, there will likely be several remedies to suggest for managing the immediate situation without needing to defend the merit of the specific course or degree requirement.

Hindsight Is 20/20

A department chair's credibility is on the line with every student encounter. Taking time to actively listen to the student's perspective and expectations before responding to a student concern or request will inevitably help set the tone for further interactions with that student. Even when students do not get the answer they want from a department chair, it is important that they leave the interaction believing that the department chair heard their concern and fairly addressed their situation. To put this another way, when students believe that their concerns are unfairly dismissed without full and fair consideration, they are less likely to perceive the department chair as a credible source of information on any matter. Moreover, when students are convinced that the department chair does not understand and fairly consider their concerns, they are more likely to take their concerns to someone else in the administration. When this happens, department chairs may find themselves needing to reestablish their leadership credibility with other members of the administration and students.

Let's Recap

There is little doubt that today's students are different from previous generations of students. Today's students arrive at college with perceptions and expectations that influence how they approach learning and how they interact with faculty and others. Today's traditional-age students are often quick to register their concerns, and many have parents who are fully prepared to help them be successful and realize their expectations for college work and life. Long-term department chairs report spending significantly more time responding to student concerns today than they did in previous decades. If not managed well, a disgruntled student or parent can become contentious opponents that consume enormous time and energy when the ideal scenario is to have students and their parents working collaboratively with faculty to enhance student learning and success.

The leadership communication strategies presented in this chapter are designed to enhance department chair effectiveness when conversing with students and parents. Department chairs can enhance their leadership effectiveness in communicating with today's students and their parents by employing the following strategies:

- Discern the real issue.
- Adapt communication to the student's perspective and expectations.
- Employ three-way communication.
- Provide professional development for faculty.

In conversing with today's students and their parents, it is rarely sufficient to cite relevant policy. When students challenge the purpose for a specific course requirement, merely affirming that students must complete the course because it is a requirement can make matters worse because students will likely conclude that their concerns are not being heard. Further, explaining the requirement being challenged is somehow good for students does not demonstrate that the department chair has heard or understood their perspective. Concerns raised by today's students and their parents are better managed when department chairs first take the time needed to discern the real issue and then adapt communication to the perspective and expectations of that student or parent. Department chairs will be able to manage interactions with students and their parents more effectively when they demonstrate that they understand the student's perspective and expectations. This is especially true when explaining the basis for denying a student's request.

Many of today's traditional-age students keep their parents apprised of daily experiences at college. Parents therefore believe they are fully informed when approaching the department chair with a concern. Employing three-way communication involving student and parents and, when appropriate, faculty members can prevent multiple and extended "he said, she said" discussions. Having all the relevant parties in the same room at the same time is often the quickest and only way to discern the facts and help everyone reach a common understanding about what has happened and what can and cannot be done to remedy a concern.

Most faculty members would benefit from coaching on how to more effectively interact with today's students. Even when faculty members have conscientiously honed teaching methodologies that work best with the way today's students learn best, they may be uncomfortable managing individual student concerns or helping students revise unrealistic expectations of what is required to successfully do college work. Even though faculty members know well their subject matter, they may be frustrated by students who refuse to detach from cell phones during class or fail to take assignments seriously and demand opportunities for extra credit. Professional development for how best to communicate and work with today's traditional-age students can help prevent faculty frustration on matters beyond the scope of teaching their subject matter. As faculty members become more proficient in hearing and responding to student concerns, the number of student concerns that require the department chair's time and attention should decrease.

2

LEADING CURRICULUM REVISION

AS EXPERTS IN THE DISCIPLINE, faculty determine what students should learn. Faculty members typically take seriously their role responsibility for curriculum revision. However, changing conditions make it impractical, if not impossible, for faculty members to be the sole catalyst for curriculum revision. Today, curriculum revision requires knowledge of employment trends and student demand beyond what most faculty members possess. Making informed revisions to the curriculum requires an understanding of such external factors as employment opportunities for graduates, employer expectations for what graduates will know and be able to do, competing programs offered at other institutions, prospective student interest in the program, and educational standards imposed by state or federal agencies and regional or discipline-specific accrediting bodies. Consequently, informed curriculum revision requires more than discipline expertise and, on occasion, may warrant involvement of the administration in curriculum revision than is historically the custom.

The goal for this chapter is to help department chairs know how to effectively lead curriculum revision. A second goal of this chapter is to equip department chairs with leadership communication strategies for minimizing the destructive conflict and resistance to change that can hinder informed curriculum revision. The scenarios presented in this chapter focus on the need to lead curriculum revision in response to external conditions, including a formal request from the central administration. Leading curriculum revision in such instances can be especially difficult when faculty members, who view curriculum revision as the exclusive purview of the faculty, reframe the discussion from one of curriculum revision to one about faculty rights and responsibilities.

Defining the Task

Because curriculum revision has historically been a faculty responsibility, it is not surprising that some faculty members feel ownership over the courses they teach or an academic program they helped to develop. When campus enrollments are strong and growing, academic departments may be inclined to hire strong faculty and allow them to teach courses consistent with their research interest and expertise. To instead hire faculty to teach specific courses developed and implemented by faculty who have retired is sometimes viewed as being more vocational than is ideal for an institution of higher learning. It is not surprising that some faculty take umbrage when administrators, business leaders, alumni, or some accrediting body requests curriculum revision. When faculty members perceive externally initiated requests for curriculum revision as discounting faculty expertise or an inappropriate circumvention of faculty authority, these attitudes can get in the way of engaging in informed curriculum revision that benefits students and the department. Moreover, when this is the faculty's reaction to suggested curriculum revision, department chairs can find themselves managing contentious situations and resistance to change. Unless negative faculty reactions are managed effectively, the department conversation typically becomes one about roles and responsibilities and faculty rights, which does little to address the need for curriculum revision.

Experienced department chairs recognize that in a number of scenarios today it is appropriate, if not essential, for constituencies beyond the department to suggest the need for curriculum revision. Yet department chairs run the risk of losing leadership credibility with the faculty when championing externally initiated requests for curriculum revision. The department chair's challenge is to frame externally initiated requests for curriculum revision in such a way that the faculty recognize and embrace the merit of the request without becoming preoccupied with assessing the legitimacy of the request or sidetracked by a perceived need to defend faculty rights. The department chair becomes the interpreter of the motive and context for externally initiated requests to revise the curriculum.

At the same time, department chairs find themselves needing to remind the administration and other external sources of the need for faculty expertise in the discipline to inform curriculum revision. In doing so, department chairs run the risk of appearing unsupportive of requests for curriculum revision that are recognized by external sources to be essential to the viability of the department and institution. The department chair's challenge is to advance legitimate faculty concerns in a manner that allows external sources to recognize the merit of the concern without hearing it as a tactic to stall or derail curriculum revision perceived to be important to the viability of the institution.

In leading curriculum revision today, department chairs often find themselves very much in the middle between faculty and administrative interests. It is imperative that department chairs maintain a neutral but informed posture in brokering a better understanding between department faculty and the administration or any other external source. If this is not done effectively, department chairs will likely find that they lose leadership credibility with one or more constituencies.

Relevant Leadership Communication Strategies

Department chairs can use specific leadership communication strategies when leading curriculum revision that will minimize the potential for destructive conflict and facilitate change. The following leadership communication strategies will aid department chairs when leading curriculum revision.

Adapt Communication to the Constituency

When department chairs find themselves in the middle between two or more constituencies, it is important to understand the perspective of each constituency and to adapt their communication with each audience accordingly. This can be an onerous task for a department chair who keeps a frenetic pace managing an ever-escalating workload. However, taking time to implement this leadership communication strategy can save time in the long run because, if done effectively, it can spare the department chair the task of mending misunderstandings and reducing unnecessary defensiveness. To adapt communication to a particular constituency, department chairs must consider the issue from that constituent's perspective. A campus goal to increase enrollment, for example, can be an essential priority for the administration and a dreaded outcome for an overworked faculty. Understanding the perspective held by each constituency will enable the department chair to adapt his or her communication accordingly. For example, an overworked faculty will more quickly support an initiative to grow enrollment if they understand how the outcome might improve their situation. Similarly, the department chair will be better able to frame a request for curriculum revision in a way that minimizes faculty resistance if the chair understands that faculty will likely perceive the requested curriculum revision as unnecessarily increasing faculty workloads.

Clarify the Need for Curriculum Revision

As with any change initiative, department chairs can reduce resistance to curriculum revision by first helping others understand the need for revising the curriculum. Change takes work, and change is uncomfortable for many individuals. Consequently, few people will support change for the sake of change. Most individuals are skeptical of, if not out right opposed to, change initiatives unless they are persuaded of the need for change. Helping others understand the larger context and the need for change goes a long way toward melting resistance to change. By taking time to build consensus around the need for curriculum revision, department chairs change the discussion from *whether* we should we revise the curriculum to *how* we should revise the curriculum. When department chairs lead curriculum revision by starting the conversation with *what* needs to be done before engaging faculty in a discussion of *why* the department should take action, they will encounter greater resistance to changing the status quo. Similarly, when department chairs forward curriculum proposals to the administration without providing appropriate explanation regarding the rationale for the proposed changes, they invite a more critical examination of their department's curriculum proposal. This is especially important when the curriculum proposal requires an investment of new resources.

Bridge Disconnects

When individuals lack an understanding of the larger context, they inevitably view requests for change from their personal perspectives. To the extent that individuals do not share common experiences that shape their individual perspectives, they will hear and interpret requests and information differently. Department chairs must help to bridge the disconnects attributable to variations in individual experience and perspective to effectively lead curriculum revision. An initiative to add a common 100-level course requirement, for example, will be perceived differently by individual faculty. Some faculty may perceive the proposed requirement as enhancing the degree program, whereas other faculty may perceive it as unnecessarily directing instruction at the upper level. Little progress will be made in leading consideration of the proposed common course requirement until all involved in shaping the curriculum revision understand the various perspectives held by members of the department. Similarly, the administration may perceive a proposal to add a new academic program as an ill-timed request for expansion during tight fiscal constraints when the department's purpose for proposing the program is to grow enrollment and revenue for the institution. Department chairs leading curriculum revision must identify and then bridge such disconnects. Failure to do so will make the task of leading curriculum revision much more difficult and time-consuming.

To bridge existing disconnects that prompt resistance to change, department chairs must first understand how others perceive the situation and the proposed curriculum revision. It is through understanding the perspectives of others that department chairs will acquire the insight needed to frame the issue in a way that enables others to more objectively consider the proposed change. For example, if senior faculty members perceive the proposed curriculum revision as adding to the workload of faculty, it will not be helpful to champion the curriculum revision because it will grow enrollment. To bridge disconnects, department chairs must understand existing perspectives, correct faulty thinking, and respond directly to legitimate concerns.

Focus on Positive Outcomes

A focus on positive outcomes will help to bridge disconnects and keep everyone involved on the same page. Positive outcomes are the tangible by-products of change. When leading curriculum revision, department chairs must clarify both the need for change and the anticipated positive outcomes from implementing the proposed change. Since few individuals embrace change for the sake of change, clarifying the anticipated positive outcome can motivate others to consider the proposed curriculum revision. Moreover, the anticipated positive outcomes become the standard against which the effectiveness of the proposed change can be measured. Consider a proposal to add an internship requirement for all students because graduates will be more marketable. One benefit of the proposed curriculum revision is the preparation of students who are better able to secure employment upon graduation, and monitoring the ability of graduates to secure employment upon graduation will be one measure of the effectiveness of this curriculum revision. When faculty are confident that the department chair will use the anticipated positive outcomes to assess the intended effectiveness of a curriculum revision, they will be more willing to consider curriculum revision.

Putting Theory into Practice

These leadership communication strategies may seem obvious to seasoned department chairs, who believe they possess a solid understanding of the faculty personalities within the department. Department chairs, however, can enhance their effectiveness in leading curriculum revision by intentionally employing these strategies. Place yourself in the role of the department chair as you read Case 2.1.

Case 2.1: Why Would We Do That?

Pat O'Malley has served as chair of the English department for 15 years and, for the most part, has been effective in motivating a group of strong-willed individuals to work together in the department's best interests. The faculty have responded constructively to a myriad of changing conditions and externally imposed mandates, including the assessment of student learning and the need to become more actively involved in the recruitment and retention of students. The faculty accepted the extra work associated with recruiting students. They developed a rotation scheme to ensure that there is some English faculty representation at all campus events aimed at recruiting new students, and most of the English faculty members welcome prospective students to sit in on the classes they teach. Pat O'Malley is also proud of the extra effort expended by English faculty to identify and assist students who are struggling in English courses. Without doubt, English faculty members have been very responsive to the institution's goal to recruit and retain greater numbers of students. For this reason, the English department chair expects the faculty, after some grumbling, to get behind the newest request from central administration that is believed to enhance student recruitment.

Declining enrollment at the university continues to be a pressing concern. Pat O'Malley understands the concern and worries about the significant decline in the number of students majoring and minoring in English. Many of the upper-level courses in English are undersubscribed. Consequently, the courses offered for students majoring or minoring in English are now offered less frequently. Teaching loads in English, however, remain stable because English faculty members staff courses that service the core curriculum and other majors. In fact, all full-time English faculty members teach more service than upper-level courses in the major.

Staff members in the admissions office report that prospective students and their parents seek a college education that will lead seamlessly to gainful employment in students academic major, and the central administration is persuaded that student recruitment and retention would be enhanced if faculty in every academic major would clearly articulate the specific and tangible employment opportunities that derive from study in the major. Subsequently, the central administration asked all academic departments to demonstrate and document how study in the major leads to gainful employment within the discipline. The employment outcomes documented by each academic department are to be used by staff in the admissions office to persuade prospective students of the long-term benefit of enrolling in their preferred majors at the university. Further, the central administration asked that the curriculum offered in each major be more explicitly linked to employment opportunities following graduation to enhance the retention of employment-focused students.

Even though Pat O'Malley recognizes that this task may be easier for disciplines like computer science or business, Pat wholeheartedly believes that the study of English prepares a student well for gainful employment. Pat is confident that the English faculty members agree with him but anticipates that a few of the more senior faculty will have an issue with being asked to demonstrate and document the value of studying English. English faculty members perceive the study of English as the heart of the core curriculum, especially at an institution that is committed to the value of a liberal arts education. Pat also expects that some of the English faculty members will hear the request to more tightly align the curriculum with employment opportunities as a request to dumb down or micromanage the curriculum. Nonetheless, Pat believes the English faculty will comply with this request because they understand the importance of enhancing student recruitment and retention at the university. Pat recognizes that the central administration's request has merit even though it may be perceived by a few to be micromanaging curriculum which is traditionally the purview of faculty. Pat has talked with students who transferred out of English to pursue an academic major that their parents believe holds more promise for employment, and expects that others in the department have had similar conversations.

Breaking the News

Department chair: I want to begin our meeting by thanking everyone for taking seriously our role in recruiting prospective students. The English department is well represented at every recruitment event hosted on campus. In addition, English faculty have opened their classes to prospective students. We have effectively and responsibly done everything asked of us. I wish the outcome were better. Despite all efforts, the institution did not reach its enrollment goal for the entering fall class. Fortunately, our retention of students has improved slightly. Nonetheless, the central administration is anxious to enhance efforts to recruit and retain students."

Suzanne: What else can be done?

Mike: Maybe the administration is going to finally bite the bullet and advertise more. I'm tired of seeing Web and TV ads during prime time for competing institutions."

Kay: You are on to something. I know the faculty cannot do any more than we are already doing.

Department chair: Unfortunately, advertising costs money, and when enrollment is down revenue is needed to cover existing operating expenses.

Suzanne: So what's the silver bullet the administration plans to use?

Department chair: I don't know if anyone believes there is a single silver bullet, but everyone agrees that growing enrollment is the institution's top priority.

John: That may be an understatement. I know of other institutions that found it necessary to eliminate faculty and staff positions following a decline in enrollment.

Department chair: That is a worry.

Marvin: At least we can take comfort in being in one of the core disciplines. There will always be an English department.

June: That's right. English *is* the essential discipline, the cornerstone of all the humanities.

Suzanne: Without English, there is no college education or bachelor's degree.

Department chair: Sadly, the number of students majoring or minoring in English continues to decline. In fact, I doubt that the current number of majors and minors is sufficient to support our current course schedule in which every upper-level course is offered once a year.

June: Wait a minute. Are you saying that some of our upper-level courses may not be offered every year?

Department chair: That is precisely what I am saying.

Lisa: Wow! I didn't realize our enrollment declined that much. It seems as if I am still teaching a lot of students.

Department chair: Actually, you are teaching a lot of students because enrollment in the core and service courses remains fairly healthy, but this, too, could decline if the university is unable to grow total enrollment.

Mike: Okay, you have our attention. What's the central administration's new idea?

Department chair: You are all aware that the admissions staff inform recruitment efforts with feedback obtained from both prospective students who enroll at the university and those who elect to enroll elsewhere.

Mike: This seems backward to me. Shouldn't we be telling prospective students what college is about rather than trying to make college into what they think it should be?

Department chair: You have a point, but we need to get prospective students to enroll to have an opportunity to educate them. The admissions staff report that prospective students are preoccupied with getting a college education that leads to gainful employment. In other words, prospective students select the institution that they believe can best help them move from graduation to gainful employment in the discipline."

Suzanne: It sounds like they expect us to promise them jobs.

Department chair: Obviously, we cannot promise them jobs. However, the central administration believes that faculty can help prospective students know the type of employment opportunities they can get after graduation. Consequently, the central administration is asking every academic department to demonstrate and document how study in the major leads to gainful employment within the discipline. This information will be used by staff in admissions in recruiting prospective students.

Mike: You've got to be kidding. This sounds like a request one would make of instructors at a technical school rather than at an institution committed to the importance of a liberal arts education. Are we becoming a vocational school? What happened to helping students learn how to think critically and write well? Isn't our job to educate students and help them to cultivate their individual abilities?

Suzanne: I agree. There is a vast difference between educating students and training a young person to assume a particular job. I cannot imagine parents would want to pay our tuition for a college education when their student is receiving only vocational training.

Department chair: I understand the point you're making. At the same time, I have talked with students and parents who are very concerned that an expensive college education may not lead to gainful employment. Today's prospective students are more aware of the unemployment rate than they are of the intrinsic value of a liberal arts education.

June: Isn't it the job of admissions staff to educate prospective students and their parents about the value of a college education? It seems to me that this request would have us competing with vocational schools, and that seems unwise, if not dangerous.

Marvin: I agree. The regional community college recruits students by telling them what job they can get in 2 years. Why would we want to sound like the regional community college?

Department chair: That may be reading more into the request than is intended. Surely, in advising current students, we have all suggested a range of employment possibilities. All we are being asked to do is list these options as possible employment outcomes so prospective students can begin to imagine how majoring in English at this university will lead to employment.

Marvin: I'm not sure about that. Repeat the precise language used by the central administration. Didn't you say we were being asked to demonstrate and document how study in the major leads to gainful employment within the discipline? What would that look like? It's sounds like the administration seeks more than a general list of possible employment outcomes.

Department chair: To be honest, I haven't had much time to think about how we might demonstrate and document the employment opportunities for students majoring in English. We might start by listing the jobs that are graduates hold.

Mike: I don't like that idea. The best thing about the study of English is that it prepares students for an infinite number of job opportunities. We teach critical thinking and writing, skills that make our graduates qualified for countless positions. I am not willing to limit employment opportunities to a finite list of job titles such as editor, writer, or journalist.

Department chair: I'm not sure we need to limit the list, but we may learn something by looking at a list of the occupations currently held by our graduates.

June: I would be curious to see a list of positions held by our graduates.
[Most in attendance indicated their agreement with June.]

Department chair: With your permission, I will take the first pass at drafting what I believe would be helpful to the admissions staff in helping prospective students know what employment opportunities derive from the study of English.

Mike: To be clear, whatever you draft will be reviewed with us before it is shared with anyone outside the department.

Department chair: Absolutely, I will want your careful review of any document that is to be shared beyond the department.

Let's Analyze the Case

The department chair anticipates that a few faculty members will grumble about the central administration's newest mandate but will comply as they have with previous requests to enhance student recruitment and retention. However, the department chair experiences more faculty resistance to the first part of the central administration's request during the meeting than was anticipated. No mention is made of the department chair doing spadework before the meeting, and the meeting discussion suggests that nothing was done to prepare the faculty for learning of the central administration's request. There is little evidence that the department chair uses knowledge of the faculty, the institution, and the issue to inform the management of the meeting.

The department chair does not become defensive and quickly acknowledges when a faculty member raises a valid concern. However, the department chair fails to facilitate a productive discussion of the request and concerns the faculty have about it. Any discussion about how the English department should respond to the central administration's request is stifled by a few vocal faculty members, who raise concerns that the department chair acknowledges have merit. Some faculty concerns are listed but are never discussed substantively. Consequently, the meeting purpose is never realized, and the department chair never informs the faculty of the second part of the central administration's request.

The resistance quiets when the department chair offers to draft the department's response to the central administration's request. Although this seems to end the debate, the department chair did not succeed in helping the faculty understand of the central administration's request or reach consensus regarding the department's response to the request. Some faculty members voice concerns, but there is no evidence to suggest that these are the only faculty concerns. In the event that they are deemed valid, the department chair has responsibility to air them within the department and possibly share them with the central administration. The department chair must facilitate an honest discussion to help the English faculty assess the merit of each.

By the close of the meeting, the English faculty members are aware of the first part of the central administration's request and concerns raised by a few faculty members. The chair makes no attempt to bridge the disconnect between what the central administration hopes to achieve through the request and the perspectives held by faculty members voicing concerns. There is no consideration of possible positive outcomes.

The department chair's offer to draft the department's response frees the faculty from further thought about the central administration's request. The meeting ends without faculty members understanding the value in the request or taking ownership for the department's reply. Although not stated explicitly in the scenario, the English faculty have reason to conclude that the concerns raised outweigh any value obtained in complying with the central administration's request.

It's Your Turn

Assume the role of department chair in this case and think through how you would have handled the meeting.

1. What, if anything, would you do in advance of the meeting to minimize the negative faculty reaction to the central administration's request? Would you have done anything prior to the meeting to help manage the anticipated reaction from a few of the more senior faculty members, and, if so, what would you do?

2. Is there anything you would have done before the meeting to prepare for the discussion? For example, would you learn how other departments in the humanities plan to approach the request? Would you share your conversation with students who have left the program to pursue other majors that they believe offer greater promise of employment after graduation? Would you share available summary information about the positions currently held by graduates?

3. What would be your goal for the meeting? How would you structure the meeting to achieve your goal?

4. How would you present the central administration's request? How might you engage the faculty in considering the substance of the issue before it is presented as a request or mandate from the central administration?

5. Review the meeting discussion and determine when you would have responded differently from the chair in the scenario. Be specific in scripting what you say and why. Based on comments made by faculty during the meeting, anticipate how Mike, Suzanne, June, and Marvin might respond to your comments.

Please Consider

The department chair offers to draft a document that will comply with the central administration's request. Although offering to do so quiets the immediate faculty resistance, it prevents the faculty from assuming ownership of the department's response. Instead, the faculty members remain passive, third-person observers who have virtually no commitment to the initiative. This course of action may be the path of least resistance in the short term, but it can prove costly on the long term if faculty support of subsequent efforts to enhance student recruitment and retention is needed. Failure to involve the faculty in shaping the department's response to the central administration's request prevents faculty from understanding the larger context and purpose for the request. It also precludes their understanding all how the information to be gathered might benefit the department.

The department chair closes the meeting without presenting the second part of the central administration's request that every department review and revise, as necessary, the curriculum to be more explicitly linked to employment opportunities following graduation. Assuming responsibility for drafting the department's response to the first request does not help manage faculty reaction to the second part of the central administration's request. The department chair acknowledges that concerns articulated by faculty during the meeting are valid. Until these concerns are addressed, the faculty can be expected to hold the same concerns when responding to the second part of the central administration's request is presented. The department chair gains little by postponing discussion of faculty concerns because the chair needs faculty to assume an active role in shaping the department's response to the requested curriculum revision.

Let's Recap

Take a moment to review your approach to handling the meeting in Case 2.1. Does your approach stem from an analysis of the faculty? How would you adapt your communication in talking with the department faculty? What disconnects did you note in Case 2.1, and what would you say to help bridge them? One significant disconnect is faculty perception of the merit of the central administration's request. Faculty perceive the request as more work for the faculty without tangible benefit for the English department. The central administration, however, perceives the request as a logical next step in the institution's ongoing effort to enhance student recruitment and retention. What use would you make of anticipated positive outcomes? Would you offer what you perceive to be the anticipated positive outcomes, or would you parrot the central administration's view? Consider the faculty reaction to either approach.

Putting Theory into Practice

Once you have thought through how you would present the second part of the central administration's request to the department, you are ready to read Case 2.2. Pay particular attention to the department chair's management of the meeting, and note every instance when you would act differently.

Case 2.2: No Way!

Pat O'Malley satisfies her commitment to draft the department's response to the central administration's request that the English department demonstrate and document how study in the major leads to gainful employment within the discipline. The result of Pat's work is a three-page summary of current positions held by graduates. Each entry lists the position held, the year graduated, and skills each graduate learned from studying English to prepare him or her for the position. To protect graduates' identities, each is assigned a code, and position titles are given without company affiliations. The following few entries illustrate the type of information provided in the document.

Graduate	Year graduated	Current position	Relevant skills
001	2000	Editor	Writing and grammar
002	2008	Unknown	Cannot be determined
003	2010	Administrative assistant	Writing and critical thinking
004	2010	Copywriter	Writing and grammar

Pat hopes her work will help to engage the faculty in crafting the department's response to the central administration. Pat is painfully aware that she needs the English faculty to embrace the request to supply admissions staff with information that will help them discuss the merit of pursuing an English degree at the university. If the English faculty cannot understand the value in helping prospective students understand the benefits of studying English, Pat has little hope of persuading the faculty to comply with the second part of the central administration's request that the curriculum offered in each major be more explicitly linked to employment opportunities following graduation. Pat understands that the faculty are overworked and are growing weary of the central administration's requests that they do more to enhance student recruitment and retention. Nonetheless, Pat believes that the faculty recognize the importance of growing enrollment at the university. Pat hopes that having spared faculty some of the initial work will help melt the resistance expressed at the previous meeting.

The Meeting

Department chair: Let's get started. I know everyone's time is tight, and we need to reach closure on some important matters. First, I hope you had a chance to review the summary table I drafted. You will recall that the central administration asked every academic department to demonstrate and document how study in the major leads to gainful employment within the discipline. The summary provides the graduation year, current position title, and relevant skill set for all English graduates in the past 10 years. Unfortunately, we do not have this information for roughly 35% of the English graduates, so these entries show the position title as unknown.

Mike: Thanks for compiling the summary, Pat. It looks great to me.

Department chair: Are you all comfortable that this summary adequately demonstrates how the study of English leads to gainful employment? Is there more we might add to illustrate the value of earning a degree in English?

Mike: It's as good as anything I could produce.

Suzanne: It would be better if we had information on all of our graduates. Do we know how to reach them?

Marvin: I have received email updates from a few of the students coded as unknown, and I can share what I know about them with Pat.

Department chair: That would be great. How about the rest of you? Do you have current employment information on any of the students coded as unknown? If so, will you send that information to me in the next few days?

[Most nodded to indicate that they are agreeable to supplying information they have on the department's graduates.]

Department chair: Great. It is important that the summary table be as complete as possible before we submit it to the central administration. What else might we add to illustrate the value of earning a degree in English?

Marvin: This does it for me.

Mike: Thanks again, Pat, for handling this newest mandate from the central administration.

Department chair: I'm glad to handle whatever I can, but believe we will all need to contribute to part B of the central administration's request.

Mike: Part B? What is part B?

Marvin: Here we go again. The other shoe is about to fall.

Department chair: The central administration is asking that the curriculum offered in each major be more explicitly linked to employment opportunities following graduation to enhance the retention of employment-focused students.

Marvin: You've got to be kidding! First, they ask us to produce job titles that our graduates can hold, which could actually limit the thinking of prospective students about the value of pursuing a major in English. Now they want us to dumb down the curriculum so English graduates are prepared to secure only a finite number of labeled positions.

Department chair: No one is asking us to dumb down the curriculum.

Mike: I have to agree with Marvin. These requests from central administration have us moving in the wrong direction. Instead of asking us to make the curriculum more vocational, the administration should be asking admissions staff to educate prospective students on the value of a liberal arts education and how it will prepare them for infinite employment opportunities.

Department chair: The central administration agrees with you regarding the value of a liberal arts education. This is a hard sell to prospective students and their parents who view a college education as a means to gainful employment.

Marvin: Are they even trying to sell it? I think we need to push back on this one.

Mike: I agree. We have done everything asked of us, and student recruitment and retention remain a serious concern at this institution. It is time to educate the central administration and admissions staff on what *they* should be doing to enhance student recruitment and retention.

June: Marvin and Mike have a good point. We all attend recruitment events, and I don't recall hearing any of the speakers delineate the long-term value of a liberal arts education to an individual's personal and professional life.

Department chair: Please remember that we attend only one session of those day-long recruitment events.

Suzanne: Yes, but if the central administration is wrong in asking us to mimic a vocational school, it could be very costly to this department and institution.

Department chair: I understand the point you are making, but I believe we cannot ignore this request.

At this point in the meeting, Pat's head is swimming. The resistance to the second part of the central administration's request is significantly greater than anticipated. She understands full well the point that her faculty colleagues are making. At the same time, she is charged by the central administration with compiling information and leading curriculum revision deemed by the campus leadership as important to the institution's goal to enhance student recruitment and retention. Pat is uncertain as to how to proceed so she decides to truncate the discussion and close the meeting.

Department chair: Please know that I understand the point you are making. It's clear that we will not be able to come to closure in the time we have remaining. I suggest we all give this important matter more thought and plan to continue our discussion at our next meeting.

Let's Analyze the Case

The faculty are very comfortable having the summary prepared by the department chair serve as the English department's response to the central administration's request that they demonstrate and document how study in the major leads to gainful employment within the discipline. Faculty are willing to provide information they have on individual graduates to help the department chair fill in information for some of the students currently coded as unknown. However, the faculty show no interest in spending more time on the request or in considering what other information might be provided to illustrate the value earning a degree in English. At two different points in the meeting, the department chair explicitly asks the faculty if other information might be added. The chair offers no examples of what might be included, and the invitation to expand on the draft summary falls on deaf ears. The faculty are comfortable having the department chair's summary serve as the English department's response. Case 2.2 illustrates how difficult it can be to convert bystanders into actively engaged contributors.

The chair is caught off guard by the negative reaction to the second part of the central administration's request. Previously, the English faculty members accepted responsibility for requests intended to enhance student recruitment and retention. This time, however, they question the merit and desirability of the request. In particular, the English faculty believe that complying with the request could prove harmful to the department. The request to revise the curriculum such that it is more explicitly linked to employment opportunities following graduation is offensive to faculty who are committed to the value of a liberal arts education. The department chair offers little context when presenting of the central administration's request, which forces the faculty to view the request from their own perspectives. Because they perceive the study of English as enhancing an individual's personal and professional life in infinite ways, they perceive a request to link the study of English to specific occupations as limiting both the employment possibilities and benefits of pursuing a major in English. The department chair listens patiently to faculty members vent their concerns about the central administration's request. Before faculty can reach consensus about the suggestion that the department push back rather than comply with part B of the central administration's request, the department chair brings the meeting to a close. This buys some time but does nothing to challenge the faculty's thinking about the central administration's request. Again, the department chair has done little to help clarify the need for the requested curriculum revision, bridge the disconnect between the central administration's intended purpose and the faculty members' concerns, and focus faculty attention on anticipated positive outcomes.

It's Your Turn

Assume the role of the department chair, and consider how you would lead the meeting in Case 2.2.

1. Would you be content with the summary document prepared by the department chair? If not, what would you add to the document? Would it be important to you that the faculty assume a more active role in drafting the department's reply to part A of the central administration's request? If yes, how would you go about enlisting faculty involvement?

2. What, if anything, would you do prior to the meeting to have the faculty more receptive to part B of the central administration's request? Would you preview the issue with individual faculty members? If yes, how would you broach the issue with faculty members? How might you uncovered faculty concerns prior to the meeting? What information or testimony would you gather to aid in

responding to the anticipated objections? If so, how might you frame and communicate the merit of the central administration's request to the faculty? To what extent would you defend the central administration's position?

3. In Case 2.2, we learn that department chair Pat O'Malley is a woman. Based on the information and dialogue presented in Cases 2.1 and 2.2, do you believe the department chair's gender influences the situation described? If yes, how?

4. Review the dialogue in Case 2.2, and substitute your own words for the department chair's remarks. How would you were approach alter the outcome?

Please Consider

Despite a history of effective chair leadership with the English faculty, Pat O'Malley is struggling to secure faculty support for the central administration's request to revise the curriculum in a way that is responsive to the employment-focused shopping mentality of prospective students. She took for granted her existing relationship with the faculty and their previous willingness to get behind initiatives that enhance student recruitment and retention. Whenever leading change it is important to take time to view the change initiative from the perspective of others. Department chairs are well served to consider how the change will affect others because this will impact their perception of the change initiative. The English faculty in this case do not perceive the central administration's request as helpful to student recruitment. Indeed, one faculty concern is that linking the study of English to specific jobs reduces the English degree to something that would be similar to vocational study rather than a liberal arts education. Similarly, the English faculty in Case 2.2 view the request to revise the curriculum such that it links more tightly with employment opportunities as inappropriate for a liberal arts education.

Understanding the perception of others helps department chairs to anticipate the sources and basis for resisting change. For example, knowing that the faculty are likely to perceive the request as placing the study of English on par with vocational programs enables the department chair to consider credible responses to the concern in advance of the meeting. By considering the issue from the perspective of the faculty, the department chair could assemble testimony and documentation that addresses specific concerns. Absent a response, the department chair allows a faculty concern to stand as a legitimate basis for pushing back on the central administration's request. In leading change, the department chair must address all substantive concerns raised regarding the change initiative. Until the faculty believe that their concerns have been heard, understood, and addressed, their resistance to change will not melt.

This does not mean that the department chair should argue against all concerns raised. To preserve one's leadership credibility, the department chair must understand and appropriately weigh all substantive concerns about the change initiative. Legitimate concerns should be investigated honestly and openly. In doing so, department chairs have an opportunity to persuade others that they are working to protect the best interests of the department. Should those opposing change raise a valid concern, department chairs are well served to acknowledge the validity of the concern. Rather than attempting to refute legitimate concerns, department chairs should work with others involved on ways to limit the anticipated negative consequences of the proposed change. If, after thorough consideration, the department concludes that the requested curriculum revision would threaten future enrollment in English should prospective students conclude that the 4-year English degree at the university is comparable to what can be earned in 2 years at the regional community college, this conclusion should help shape the English department's response to the central administration's request. This might be done by adding text to the catalog copy that makes clear the added value of earning a 4-year degree in English. Or the English faculty might request time with the admissions staff to help them understand how best to explain the added value of earning a 4-year degree in English at the university to prospective students and their parents.

Putting Theory into Practice

The department chair works hard to gather information before the next department meeting. In Case 2.3, the department chair takes a more proactive approach to leading the curriculum revision requested by the central administration. As you read Case 2.3, note instances when you, as department chair of this English department, would speak or behave differently.

Case 2.3, Take Two: A Proactive Approach

Before the next meeting, Pat O'Malley gathers information. She talks with admissions staff to learn more precisely what they say when persuading prospective students of the value of pursuing a liberal arts education. She gathers all printed and online references to the study of English at the institution, including the narrative found in promotional materials, the college catalog, and advising documents. Pat talks with other department chairs on campus to learn how they plan to respond to the central administration's request. She writes to English department chairs at comparable institutions to inquire of their experience and solicit ideas that might be considered by her department faculty. Whenever possible, she brainstorms with individual faculty members about the central administration's request and the English department's options.

All of this work took an enormous amount of time. Fortunately, Pat senses that the initial, irate reaction to the central administration's request has softened. Every informal conversation with a faculty member helps to evidence that the department chair heard the faculty's concerns and is genuinely assessing the advisability of the central administration's request. Although Pat's preparation for the next meeting was time-consuming, it did much to relieve her stress and pave the way for a constructive discussion.

The Meeting

Department chair: I hope everyone has had an opportunity to think seriously about the central administration's request that the curriculum for every academic major be more explicitly linked to employment opportunities following graduation. I also hope we can discuss how best to increase enrollment in English study without getting sidetracked by what we wish the central administration would or would not do.

Mike: I have given this a lot of thought, and I continue to believe that the administration is asking us to dumb down our curriculum.

Department chair: Please put aside the request made by the administration and focus on what we can do to recruit more English majors and minors.

Mike: I'm happy to dismiss the central administration's request.

Marvin: Yeah, if we can dismiss their request, we don't need to waste another minute talking or thinking about curriculum revision.

Department chair: Perhaps one benefit of the central administration's request is that it started us thinking about something that I am persuaded is important. We know full well the lifelong value of studying English, whereas the typical high school graduate and their parents may not. What can we do to help prospective students recognize and appreciate what they can gain through coursework for a 4-year degree in English?

Mike: But is that our job?

Department chair: Who is more knowledgeable than us about the value of our discipline?

Marvin: True, but we should not have to defend the value of our discipline. It should be obvious.

Department chair: I've heard many of you lament that incoming students lack the level intellectual and educational abilities evident in previous generations of students. Do you believe it wise to rely on the typical 18-year-old's understanding of the value of our discipline?

Marvin: Probably not, but it should be their course work and not a marketing campaign that educates them.

Department chair: I agree, but we need to get them enrolled to educate them.

Marvin: No argument there, but it simply is not possible to convey to prospective students what our graduates took 4 or more years to understand.

Mike: Wait a minute. I thought the request was to revise the curriculum so it links to jobs?

Department chair: I believe it's all the same issue. If there are features to our curriculum that will improve employment opportunities for our graduates, it will help to persuade students to enroll in the English program at this institution.

Mike: What happened to using the strength of the faculty to recruit students?

Department chair: A quality faculty that is committed to student learning will always help to recruit bright students. Perhaps we should look at this curriculum revision as a vehicle for bragging about how our faculty teach and prepare students for infinite employment opportunities.

Suzanne: I like that.

June: Me, too.

Department chair: I talked with English department chairs who I thought may be facing a similar issue at a few other institutions. One program has had some success by incorporating experiential learning components in the upper-level courses for majors. The experiential learning modules include such things as internships in campus offices and area businesses. For example, an English major might spend a semester shadowing the editor of at a publishing company. The idea is to make the experiential learning opportunity appropriate for the individual student's academic preparation and professional interests. The English major who is interested in politics, for example, might do an internship working on a political campaign, whereas the English major planning to teach after graduate school might do an internship serving as a course assistant to one of us.

Suzanne: That sounds ideal, but who arranges for the internships?

Department chair: The internships could come about in a variety of ways. Some would derive from faculty contacts on and off campus. Or a student might propose an internship experience that we would find acceptable. I learned that area businesses sometimes call an institution to seek students with a particular training. One department chair I talked to said his department had six students serving in internships at public relations agencies. He volunteered that he would not have considered public relations as a career path for English graduates before a public relation agency approached him to inquire if the department knew of upperclassmen with strong critical thinking and writing skills who might wish to work at the agency in exchange for a nominal wage and professional experience.

Mike: It seems like a lot of work. We would be essentially running our own employment agency to place every student in an internship.

Department chair: I would not propose that we begin by promising internships to all majors. Instead, the internship experience might be something that a student earns with a minimum GPA or other criteria. In other words, these experiential learning opportunities would be reserved for our very best students.

June: Would that satisfy the central administration?

Department chair: First of all, internships are only one type of experiential learning opportunity and we may decide to add others. But even the addition of a few professional internship experiences would enable the admissions staff to talk about how our curriculum prepares students for employment through professional internships that are available to qualified students.

Suzanne: What are some other types of experiential learning opportunities?

Department chair: The possibilities are infinite, and I would encourage all of you to talk with colleagues at other institutions about what they are doing. For the English majors and minors who aspire to be writers, we might institute a writing competition or a literary publication that would provide students with the opportunity to enhance their credentials prior to graduation. We could require students enrolled in the 400-level writing courses to submit one piece for publication. The process of receiving and digesting an outside review on one's writing can be very informative, and it is a professional experience that could set our creative writing curriculum apart from the English curriculums offered at other institutions.

June: That's exciting, but I am overwhelmed by the work involved.

Department chair: Fortunately, the central administration recognizes that sound curriculum review and revision take time. I suggest that we begin by brainstorming the options that make sense for this department. Over the course of the next month, let's meet as two groups: one focused on literature, and the other focused on creative and technical writing. The task before both groups is to brainstorm possible experiential learning opportunities. I will meet with both groups and keep notes of your ideas. One month from today we will meet to hear and consider the best ideas from both groups. Does this sound like a reasonable way to proceed?

Sensing general agreement from the faculty, the department chair brings the meeting to a close.

Let's Analyze the Case

In Case 2.3, the department chair takes a proactive approach in addressing faculty concerns. The central administration's request to revise the curriculum is reframed to an issue that warrants department consideration. This helps to focus the conversation on what, if any, curriculum revision would make most sense for the English department at this university. Notice how the department chair begins the meeting by asking faculty to focus the discussion on what the department might do to increase enrollment in English study. By doing this, the department chair reframes the issue into one that the faculty recognize as salient. This steers the conversation away from faculty rights versus administrative prerogative. The department chair goes one step further by stating explicitly that she does not wish the conversation to be sidetracked by discussing what the central administration should or should not do. By establishing the parameters for discussion at the beginning of the meeting, the department chair will be better able to guide the discussion toward a constructive outcome. The department chair uses her knowledge that the English faculty perceive themselves as the best possible experts on the English discipline to frame the issue in a way that persuades the faculty to consider revising the curriculum.

In Case 2.3, the department chair responds to faculty concerns. Notice how this helps to move the conversation forward. When a faculty member attempts to dismiss the issue by contending that it is not the job of English faculty to help prospective students understand the value in studying English, the department chair emphasizes the expertise of the English faculty by asking who else would be better suited to make the case. Similarly, when a faculty member attempts to reject consideration of adding internships by pointing out how much work would be involved, the department chair responds by pointing out that the initiative could be phased in overtime. With each faculty concern raised, the department chair demonstrates that she has heard the concern and offers a response that addresses the specific concern raised. This proactive approach helps to keep the conversation on topic and helps faculty perceive the task as more manageable. Moreover, the approach helps to melt resistance to revising the curriculum. By the close of the meeting, there appears to be the general consensus that the English faculty should seriously consider how they might revise the curriculum to enhance student enrollment in English study. One by-product of the initiative will be a curriculum that more clearly links to employment opportunities following graduation.

It's Your Turn

Consider how the department chair's approach to the meeting compares with how you would manage this situation.

1. Is there other preparation you would do before the meeting? If so, what would you do and why? What, if any, preparation done by the department chair do you consider unnecessary and why?

2. Review the department chair's management of the meeting, and edit her remarks where your approach would differ from the one used in Case 2.3.

3. Consider whether the department chair's goal for the meeting is appropriate. Would you have the same goal? If not, what would your goal be? Please script how you envision achieving your goal.

Please Consider

The department chair in Case 2.3 very intentionally asks the faculty to consider a curriculum revision that has value to the English department. Typically, faculty are more willing to work on initiatives that benefit the department than requests or mandates from the central administration that may be viewed as unnecessary bureaucratic requests that absorb scarce faculty time and department resources. In this scenario, the department chair perceives some merit in the central administration's request.

The department chair's challenge is to lead a curriculum revision that benefits the English department and also supports the central administration's goal to enhance student recruitment and retention. Even though the department chair reframes the issue for the English faculty, the product will enable the department chair to comply with the central administration's request that every academic major revise its curriculum to be more explicitly linked to employment opportunities following graduation. In reframing the formal request in a way that captures faculty interest and support, the department chair bridges the existing disconnect between administration and faculty perspectives. This strategy can be very helpful when leading change. However, it is impossible to successfully employ this strategy without analyzing the audience and using language that clarifies the need for change and anticipated positive outcomes. The positive outcomes often encompass more then the curriculum revision. For example, in this scenario, one positive outcome is that the best experts on the value of English study will drive curriculum revision.

Putting Theory into Practice

Case 2.4 presents a very different scenario involving curriculum revision. In this situation the department chair needs to bridle unrealistic enthusiasm for developing a new program that is not feasible in light of current conditions and fiscal constraints. As you read, give some thought to how you manage the situation.

Case 2.4: Build It and They Will Come

Four months later, Pat O'Malley is again pleased with the work being done by the English faculty to revise the curriculum. Faculty members now embrace curriculum revision as a way to make students majoring or minoring in English more competitive in the job market. They have made great progress in identifying professional internship placements for students. Faculty efforts are buoyed by the positive student response to the availability of professional internships. In addition, the department received support from the central administration to launch a literary publication that will invite articles from undergraduate students nationally. The publication is expected to heighten visibility of the master's program in creative writing and give bright undergraduate students an opportunity to publish. There is a lot of positive energy around the new initiatives, and everyone is hopeful that curriculum revision will increase enrollment in English.

A New Program Idea

The heightened energy for curriculum revision spawned an idea for a new program. Convinced that the study of English is essential for all students, a few faculty members took the initiative to draft a proposal for a new writing specialist minor. As proposed, the new 18-credit minor requires students to take a core of 12 credits that encompass courses in advanced writing composition, technical writing for the professional, writing to communicate, and understanding proper citation and plagiarism. After completing the core, students can elect two courses from the following topics: writing for the health professional; writing for the legal professional; writing for the business professional; writing for the nonprofit sector; grant writing; and personal professional writing.

Pat is surprised to have faculty members develop and champion a proposal that, a few months ago, they would have resisted as being too vocational. Pat appreciates the earnest enthusiasm that faculty now evidence for curriculum revision. They have bought into the importance of helping students transition to gainful employment after graduation. This is admirable, and Pat does not wish to dampen their newfound enthusiasm.

The Problem

If approved, the new minor would require the addition of eight new courses in the English department. Beyond the work to develop these courses, it would take the addition of at least one new faculty to incorporate the staffing of the new courses in department's curriculum, and fiscal constraints at the university make it highly unlikely that the central administration would consider a request to add a full-time faculty position in English in support of a new minor. To add the minor with existing faculty would further erode the department's offering of existing upper-level courses for English majors and minors. Pat is not certain how to raise these concerns with the faculty without dampening their enthusiasm for curriculum revision.

Pat appreciates the faculty work to develop the proposed minor. However, she is not certain that there would be sufficient demand for the minor. On one occasion, Pat gently raised the issue of prospective demand for such a minor with a few faculty members. She learned that faculty members are persuaded that the proposed minor would be hugely popular with undergraduates who are anxious to enhance their marketability in the labor force. When Pat points out that majors in other disciplines such as business, health, and prelaw already include coursework that sounds similar to the courses in the proposed minor, the English faculty dismiss the concern adding that other departments probably took a stab at teaching these subjects only because the courses were not already offered by the English department. Further, the English faculty believe that when the proposed courses and minor are added, other departments will quickly drop their courses and send their students to the English department. The English faculty, however, have not discussed their plan with other departments, so it is uncertain as to how other departments might respond to the proposed minor.

The Department Chair's Challenge

Pat must help the English faculty investigate the feasibility of the proposed minor without dampening their enthusiasm for curriculum revision or weakening their commitment to help students transition successfully into gainful employment after graduation. Pat considers the English faculty belief in a "build it, and they will come" perspective to be risky. Pat is convinced that this is not a sound basis from which to develop new academic programs. Still, she is not certain how to get the faculty to take a more realistic approach to program development.

Let's Analyze the Case

The English faculty are committed to revising the curriculum in ways that help students transition to gainful employment after graduation. This is admirable, and it is understandable that the department chair would not wish to dampen the enthusiasm or energy of faculty. It is, after all, important that faculty remain forward thinking and committed to a curriculum revision that serves the ever-changing learning needs of students. The proposal for a new minor, however, does not incorporate the fiscal realities faced by the department and university.

When leading change, it is important to make certain that everyone understands the context in which change will take place. Department chairs can do much to prevent and bridge existing disconnects between the faculty and the administration by keeping faculty informed of the larger context. For example, the better faculty members understand the fiscal constraints of the institution, the less likely they are to initiate proposals that cannot realistically be funded. Most faculty prefer to spend time on initiatives that can move forward and be successful. To the extent that department chairs help faculty remain cognizant of the larger context and the challenges being faced by the institution, the easier it will be to lead faculty in relevant curriculum revision.

It's Your Turn

Put yourself in the department chair's role in answering the following questions:

1. How would you broach the subject of fiscal constraint with the faculty? Would you talk first with only those faculty members who developed the proposal for a new minor? Or would you invite the entire department to discuss the proposed minor?
2. How would you help the faculty understand the larger context that will govern how the proposal is viewed beyond the department without appearing to dismiss or devalue the faculty proposal?
3. Believing that the proposal will not be approved, would you work to persuade the faculty that the proposed minor is not a good idea? Or would you forward the proposed minor and wait to receive the anticipated negative feedback from the central administration? How would you protect your leadership credibility with the faculty and administration in each of these alternatives?

Hindsight Is 20/20

The department chair in the scenario is surprised first by the level of faculty resistance to an administrative request intended to enhance student recruitment and retention and second by faculty initiative to develop a program that is unrealistic in light of current fiscal constraints. Department chairs can avoid being surprised by faculty perspectives and reactions by remaining in touch with current faculty thinking. This can be difficult to do for several reasons. First, department chairs are busy, and it takes time to touch base and remain current on where faculty thinking is regarding particular issues. Second, faculty are busy. Although faculty members no doubt have perceptions of the decisions being made at the institution, they are most likely too busy to volunteer when and how their perspectives change. Third, the existence of cordial relationships can mask disconnects on particular issues. As in the case, the department chair's existing rapport and familiarity with the English faculty prompted her to miscalculate the level of resistance she experienced to the central administration's request.

Much time and energy can be saved when department chairs remain abreast of faculty perspectives. Having information about current faculty perspectives on particular issues will enable department chairs to adapt their communication appropriately when leading curriculum revision or other change. This can be done fairly efficiently at department meetings by inviting faculty members to comment on information and perspectives shared about such important things as the challenges facing the department and the institution, external changes that impact higher education, and changes in the learning needs and expectations of students. Inviting faculty members to share their perspectives either formally at the department meeting or informally over coffee will help guide department chair leadership by helping department chairs know how best to adapt their communication when leading change.

Let's Recap

Many of the challenges facing higher education make ongoing curriculum revision important to the viability of the institution. To remain competitive, institutions of higher education need to offer academic programs that serve the learning needs of today's students and prepare college graduates who can satisfy employers' expectations. Moreover, economic challenges alter how prospective students shop for a college. Increasingly, prospective students seek to know how a program of study will lead to gainful employment upon graduation. With finances stretched at home, fewer prospective students have the luxury of pursuing a college education for the sole purpose of becoming educated. These trends force some institutions to consider the addition of new academic programs that appear to faculty to be beyond the scope of the institution's mission. For example, a small private liberal arts college may add degrees in such professional occupations as nursing and physician assistant to generate revenue when the existing program inventory is insufficient to recruit needed enrollment.

Leading change can be difficult because change is uncomfortable for many people. Leading curriculum revision can be especially challenging because faculty members often assume ownership of the courses they teach and the programs they helped to develop. In addition to the customary resistance to change, department chairs leading curriculum revision must manage faculty attitudes about such things as faculty autonomy, administrative mandates, and faculty rights and responsibilities. Concerns about preserving faculty autonomy or faculty rights can quickly derail department discussion about curriculum revision. Similarly, the value of a proposed curriculum revision can be sacrificed when faculty are intent on resisting an administrative mandate on the basis of principle. Consequently, department chairs frequently find themselves in the middle between faculty and administration when leading curriculum revision.

To effectively lead curriculum revision, department chairs must interpret and balance the perspectives and interests of faculty members and the administration. This leadership work requires a skilled communicator who is able to do the following:

o Adapt his or her communication to the constituency.
o Clarify the need for curriculum revision.
o Bridge existing disconnects.
o Focus on positive outcomes.

In exercising these leadership communication strategies, department chairs can help all involved to understand the need for, and anticipated benefits of, curriculum revision. Without employing these strategies, department chairs will most likely spend more time managing conflict then leading curriculum revision. By using these leadership communication strategies, department chairs can enhance their effectiveness in leading curriculum revision.

3

REVISING ORGANIZATIONAL STRUCTURES

THERE IS NO STANDARD or uniform organizational structure for institutions of higher education. Each institution's organizational structure is the product of previous responses to experienced external and internal conditions. The campus culture and leadership influence how academic departments are organized and the placement of specific functions such as instructional technology, career services, or athletics within the organizational structure of the institution. Consequently, it is possible to find a particular academic department such as communication studies housed with the humanities at one institution and with the social sciences at another institution. Similarly, it is possible to find athletics reporting directly to the president at one institution and reporting to a vice president at another institution. What makes the organizational structure a good or poor fit for the institution is whether it supports the mission of the institution by serving the function of those working to fulfill the mission. As institutions of higher education face increasingly complex challenges, it is essential to continually assess the viability of the organizational structure and be willing to revise organizational structures that no longer support mission and function.

The goal of this chapter is to help department chairs understand how to propose and lead organizational change without sacrificing their leadership credibility. A second goal of this chapter is to equip department chairs with leadership communication strategies for determining whether the organizational structure supports mission and function and for managing the conflict that can develop when faculty and staff consider revisions to the organizational structure. Although the cases presented in this chapter focus on reorganization at the departmental level, the leadership communication strategies presented have relevance when proposing or leading reorganization at any level of the institution.

Defining the Task

The number and significance of the challenges facing institutions of higher education will inevitably require many institutions to revise both *what* and *how* work is done. Fifteen years ago, efforts to recruit and retain students seldom involved continuous communication with parents. Today, many institutions have an organized parents' council and communicate regularly with parents. This represents new work that some institutions believe is important for the recruitment and retention of traditional students. When such new work is implemented, the organizational structure of the institution changes to absorb the new work. Reporting lines for the new work are established in a way that either creates new positions of leadership or changes the responsibilities assigned to existing positions of leadership.

Reorganization is sometimes a remedy for fiscal constraint. An institution might outsource food or custodial services because doing so is cost-effective. The consolidation of two vice presidential areas into one may be motivated by a need to cut expenses. The addition of lacrosse at a small, private, liberal arts college may be motivated by a need to increase revenue through the recruitment of a new market of students. Such decisions are fiscally motivated, but they inevitably require some reorganization at the institution to incorporate the new work or entity.

Department chairs and other academic leaders often have a central role in leading organizational change. At times, department chairs need to initiate organizational change that would benefit faculty and students in the discipline. The department chair, for example, might propose moving the department to a different college at the institution or merging the department with another department to create a larger, more effective academic department. At other times, department chairs find themselves responsible for implementing organizational change initiated outside the department. This in-the-middle position can be especially difficult for department chairs who, to be effective leaders, must maintain their leadership credibility with both faculty and the administration. It can be difficult to lead organizational change that one initiates, but it can be even more difficult to oppose or implement organizational change that is initiated elsewhere on campus.

Because most people find change uncomfortable, there is the potential for destructive conflict when leading organizational change. Leading organizational change can be especially challenging when working with faculty and staff members who resist any change in the status quo. The challenge for department chairs is to help others recognize the need for change to remedy a very real problem and to demonstrate how revising the organizational structure addresses the problem and advantages the department and institution. The challenge is the same whether department chairs are talking with faculty or the administration. Moreover, effective department chairs navigate the task of leading organizational change in a way that enhances their leadership credibility with both the faculty and the administration.

Relevant Leadership Communication Strategies

Department chairs can use some leadership communication strategies to assess and effectively lead organizational change and manage the conflict often experienced when changing organizational structures. The following leadership communication strategies will aid department chairs in leading organizational change while minimizing destructive conflict.

Assess the Potential Benefits and Liabilities Associated with Reorganization

When leading structural change, it is important to thoroughly understand the proposed organizational change and the potential benefits and liabilities of the reorganization. Possessing an accurate understanding of the pros and cons of the proposed organizational change enables department chairs to respond directly to faculty and administrative concerns. When individuals are resistant to change because the status quo is familiar and they fear change in general, department chairs will hear objections that lack substance. Faculty may, for example, argue that a matter has always been handled a certain way as a sufficient reason to reject change. Or the administration may contend that there is too much going on to consider the proposed reorganization. When faced with such nonsubstantive concerns, department chairs will be better able to steer the discussion to substantive issues if they have a firm understanding of the reasons for considering organizational change and the potential benefits of implementing that change. Armed with information about the need for change and the anticipated benefits, department chairs can manage nonsubstantive objections by describing a very real problem that did not exist when the current structure was put in place and by showing how the proposed reorganization will yield concrete benefits for the department and the institution.

When individuals get stuck defending the status quo because change is uncomfortable, they forget that organizational structures exist to support the mission and function of the institution. When the organizational structure no longer supports the mission and function of the institution, effective leadership should consider the potential benefits of some reorganization. Failure to consider reorganization when the current structure no longer supports the mission and function of the institution will inevitably compound the problem being experienced. This does not mean that the potential liabilities of reorganization should be ignored. In the same way that it is unwise to resist all change, it is not prudent to change for the sake of change. The potential benefits and liabilities of any organizational change should be weighed carefully. Moreover, department chairs can enhance their leadership credibility when they are careful to communicate both the potential benefits and liabilities associated with the proposed organizational change. Careful consideration of the potential benefits and liabilities will yield more informed decision making and greater trust in leadership.

Understand Relevant Perspectives

It is important to understand the perspectives of all relevant constituencies, that is, those that would be affected by the proposed organizational change. Assume, for example, that a dean wishes to relocate the writing lab from the Department of English to the newly created Office of Academic Support, which oversees all other student tutoring and learning support on the campus. The English faculty and staff in the academic support office are two relevant constituencies. Students who use the writing lab are another relevant constituency. Should the writing lab be staffed with adjunct faculty, they are a relevant constituency who may possess a different perspective than the full-time English faculty. The individuals responsible for leading the English department and the academic support office represent other relevant constituents whose perspectives can influence the implementation of the proposed change. Should admissions staff use the placement of the writing lab and academic support services when recruiting students, they represent another relevant constituency.

Department chairs may not know the perspectives held by each relevant constituency without discussing a possible reorganization with each. If this is the case, department chairs should actively seek the perspectives of all relevant constituencies early in the process of considering reorganization so the perspectives of relevant constituencies can be considered in shaping the most beneficial reorganization. When department chairs present formal proposals for organizational change to others without first knowing their perspective, reaction to the proposed change will be more difficult to manage. Individuals who are resistant to change tend to take greater umbrage when presented with a formal request to support a specific change without being given an opportunity to comment on the need to make changes and how best to reorganize. Department chairs who move too quickly to present others with a formal proposal for structural change are likely to persuade others that they have little regard for perspectives other than their own. The inevitable outcome will be even greater resistance to change. However, department chairs can demonstrate their high regard for the perspectives held by others by actively seeking their input before developing a formal proposal for organizational change.

Link the Proposed Reorganization to Shared Priorities

When advocating structural change, it can be helpful to connect the anticipated benefits of the proposed change with commonly shared priorities. For example, if increasing student enrollment is a commonly shared priority at the institution, demonstrating how the proposed organizational change can fuel enrollment growth will help melt resistance to change. Similarly, if gaining national visibility for academic programming is a priority of the administration, showing how the proposed organizational change will yield heightened visibility for the program and the institution will help to garner support for the change.

When the initial resistance to the organizational change is great, department chairs should begin by building consensus around shared priorities. This may be the case when external circumstances threaten the viability of an academic program. For example, department chairs will garner more support for an organizational change designed to rescue a program whose precipitous drop in enrollment threatens the program's continuation if they first help to build consensus among those involved around the need to take action to revive the program.

At times, campus priorities surface in response to specific challenges. These priorities may or may not be related to the institution's mission but are likely perceived as important to the health and viability of the institution. The mission of a small, private, liberal arts institution, for example, may speak to the institution's commitment to educate young minds through an education grounded in the liberal arts tradition. The same institution, however, may be quick to add professional degree programs in nursing and other career destinations to protect the fiscal health of the institution. Whether the shared priority proceeds or follows organizational change, there should be a connection between shared institutional priorities and the organizational structure. Remember that organizational structure is to serve the mission and function of the institution, making it essential that the organizational structure of the institution supports the fulfillment of shared institutional priorities.

Assess Initial Leadership Credibility for Leading Organizational Change

A department chair's leadership credibility for leading organizational change can make the task easier or more difficult. Generally, the higher a person's leadership credibility, the easier it is to lead change because individuals perceiving a leader as highly credible have more trust in that person's leadership. Leadership credibility is the confidence that others have in a particular person to lead effectively. The confidence for a leader derives over time and is based on perceptions of that leader's decisions, actions, and communication. In other words, leadership credibility is an assigned attribute in that it resides in perceptions held by others. A department chair's leadership credibility can vary with the particular issue or situation. For example, faculty members may perceive a department chair as highly credible when handling personnel matters and as having low credibility when managing fiscal matters. Similarly, a person may be perceived as a highly credible department chair but not be perceived as having the requisite knowledge, experience, or skill (low credibility) to lead a new school or division created by merging two smaller departments. For this reason, it is prudent to take stock of one's leadership credibility when leading organizational change.

Department chairs generally know how others perceive their leadership. If there is ambiguity, department chairs should proactively seek to learn the perceptions of others. This can be done informally by soliciting the reaction of others to specific ideas. For example, a department chair might ask faculty members to comment on the feasibility of a particular organizational change. The faculty reaction will provide the department chair with information about the faculty members' confidence in the department chair's ability to lead the change. Because leadership credibility is an assigned attribute, department chairs need to take stock of their leadership credibility with every relevant constituency that will be impacted by the organizational change.

Putting Theory into Practice

These strategies may seem to make good intuitive sense to most department chairs, but they can be difficult to implement. In Case 3.1, the department chair hopes to craft a proposal to divide the Department of Math and Computer Science into two separate departments. Place yourself in the role of department chair as you read.

Case 3.1: Making the Case for Dividing the Department

When Jonathan Anker became chair of the Department of Math and Computer Science 4 years ago, he replaced a math faculty member, who had chaired the department for more than 25 years. Although Jonathan holds a doctorate in mathematics, he identifies with the faculty teaching computer science primarily because he was hired to fill a tenure-track position in computer science.

The Department of Mathematics became the Department of Math and Computer Science a few years after a math faculty member became interested in offering computer science courses. Student interest grew and fueled the development of a degree program in computer science, and the department's name was changed to include math and computer science. Currently, enrollment in computer science is five times the enrollment in mathematics. The computer science faculty members are innovative about enhancing the program's positive reputation on and off campus. The computer science faculty members run programming competitions for area high school students so they can identify and recruit strong students. They also identify professional internship experiences for students majoring in computer science, which helps to recruit students seeking a strong, professionally focused program that can lead to employment after graduation. In contrast, math faculty members boast a traditional curriculum and take great pride in knowing that roughly 60% of the graduates in mathematics go on to teach math, and almost 10% decide to do graduate work in mathematics.

Although faculty in the math and computer science department maintain a good rapport, the two programs are managed separately with virtually no collaboration between them. Jonathan is convinced that the same company could very well be interested in both students with training in computer science and students knowledgeable of mathematics, so in his first year as department chair he suggested that both computer science and math faculty pursue professional internships for students in both majors. He thought that sharing the task of reaching out to area businesses would prove beneficial to both programs. Jonathon quickly learned that math faculty have no interest in experiential learning and, in general, are very resistant to change.

As chair of the department, Jonathan is responsible for leading and implementing all change initiatives, including changes requested by the administration and those he believes will benefit the department. Since the math faculty members remain steadfastly opposed to all change, Jonathan spends a lot of time and energy leading change and managing the conflict that often accompanies change. He is weary and, quite frankly, tired of trying to help the math faculty understand the challenges faced by the institution that warrant consideration of change. Chairing the math faculty consumes the majority of Jonathan's time with no tangible benefit. Jonathan, however, enjoys chairing the computer science portion of the department. The computer science faculty members are bright and energetic. They embrace change and are skilled in collaborative problem solving. Jonathan is not surprised that enrollment in mathematics is declining while enrollment in computer science continues to grow. Moreover, Jonathan expects the enrollment in mathematics to decline more sharply as the number of students pursuing degrees in education with plans to teach math decrease in response to a dramatic reduction in employment opportunities for K–12 math teachers in the region.

Jonathan is preoccupied with the idea of separating math and computer science into two separate departments. Since the programs have always operated individually, he can see no benefit to having both programs housed in the same academic department. He is confident that the math faculty members who prefer to be left alone would support separating math and computer science into two departments. Jonathan also realizes that at least the previous chair understood the advantage of having a low-enrolled program combined with a high-enrolled program when generating department data. As a stand-alone department, mathematics would likely experience greater pressure from the administration to increase enrollment and possibly experience budget cuts. The computer science program, however, would have a much stronger profile if its data were not combined with mathematics. Although Jonathan is convinced that dividing the Department of Math and Computer Science into two separate departments would best serve computer science, he is less certain how to make the case for breaking the department into two separate entities to the mathematics faculty and eventually to the central administration.

Let's Analyze the Case

Jonathan believes that chairing only computer science would spare him frustration and time that would be better spent enhancing the computer science program. He is energized by working with the computer science faculty and disheartened that the time and energy spent chairing the math faculty yield no tangible benefit. As department chair, Jonathan finds himself responsible for leading change initiatives. Whereas computer science faculty embrace change and engage in collaborative problem solving, the math faculty resist change. Although Jonathan would prefer to divide math and computer science into two separate departments, he is not certain that his idea would be supported by the math faculty or by the central administration.

To effectively make the case for dividing the Department of Math and Computer Science in two, Jonathan must persuade both the computer science and math faculty to support the proposal. Unless the plan has the unanimous support of both math and computer science faculty, Jonathan will be hard-pressed to persuade the administration that dividing the department would benefit both math and computer science programs. Especially with the math faculty being resistant to any change, Jonathan will need to frame the proposal in a way that enables the math faculty to perceive tangible benefits from becoming a stand-alone department. To do this, Jonathan needs to understand the perspective and priorities of the math faculty. If a top priority for the math faculty is securing unilateral control over their own work and future, then Jonathan will want to frame the proposed reorganization as a mechanism toward that end. If a priority for the math faculty is retaining the security that comes from being housed with a high-enrolled program, then Jonathan will need to address that concern in his framing of the proposed reorganization. Jonathan might, for example, argue that enrollment in math could increase if the program was not linked with computer science because the blended department likely undermines the successful recruitment of students who are seriously interested in the study of mathematics.

Assuming that Jonathan is able to obtain unanimous department support for a proposal to divide the Department of Math and Computer Science into two separate departments, his proposal to the administration must clearly articulate the benefits to be realized by replacing one department with two departments. This requires Jonathan to have an accurate sense of institutional priorities. If the institutional priority is growing enrollment, Jonathan could frame the proposed reorganization as a change that would enhance enrollment growth. If, however, the institutional priority is cutting costs, Jonathan needs to demonstrate that the proposed reorganization would be cost neutral, save the institution money, or be worth a modest investment of additional resources.

It's Your Turn

Assume the position of department chair in the case and think through how you would approach the math faculty.

1. Would you first raise the issue informally or draft a full proposal for faculty review? If you decide to raise the issue informally, how and when would you raise the issue? Be specific in saying how you would frame the issue. For example, would you begin by describing the benefits of having separate departments for math and computer science? Or would you begin by involving the faculty in a discussion of similarities and differences between the math and computer science programs? How else might you introduce the issue?

2. Currently, math and computer science faculty meet together as one department. Would you raise the issue at the department meeting or talk separately with math and computer science faculty? What factors would help you decide on a particular approach? For example, would the level of collegiality between math and computer science faculty influence your thinking? Would the differing perspectives held by the math and computer science faculty members influence your approach?

3. If you would begin by preparing a proposal for faculty review, delineate the content you would include in the proposal. Would you, for example, limit the proposal to anticipated benefits of the proposed reorganization or would you include comparative data for each program on enrollment, faculty positions, operating budget, and other such variables? Under what circumstances would it make sense to begin the department discussion with a written proposal? For example, when faculty are quick to dismiss suggestions for change without consideration, preparing a full proposal might be a way to have them consider the merits of a proposed change before resisting any and all change without informed discussion.

4. Assume you secure unanimous support from the math and computer science faculty for the proposed reorganization. Consider what, if any, changes you would make to the proposal before forwarding it to the central administration. What concerns, if any, would the central administration have that may not be raised by the faculty? For example, would implementation of the proposal accrue additional costs for the institution? If yes, does your proposal demonstrate the benefit to the institution that would be realized from making the requested investment of additional funds?

Please Consider

Jonathan is in his fourth year as department chair. We also know that he was hired on a tenure-track position in computer science. We do not know if he is tenured at the institution. Increasingly, faculty members are asked to serve as department chair before being granted tenure. Not holding tenure can alter a department chair's leadership. Untenured department chairs may not believe that they possess the same freedom to exercise strong leadership in the face of resistance to change.

Although being untenured does not exempt department chairs from exercising their leadership responsibility, it can shape how department chairs proceed when leading change. In particular, more time will be spent discussing issues and weighing the pros and cons of any proposed change because untenured department chairs may perceive it dangerous to appear cavalier or to make unilateral decisions for the department. This dynamic can make leading change painstakingly slow and challenging when department faculty are committed to supporting the status quo at any cost. Review your plan for proposing that the Department of Math and Computer Science be divided in two. What, if any, changes will you make if you as department chair are untenured?

Let's Recap

Take a moment to finalize your plan for leading the structural change desired by the department chair in Case 3.1. Does your approach

- o Address the potential benefits and liabilities of the proposed reorganization?
- o Incorporate an understanding of the relevant perspectives?
- o Link the proposed reorganization to shared priorities?
- o Take into account your leadership credibility for leading organizational change?

Putting Theory into Practice

In Case 3.2, the director of the School of Art has an opportunity to absorb two tenured faculty members from another department and college on the campus. Although the provost and two college deans believe the transfer of two faculty members to the School of Art makes good sense, the art director is not certain that the plan would benefit the School of Art. Place yourself in the role of the director of the School of Art as you read, and consider how you would respond to the proposed reorganization.

Case 3.2: A Round Peg in a Square Hole?

The School of Art, which is housed in the College of Fine Arts at Southwest Research University, enjoys a strong reputation both on and off campus. With an emphasis on studio arts, the school offers BFA and MFA programs in fibers, glass blowing, large metal sculpture, ceramics, jewelry making, painting, drawing, and watercolor. At the close of each semester, art students exhibit their work on campus. The caliber of student work supports the common perception that art faculty members are skilled teachers. In addition, the art faculty members are productive studio artists. All create pieces for juried exhibits and one-person shows of their work. Several of the faculty members have had their work featured in national publications and PBS programs, and all faculty members are at times commissioned to create pieces.

Ben Herzog, the longtime director of the School of Art, is respected on the campus as an internationally known artist and strong academic leader. He is known for running an efficient but collegial School of Art. Other school directors and department chairs on campus often seek Ben's perspective on issues. He has a direct, no-nonsense style of leadership. He prides himself in involving faculty when appropriate and sparing faculty when a bureaucratic task can be handled more efficiently by his taking unilateral action. Ben makes good use of the high regard and trust that the art faculty members have for his leadership.

Elsewhere on Campus

The university houses a College of Technical Careers that offers 2-year associate's degrees in a range of technical fields. The Technical Careers College was instituted many years ago for the express purpose of providing vocational education in a part of the state that did not have a community college. With the creation of a credible community college nearby, the College of Technical Careers has narrowed its focus to associate's degrees not offered at the regional community college. Although many of the associate's degree programs boast healthy enrollments, the program in visual art and design is unable to recruit sufficient enrollment to remain viable as a stand-alone degree program. With declining enrollment, retiring faculty were not replaced, leaving only two full-time tenured faculty members in visual art and design. Sadly, enrollment is no longer sufficient to support the two remaining faculty members.

The college dean and provost have discussed the options. Neither is anxious to close the program and terminate two tenured faculty members even though policy allows for the dismissal of tenured faculty should a program be closed. At the same time, no one expects the demand for a 2-year degree in visual art and design to increase because the better jobs for students with training in visual art and design typically require a baccalaureate degree. The two faculty members in visual art and design are strong teachers. However, they lack the expertise to develop a baccalaureate program, and the provost prefers to offer only 2-year associate's degrees through the College of Technical Careers. With much thought, the college dean and provost agree that the preferred outcome would be to transfer the two tenured faculty members in visual art design to the School of Art. The School of Art, under Ben Herzog's leadership, could then decide how best to integrate the faculty in visual art and design into the existing art curriculum and determine whether the addition of these faculty members would enable the School of Art to develop a BFA in design.

Pitching the Idea on Campus

The provost communicates the idea to the dean of the College of Fine Arts. The College of Fine Arts is composed of two schools (i.e., art, music) and two departments (i.e., photography, film studies and digital media). The Fine Arts dean wholeheartedly embraces the provost's plan, believing that adding design to the curriculum would further bolster the School of Art's stature. The Technical Careers dean assures the Fine Arts dean that the two faculty members in visual art and design are very willing, indeed eager, to have their positions transferred to the School of Art. The Fine Arts dean agrees to discuss the idea with Ben as soon as possible to learn his reaction but volunteers that he will likely relish the opportunity to acquire two additional faculty members.

School of Art's Reaction

Upon hearing the idea, Ben is skeptical. He knows the two faculty members in visual art and design and believes they do not share the same work ethic or professional credential as the art faculty members. Although the School of Art might benefit by adding a BFA in design, the credentials of the two faculty members would not be sufficient to staff a BFA in design. Moreover, developing a program in design would take enormous time and require expertise beyond that which resides in the School of Art. Ben asks for time to discuss the idea with the art faculty before reaching a decision. The Fine Arts dean agrees and encourages Ben to help the art faculty understand the benefit of receiving two additional faculty positions during a time of tight resources.

Let's Analyze the Case

Ben Herzog, director of the School of Art, is in a difficult position. He is being presented with the plan that others believe is the preferred outcome to a troubling situation. The provost and two college deans are persuaded that the best remedy to declining enrollment in a 2-year associate's degree program in visual art and design is to eliminate the 2-year program in visual art and design and transfer the two remaining tenured faculty members to the School of Art. Both the problem and the solution being presented, however, are new issues for the art school director. It is likely that the provost and college deans understand the director's desire to discuss the plan with art faculty members, but it is also apparent that they do not expect the art school director and art faculty members to oppose the plan. There is no evidence that the provost and college deans intend to be heavy-handed with the School of Art. From the provost and college deans' perspectives, the plan would net two additional faculty members for the School of Art while sparing them from dismissing two tenured faculty members. In other words, the provost and college deans perceive the proposal as win-win for the two visual arts faculty members and the School of Art.

The director of the School of Art is not persuaded that the plan is a good idea. Having just learned of the proposal, the director has several reservations. First, he doubts that the two tenured faculty members in visual art and design share the same work ethic common to faculty in the School of Art. Second, the director recognizes that the two tenured faculty members lack the professional credentials needed to develop a BFA in design. Consequently, the director doubts that the benefit perceived by the provost and college deans can be realized through the transfer of the two tenured faculty members. Rather than raise his reservations when first hearing about the plan, the director asks for time to talk with the art faculty. The magnitude of the issue makes it one that the art director wants to discuss with the art faculty. At the same time, the art school director recognizes the art faculty members trust his leadership and will likely ask his opinion of the proposal. Consequently, he needs to give the proposal serious thought before involving the art faculty.

It's Your Turn

1. Do you agree that the director should study the proposal and its implications for the School of Art before discussing it with the faculty? If not, why not?

2. The art faculty members have a high regard for the director's leadership ability. Place yourself in the role of art school director, and describe how the faculty members' trust in the director's leadership would influence your handling of the situation. For example, would you use it as license to guide to faculty toward a particular response? Or would you use it to engage the faculty in a thorough examination of the proposed organizational change?

3. What information would you gather to consider the merits of the proposal? For example, would you request the professional credentials of the two faculty members in visual art and design? Would you talk with the two faculty members in visual art and design? If yes, what would you hope to accomplish in talking with the faculty members in visual art and design? What, if any, data would you gather regarding BFA programs in design?

4. How would you frame the issue when presenting it to the art faculty? For example, would you share that the provost and college deans believe it is a good plan for all involved? Would you share your opinion of the proposal? If yes, would you share your thoughts early or later in the discussion, and why?

5. Assume that the faculty share the director's reservations about the proposal, and give careful consideration to how you would report this perspective to the administration. Would you, for example, present the reservations as your own, the art faculty's, or both? How might you object to the proposal while enhancing your leadership credibility with the administration?

Please Consider

The director of the School of Art enjoys positive leadership credibility. Both the art faculty and the administration perceive the director as being an experienced and skilled leader. Nonetheless, the director needs to consider his leadership credibility for managing the possible assimilation of two tenured faculty members currently housed in the College of Technical Careers. Leadership credibility can be specific to the issue and situation. In other words, an academic leader may have high or positive leadership credibility when managing operational issues and low or poor leadership credibility when managing personnel issues. Even academic leaders with high leadership credibility can discover that they have little initial credibility when managing a new responsibility. Unless the director in the case has managed a similar matter previously, the director may not possess the same high level of positive leadership credibility that he enjoys on tasks he routinely manages.

It is important for department chairs and other academic leaders to assess their initial leadership credibility for leading the specific change issue. This assessment will help to inform how to proceed. The art school director in the case can help faculty relate the immediate task to similar situations that were handled well. The director might, for example, compare the acquisition of two tenured faculty members from technical careers to the successful assimilation of new faculty hired from outside the institution. When department chairs possess positive leadership credibility, they will want to help those they lead link past success to the current change initiatives. However, when department chairs have low or poor leadership credibility, they will want to distinguish the current change initiative from previous unsuccessful efforts.

The director in the case could find himself needing to persuade the administration that the proposed organizational change is not a good plan. If not managed well, resisting a plan that the provost and two college deans find beneficial could damage the director's leadership credibility with the administration. The challenge is to reject the proposal in a way that enhances the director's leadership credibility. To do this, the director needs to recognize the benefit that the administration believes can be realized through the proposed reorganization when delineating specific concerns about the proposed reorganization in relationship to the anticipated benefits. For example, the administration believes that the two tenured faculty members in visual art and design would enable the School of Art to add a BFA in design. Rather than rejecting the proposal out of hand, the director might document all that would be needed to realistically pursue the addition of a BFA in design. This approach could further enhance the director's leadership credibility with the administration because it demonstrates his knowledge of the discipline and his willingness to inform the administration of the total cost of adding a BFA in design before developing the program. At this point, the administration can decide if the resource needs for adding a BFA in design are feasible before implementing the proposed the organization believing that something is possible when it/is not.

Putting Theory into Practice

The department featured in Case 3.3 is committed to taking action that helps the institution increase enrollment. The department's plan proposes evolving it into a school and requires the infusion of additional resources. This could be a prudent investment for the institution. How the department chair makes the case will influence whether or not the proposed reorganization is accepted. Put yourself in the role of department chair, and consider how you would craft the proposal as you read.

Case 3.3: Making the Case for Expansion

The Department of Communication Arts and Sciences (DCAS) is realizing enrollment growth at a time when the campus is experiencing declining enrollment. The administration stresses that enrollment growth is essential to the institution's fiscal health and often references the increasing enrollment in DCAS as evidence that enrollment growth is possible despite increased competition for students. DCAS offers academic programs in public relations, communication disorders and sciences, communication studies, and media arts. All four academic programs report a growth in enrollment such that most courses are running at capacity, and the department is using more adjunct faculty to staff additional sections in every program.

Faculty members in DCAS believe that the department can do even more to bolster enrollment at the university with a few curriculum and organizational modifications. Under the leadership of department chair Sue Karnes, the faculty develop a proposal for evolving the Department of Communication Arts and Sciences into a School of Communication (SC) that would encompass new program offerings in each of the four academic programs currently housed within DCAS. The department's plan is outlined in the following proposal.

DCAS Proposal to Create the School of Communication

The Department of Communication Arts and Sciences (DCAS) spent the past year examining the possible development of a School of Communication to increase DCAS's contribution to the university's priority to grow enrollment. Faculty examined current curricular and co-curricular offerings and assessed how each might be enhanced to recruit more students to the institution. This assessment takes into account current student interest and labor demands for graduates. It also considers other programming on the campus and allows for collaboration with faculty in other disciplines. The proposed program expansions are described in the following section.

PUBLIC RELATIONS   The existing program in public relations is hugely popular with students, making it the fastest-growing degree program at the institution. Currently, two full-time faculty and several committed professionals from industry, who serve as adjunct faculty, support a program with 125 majors. Additional program growth is possible with the addition of specializations in strategic communication and health public relations. Strategic communication would combine course work in public relations and business to equip students with knowledge and skill to communicate strategically. The health public relations specialization responds to the regional focus on health care and the addition of several new programs in the health professions at the institution. The strategic communication and health public relations specializations would be attractive to both adult and traditional day students.

COMMUNICATION DISORDERS AND SCIENCES   Currently, the institution offers only a bachelor's in communication disorders and sciences. However, graduates must complete a master's to be qualified for clinical work. Given the increasingly competitive nature of seeking admission to graduate programs in speech-language pathology and audiology, students interested in this major may elect to earn their baccalaureate degree at institutions that offer a master's in communication disorders and sciences to enhance their chances of being admitted to the graduate program. The faculty propose the addition of a master's in communication disorders and sciences to protect against enrollment decline and pave the way for increased enrollment. Faculty from two other institutions that recently added graduate programs in communication disorders and sciences report an increase of more than 30% in their undergraduate enrollment. The proposed master's in communication disorders and sciences would provide a graduate program for students earning their baccalaureate degree at this institution and would attract prospective students from other institutions that offer only the bachelor's.

COMMUNICATION STUDIES Currently, communication studies offer a generalist degree with emphasis on communication skill development, theory, and research. To attract more students, the faculty members propose the creation of two specializations that would permit study in the specific emphases of health communication and relational and conflict communication. These specializations would be very attractive to students planning to work in health care and business.

MEDIA ARTS AND STUDIES Currently, the department offers programs in broadcasting, film studies, and digital media and design. To grow enrollment, the faculty propose the addition of a new major in sports communication. With four professional sports teams in the immediate region, the proposed program would be able to distinguish itself from other comparable programs through the inclusion of internships within the sports industry.

Resources Needed

All programming would be developed and implemented within the next 3 years. Although current faculty have the requisite expertise to develop the proposed programs, additional faculty will be needed to staff new courses. Because the program expansions in public relations, communication studies, and media arts link closely with area industry, new courses in these programs would be staffed by professionals in the field who would teach as adjunct faculty. This has the added benefit of introducing students to practicing professionals who can help them secure employment in the industry after graduation.

To support the new master's in communication sciences and disorders, one additional full-time tenure-track faculty position is needed. In addition, the part-time speech lab director would need to be employed full time. This person would supervise more students, offer clinical support to families in the community, and train graduate students to work with and help train undergraduate students working in the speech clinic. The additional faculty position would need to be in place when the first class of master's students begins their work.

Finally, we propose that the Department of Communication Arts and Sciences be renamed the School of Communication. The school designation is appropriate given the expanded program inventory and would greatly aid faculty members in seeking external grant funding and when approaching professionals in industry to secure student internships. The proposed school designation would secure important visibility for the programs housed within the School of Communication.

Let's Analyze the Case

Faculty in the Department of Communication Arts and Sciences recognize that they teach programs of interest to a growing number of students. Consequently, the department is in a unique position to help the institution grow its enrollment. The department faculty members developed a proposal that would add two new degree programs and four new specializations to the existing curriculum inventory for the express purpose of growing enrollment. The proposal clearly articulates the proposed additions to the academic program, but virtually no documentation is presented to demonstrate how these program additions would help the institution recruit greater numbers of students. Further, the proposal mentions the opportunity for collaboration with faculty in other disciplines, but no mention is made of having discussed the proposed program additions with the prospective collaborating departments. Ideally, the proposal should include letters from key collaborators indicating their support of the proposed curriculum. The proposal should also include documentation that evidences why the addition of these particular degree programs and program specializations will fuel enrollment growth.

The proposed evolution of the department into a School of Communication comes across as an afterthought. The proposal asserts that the school designation is appropriate and would greatly aid faculty when securing professional internships for students and grant funding. Absent a more detailed rationale of the benefits for the proposed the reorganization, there is no reason to believe that making the department a school is essential to the proposed program expansion. It is possible that this proposal is the product of brainstorming and intended to test the administration's reaction to the general idea before more work is done by the faculty to document the case for developing new programming and reorganizing the department. This approach may appear to save time, but it could yield a negative response to a good idea because the administration does not have sufficient information to recognize the true merit of the proposal. Moreover, if the administration perceives the proposal as primarily an effort to elevate the organizational status of the department, it could hurt the department chair's leadership credibility with the administration.

It's Your Turn

Assume the position of the department chair in Case 3.3 in answering the following questions:

1. How might you get a preliminary sense of the administration's receptivity to the proposal? Would you, for example, inquire whether the institution is in a position to invest in new programming that holds promise for increasing the institution's enrollment?

2. How would you document the need for additional resources? Would it be sufficient to show the additional staffing needed to offer the proposed program expansions? When institutions experience declining enrollment, it is insufficient to argue the need for additional staffing to staff new courses. Instead, department chairs must illustrate how the additional expense will generate additional revenue.

3. What factors would you examine to determine the feasibility and desirability of reorganizing the department into a school? Would you, for example, need to know the current institutional distinction between department and school status? Would you assess your department's similarity to other schools at the institution? Where might you identify support from on or off campus for reorganizing the department into a school?

4. What arguments would you make for making the department into a school? Do your arguments take into account the administration's current perspective and priority for growing enrollment at the institution? Do your arguments take into account current fiscal constraints?

Please Consider

Department chairs are expected to lead faculty in responding to pressing institutional priorities such as increasing enrollment. Unless department chairs fully understand the context and governing parameters for the institutional priorities, efforts to lead faculty in responding to specific institutional priorities will likely waste faculty time and damage department chair leadership credibility. Consider, for example, the institution for which increasing enrollment is the top priority. This does not mean that the administration will embrace every idea to increase enrollment. The administration must consider the anticipated net revenue from any plan designed to increase enrollment. Although adding a new program may attract new students, the administration must consider the cost involved in adding the new program. For a proposal to be perceived as supportive of the institutional priority, the revenue generated through the recruitment of new students must exceed the sum needed to develop and implement the new program.

Sometimes the administration has specific parameters that guide how a particular institutional goal is to be met. The institution, for example, may need to increase enrollment in online courses because the current size of the campus facility will not support increased enrollment on campus without the construction or rental of additional classroom space. The needed enrollment growth may need to be in the evening and weekend program to optimize the use of campus facilities, whereas increasing the number of residential students would require the construction of a new residence hall. At times, adding new academic programs is not the best way to increase institutional enrollment. A new program may enjoy healthy enrollment, but the addition of the new program will not support the institutional priority to grow enrollment if the new program siphons enrolled students away from other existing programs. When the institutional priority is to grow revenue through increased enrollment, program additions that enabled the institution to recruit new markets of students will be more helpful to the institution's goal than new programs that serve to give students already recruited to the institution more choice of study.

Department chairs can save faculty time and frustration by understanding the context and specific parameters for institutional priorities. Becoming fully informed about the institution's priorities is a necessary first step before leading change. Department chairs who skip this step jeopardize their leadership credibility with both the faculty and the administration because proposals developed under their leadership are less likely to respond to the specific circumstances that spawned the institutional priority. In Case 3.3, the proposal to add two new specializations to the public relations program that would attract adult students will be more appreciated if the institution believes that increasing the adult student enrollment is advantageous. Similarly, the proposal to add a master's in communication disorders and sciences will be more favorably received if current graduates have limited access to comparable master's programs. However, if students completing the baccalaureate in communication disorders and sciences have access to a number of quality master's programs, then the proposed master's will be in competition with other institutions when recruiting students. If this is the case, the cost of adding the master's must include some budget for student recruitment.

Consider whether your plan for developing the proposal in Case 3.3 involves learning more about the context and parameters guiding the institutions goal to increase enrollment. If not, how you would go about gathering information that would guide your leadership of the faculty in developing a proposal to expand the academic program.

Putting Theory into Practice

Case 3.4 describes a scenario in which faculty from the several disciplines and their department chairs are asked to consider changing the organizational structure and leadership of their respective divisions. Examine the issue presented in Case 3.4 and consider how you, as department chair, would lead the faculty in considering the recommended reorganization.

Case 3.4: The Cost of Protecting the Status Quo

The dean of the college is concerned about the unequal representation of faculty interests across the institution. The small, private, liberal arts college is organized into six academic divisions. Three academic divisions (business, education, and music) are led by full-time appointed directors on 12-month administrative contracts. The remaining three divisions (humanities, social sciences, and natural sciences) rotate the division director title each year among the chairs of the departments housed within the division. Department chairs serving as division director call meetings of the division faculty when needed but exercise no other leadership responsibility on behalf of the division. Instead, department chairs within the humanities, social sciences, and natural sciences divisions have full and exclusive leadership responsibility for their individual departments. Department chairs in the humanities, social sciences, and natural sciences divisions hold 9-month faculty positions and earn an additional stipend for serving as department chair.

The dean of the college recognizes that the current structure is the only one that faculty in the humanities, social sciences, and natural sciences know. The faculty are comfortable with the current organizational structure, which allows the faculty in each discipline to have a department chair who shares their discipline expertise and has direct access to the college dean. At same time, it is painfully clear to the college dean that faculty in the humanities, social sciences, and natural sciences divisions are not represented as well as faculty in the divisions with full-time directors. The 12-month division directors are invested full-time tending to and championing the needs of their divisions. Whether competing for faculty positions, operating budget, renovations, or other resources, the 12-month division directors advocate the needs of their respective divisions with a level of leadership skill and commitment that is unmatched by the department chairs in the humanities, social sciences, and natural sciences divisions. Although the budget would not support the conversion of all department chairs to full-time 12-month administrative appointments, it would support the appointment of full-time 12-month division directors in the humanities, social sciences, and natural sciences divisions if the three newly created division director positions replaced the elected part-time department chairs. The college dean recognizes that this would be a dramatic change for faculty in the humanities, social sciences, and natural sciences. The college dean is certain that faculty, for example, in the departments of psychology, sociology, communication studies, and economics will be apprehensive about reporting to a division director appointed by the college dean to lead the social sciences instead of to a colleague within the discipline that they elect to serve as department chair for a 3-year term.

The college dean decides to meet separately with faculty in the humanities, social sciences, and natural sciences divisions to explain how the current organizational structure places faculty in these Divisions at a disadvantage. The college dean is careful to stress that the inequitable representation of faculty interests and resource needs is a by-product of the organizational structure and is in no way a reflection on the quality of leadership exercised by department chairs in the humanities, social sciences, and natural sciences divisions. The college dean points out that divisions with full-time 12-month administrative directors enjoy leaders who are paid to spend their entire time tending to the needs of their divisions, whereas faculty in the humanities, social sciences, and natural sciences have an organizational structure that limits their leadership to a part-time responsibility compensated with an extra pay stipend. The college dean points out that organizational structures should be designed to benefit the people they serve and encourages the faculty to resist holding fast to an organizational structure designed decades earlier under different circumstances. After making clear that the budget would support replacing department chairs with a full-time 12-month administrative director in each division, the college dean asks faculty to spend a few weeks discussing the invitation to remedy the inequitable organizational structure.

Let's Analyze the Case

The college dean recognizes that faculty in three of six academic divisions are disadvantaged by the current organizational structure. Simply put, faculty in the humanities, social sciences, and natural sciences are led and represented by part-time leaders in term appointments who manage department chair responsibilities that are compensated by extra pay. In contrast, faculty in the business, education, and music divisions are led and represented by full-time directors who were hired on the basis of their leadership skill and experience. The college dean believes that the current organization structure yields an inequitable representation for faculty across the divisions. At the same time, the college dean realizes that changing current organizational structure will be uncomfortable for faculty in the humanities, social sciences, and natural sciences divisions. The college dean likely realizes that proposing an organizational change will adversely affect her leadership credibility with faculty in the humanities, social sciences, and natural sciences. To the extent that the full-time directors in education, business, and music value the uneven playing field that the current organizational structure affords their divisions, proposing the organizational change could damage the college dean's leadership credibility with the education, business, and music division directors.

Support for change is more easily obtained when those being asked to embrace change are experiencing some hardship. In the scenario described in Case 3.4, faculty members adversely affected by the current structure are unaware of the liability that exists. As a result, faculty who should embrace the proposed reorganization that would benefit them are more likely to resist it in favor of a familiar organizational structure. To obtain support for the proposed reorganization, the college dean will first need to persuade the humanities, social sciences, and natural sciences faculties that the current organizational structure imposes a real hardship for them. The college dean explains that the full-time directors devote all their time to championing the needs of their faculty, whereas department chairs, through no fault of their own, manage leadership responsibilities on top of their full-time faculty work. This could be sufficient to persuade the benefit of organizational change if faculty are concerned only about having full-time leadership. Should the faculty be concerned about having a division director that does not share their discipline, then the concern over having a full-time director that may not understand their discipline might outweigh the leadership advantage of having a full-time director. If faculty find comfort in knowing they can elect a different chair every 3 years, then the appointment of a full-time director could be viewed as a liability.

The College Dean in the case scenario asks the faculty in the humanities, social sciences, and natural sciences to give the suggested reorganization some consideration. At least in the meeting described in the case scenario, the College Dean makes no effort to address likely concerns of the faculty or to document the hardship the experience in a concrete way. Given existing perceptions and the Dean's framing of the issue, it is unlikely that faculty in the humanities, social sciences, and natural sciences will embrace the proposed reorganization.

It's Your Turn

Assume the position of college dean, and decide how you would present the issue to faculty in the humanities, social sciences, and natural sciences divisions.

1. How would you demonstrate the hardship resulting from the current organizational structure? It could prove detrimental to document that the 12-month administrative directors are more successful in obtaining resources for their divisions than are the 9-month department chairs. Similarly, it would not be prudent to offer a comparison of resource requests received from full-time directors and department chairs who manage leadership responsibilities on an extra work model. What, if any, constructive evidence might you present to help document the existing inequity in leadership? For example, would it help to share perceptions and experiences of faculty in the better represented divisions?

2. What might you do to identify and address the other faculty concerns? Would you ask faculty to list their concerns? How would you respond to the fear of having a division director who is not from the discipline? How would you address the faculty who enjoy the power of electing a department chair who serves at the pleasure of his or her colleagues?

Now assume the role of a department chair in the social sciences division, and consider how you would present the college dean's proposal to the department faculty.

1. Would you allow the anticipated faculty resistance to the proposed reorganization temper your presentation of the college dean's comments? Why or why not?

2. Would you offer an assessment of the pros and cons of the proposed reorganization when discussing the issue with the faculty? If

yes, what evidence would use to assess the college dean's proposal? Would you, for example, seek the perception of faculty colleagues in the education, business, and music divisions? Would you request time to discuss the issue further with the college dean? Specifically, what insight would you seek to obtain about the proposed preorganization?

3. If you were persuaded that the proposed reorganization would be advantageous to the department faculty, would you attempt to persuade faculty who are opposed to the proposed reorganization to consider the college dean's proposal? If yes, how would you address their existing concerns about the proposed reorganization?

4. Is there a way you might champion the proposed reorganization without losing credibility with the faculty? As department chair, you have a credible perspective from which to describe the difficulty of tending to leadership responsibilities as one might manage teaching or other overload assignments.

Hindsight Is 20/20

Proposing reorganization or leading structural change can be a daunting responsibility because most people prefer the comfort of a structure that is familiar even when that structure is no longer serving mission or function. This fact might discourage department chairs from considering the feasibility of organizational change as a possible solution to pressing challenges. Yet institutions can be effective only when the organizational structure supports mission and function. Consequently, department chairs and other academic leaders are not exercising effective leadership when they accept and make do with an organizational structure that does not serve mission and function because it would be unpopular and faculty would resist considering the benefit of reorganization.

Generally, department chairs with high or positive leadership credibility are more effective in leading change and managing difficult situations. However, unless leaders are observed managing difficult tasks, they cannot possibly enhance their leadership credibility. It is when department chairs step up to difficult situations that they have the opportunity to enhance their leadership credibility because the acquisition of this essential leadership trait relies on others' perception of how a department chair handles difficult situations like leading an organizational change. Leadership credibility is built on *how* department chairs and other academic leaders manage difficult situations and can be lost when department chairs and other academic leaders avoid exercising leadership responsibility to keep peace or avoid making waves.

Let's Recap

As frontline managers, department chairs can find themselves leading organizational change. Department chairs will find the task of leading organizational change less difficult if they begin by assessing the anticipated benefits and liabilities of the proposed reorganization. When department chairs fully understand the nature and scope of a proposed reorganization, they are in a stronger position to discuss the proposed change with faculty and other relevant constituencies. Being knowledgeable of the proposed organizational change and its ramifications will enable department chairs to address faculty concerns directly and honestly. Using this process to discuss the proposed reorganization can enhance a department chair's leadership credibility even when the faculty or other constituencies do not favor the proposed change.

When leading organizational change, it is important for department chairs to understand the perspectives of all relevant constituencies. This information is essential to identifying shared values or priorities and facilitating a compromise between and among the various constituencies. Understanding the perspectives held by relevant constituencies also enables department chairs to frame the proposed organizational change in a way that is conducive to constructive discussion without inciting unnecessary defensiveness. For example, if a department chair understands that the faculty members in a smaller department fear being outvoted once merged with a larger department, the department chair can introduce the issue of department governance as something that would be considered and ironed out as part of the discussion about how a merger of the two departments would work.

Whenever possible, building consensus around shared values and priorities can help department chairs lead organizational changes that benefit the department and institution. The more faculty and staff are stuck defending the status quo, the more important it can be to identify commonly shared values and priorities. For example, if faculty are resistant to a proposed reorganization intended to help grow student enrollment, presenting the proposed change as action that would help address the commonly shared priority to grow enrollment should help to soften resistance to the proposed reorganization.

Finally, because positive leadership credibility is a tremendous advantage when leading change, it is prudent for department chairs to take stock of their leadership credibility regarding the specific proposed organizational change. This assessment should guide the department chair's approach to the relevant constituencies. For example, should the department chair sense that faculty perceive him or her as ill-equipped to propose a reorganization of the department to the administration, he or she can proactively suggest that a proposal would not be submitted to the administration unless and until it carried the full support of the department faculty. This approach would address the faculty concern that the department chair might forward an ill-conceived or ill-advised proposal. The approach also invites the faculty to become actively involved in shaping the proposal and to serve as gatekeepers for the final product. Handled well, this approach could enhance the department chair's leadership credibility with the faculty.

4

DEVELOPING A NEW PROGRAM WITHOUT FACULTY SUPPORT

SOME INSTITUTIONS FIND IT necessary to add high-demand academic programs for which there is no existing faculty expertise on the campus to recruit new markets of students to the institution. Likewise, institutions might add a specific sport, student activity, or service in an effort to be more competitive in recruiting students. These additions represent change, and their anticipated value may not be initially apparent to faculty and staff. In such situations, the administration will likely need to be more involved in the development and implementation of the new program than is typically the custom in higher education.

The goal of this chapter is to help department chairs and other academic leaders know how to gather information and perspectives that help inform how best to move forward when responding to challenges that cannot be managed through existing policies and procedures. The second goal of this chapter is to equip department chairs and other academic leaders with leadership communication strategies for garnering support for new programs, support services, and activities that break with tradition. The case presented in this chapter focuses on developing a new academic program for which there is no existing faculty expertise or initial faculty support. However, the leadership communication strategies presented can be used to lead change whenever the institution seeks to implement a program, activity, or service that cannot be developed by existing faculty and staff.

Defining the Task

Developing a new program, support service, or activity without faculty support can require leading change against formidable resistance. The task can be challenging, time-consuming, and potentially damaging to the department chair's leadership credibility. Typically, faculty develop new academic programs. When department chairs initiate new program development, some faculty will likely view the chair's action as an affront to the faculty's role and responsibilities. It is also possible that some faculty will view the department chair's action as a criticism of the existing curriculum in which the faculty members are vested. Consequently, department chairs risk damaging their leadership credibility with faculty when they develop new programs that lack initial faculty support.

Institutions of higher education sometimes face challenges that require department chairs and other academic leaders to develop new programs that may lack initial faculty support. For example, institutions must sustain enrollment to safeguard institutional viability because tuition revenue is needed to afford salary increases and cover increasing operating costs. Given increasing competition among institutions to recruit and retain students, the administration may seek to add academic programs that will enable the institution to recruit new markets of students. For example, a small liberal arts institution may seek to add programs designed to prepare students for work in a specific occupations such as nursing or physicians assistant for the express purpose of recruiting new markets of students. Because new academic programs cannot be developed by the central administration, the task typically falls to department chairs or academic leaders that work more closely with the faculty.

Department chairs occupy challenging positions of leadership. Department chairs are simultaneously a champion for faculty and a representative of the administration. Even when department chairs recognize the need to develop new programs to ensure institutional viability, to move forward it will require careful consideration because developing a new program without faculty support can irreparably damage the department chair's leadership credibility. Moreover, because department chairs represent both the administration and the department faculty, they must look at the resource needs and perspectives of both the institution and the department when leading change.

Relevant Leadership Communication Strategies

Department chairs and other academic leaders can use some specific leadership communication strategies to develop and implement new programs without initial faculty and staff support. The following leadership communication strategies will aid in managing this leadership task while minimizing the potential for destructive conflict.

Take Stock of the Context

It is virtually impossible to fully assess the pros and cons of any change initiative without taking stock of the larger context. The context encompasses the actual condition and a range of perspectives about that condition. The actual condition is represented by factual data including retention rates, entering class size, total enrollment, graduation rates, budget, major head count, class size, and percent of tenured faculty. The factual data that describe the actual condition are measurable and concrete information. Much of the data that describe the campus condition is accessible to accrediting bodies and other outside constituencies including government, industry, prospective students, granting agencies, and alumni. Although it is possible that organizations on and off campus can access factual information to inform their perspective of the institution, it is also possible that organizations on and off campus possess impressions of the institution that are not derived exclusively from factual data.

The context encompasses a range of perspectives that can vary greatly. Differing perspectives can exist between and among constituencies that review the same factual data. For example, a downward enrollment trend might fuel the faculty perception that the institution should invest more resources to rebuild a waning program. That same downward enrollment trend, however, might prompt the administration to believe that a program should be downsized or possibly eliminated. The context also encompasses perspectives that are not based on factual data. Individuals typically possess opinions on what has or has not happened and on what should and should not be done. It is possible for individuals within the same constituency to hold very different perspectives regarding what has happened and what should be done. For example, faculty members within the same department can disagree on whether a declining enrollment trend is sufficiently worrisome to warrant action.

An important part of taking stock of the context is assessing one's leadership credibility. It should be stressed that leadership credibility is an assigned attribute. In other words, a department chair may be knowledgeable of the chair's role and responsibilities and may possess the leadership skills needed to exercise those responsibilities. However, that department chair will enjoy the benefits of positive leadership credibility only if faculty members perceive the chair as possessing these qualities. Taking stock of one's leadership credibility can be challenging because it is unlikely that all faculty members assess the department chair's leadership credibility in the same way. Department chairs also need to take stock of their leadership credibility with the dean and others who may be instrumental when developing a new program. The assessment of one's leadership credibility is especially important when leading a change that will be initially unpopular because it is easier to lead change when faculty and staff trust the department chair's leadership. Consequently, department chairs are well served to take stock of the context when initiating change that will likely be resisted.

Link Change Initiatives to Existing Concerns

Individuals are more likely to embrace change if they first understand the need for change. Because change is uncomfortable for the majority of people, few individuals embrace change for the sake of change. When persuading others of the need for change, department chairs will find it helpful to relate the change initiative to existing concerns held by those from whom support is needed. When faculty perceive the change initiative as constructively addressing existing concerns, they are more likely to support the proposed change. For this strategy to work, those who the department chair wishes to persuade to embrace the change initiative must perceive the proposed change as addressing concerns that they have. If faculty are concerned about faculty workloads, the department chair will need to demonstrate how the proposed curriculum revision will address the faculty concern about workloads. If the curriculum revision serves to streamline course offerings or help ease faculty workloads in some other way, the proposed change will be perceived as a remedy for the existing concern. Should the department chair advocate the proposed change because it would address some other issue that is not a faculty concern, the chair will be less successful in garnering the desired faculty support.

Department chairs must document the relationship between the change initiative and existing concerns using evidence that is credible to those they hope will embrace the proposed change. Consider, for example, department faculty who are concerned about preserving academic quality with entering students who are unprepared to do college work. If this is the primary concern of faculty, the department chair will not be successful in getting faculty support for changing the degree requirements unless the department chair documents how the proposed change would address the specific faculty concern.

Take the Temperature Early and Often

When leading a change initiative that lacks initial faculty or staff support, it is imperative to take the temperature of those involved early and often. Department chairs and other academic leaders can take the temperature by learning the perspectives held by those involved. This includes both the proponents and opponents of change and especially those needed to help implement the change. When department chairs are asked to implement change mandated by the administration, they need to take the temperature of both department faculty and administration. The temperature reveals an individual's perspective on the change initiative and that person's flexibility for hearing opposing views, accepting suggested modifications to the change initiative, and investing in the implementation of the proposed change. Take, for example, the situation in which department chairs are asked by the administration to implement a program of ongoing curriculum review. Before presenting the mandate to the department faculty, the chair should take the temperature of both the administration and the department faculty. Knowing what flexibility exists within the administration for modifying the mandate outcome or deadline will be helpful to leading the change initiative. Similarly, knowing the perspectives held by department faculty will help the department chair know how to frame and present the issue for department consideration. Department chairs should also take the temperature of any and all constituencies that may be impacted by the change initiative. For example, should the mandate for ongoing curriculum review stipulate the review of specific data, it will be important to take the temperature of those who would be asked to supply the needed data.

At times, department chairs can predict the reaction that various constituencies will have to a change initiative. If not, department chairs can save time and anguish by taking temperatures before moving forward. This can be done in a number of ways including formal inquiry, informal conversation, and straw polls. The specific method will depend on the issue, the culture and climate, and other such factors. Certainly, department chairs will want to clarify with the administration any aspect of an administrative mandate that is not clear before presenting it to the department faculty. Similarly, before acting on an accrediting body's recommendations, department chairs must understand fully the action being requested and the outcome expectations of the agency making recommendations for change. It is possible that the department faculty hold varying perspectives of a single change initiative. Department chairs will find it easier to lead change when they account for faculty perspectives in framing the change issue for department consideration.

It is important to take the temperature of those involved throughout the change process. Doing so will inform the process by helping department chairs take stock of remaining concerns and existing commitment to the proposed change. When appropriate, taking the temperature can be done in a way that enhances leadership credibility. Consider the situation in which the department chair is leading the faculty in revising the common core course. Faculty discussion becomes stuck on the issue of whether or not any portion of the common core course should be delivered online. The chair realizes that department deliberations are stymied because faculty members are merely repeating their views without advancing the discussion to closure. In this circumstance, the department chair might take a straw poll regarding the specific issue of incorporating online instruction. The outcome would make evident the will of the majority and enable the department chair to move the discussion forward without appearing to arbitrarily dismiss either of the faculty perspectives. By taking a straw poll, department chairs evidence their desire to learn and honor the perspective held by the majority of the faculty.

Reduce the risk to leadership credibility

When leading a change that lacks initial faculty or staff support, it is prudent for department chairs and other academic leaders to take every possible measure to reduce the risk of damaging their leadership credibility. One's leadership credibility is comprised of the perception that others hold of that leader's knowledge, good intentions, and trustworthiness. Department chairs and other academic leaders can reduce the risk to their leadership credibility by using a process that evidences their knowledge, good intentions, and trustworthiness. A number of specific techniques can be used for this purpose.

OFFER CREDIBLE EXPERT TESTIMONY Anyone with relevant experience is a potential expert whose testimony can help address concerns. The pool of available experts therefore derives from the specific issue under consideration. It is imperative that the testimony is credible to those being led. For example, faculty and staff at another institution who experienced a similar change initiative to the one being considered are likely to be more credible to the department faculty than an administrator's testimony on the same experience.

USE RELEVANT DATA When a department chair considers data and other factual information produced by an independent source such as institutional research, advisement, or the alumni office, he or she demonstrates that he or she is not attempting to filter information or guide the department toward a specific outcome or plan. Using relevant data also helps to educate faculty and staff about the context, which can go a long way in helping them understand the need for change. Comparative data can be especially useful in helping faculty understand where the department stands vis-à-vis other departments at the institution. Without information about the context, some faculty members may get stuck reliving past events in ways that are not helpful to the department or the institution. Consider, for example, the senior faculty member who argues against cooperating with the wishes of the administration because 15 years earlier the administration denied a department request to replace a retiring faculty member. Out of context, this faculty member's recollection of an earlier decision will likely be viewed as some injustice in need of correction. However, the loss of a faculty position 15 years earlier may be viewed very differently against a backdrop of current enrollment trends for every academic major.

AUGMENT EXISTING POLICY AND PROCESS Given the serious challenges facing higher education, department chairs and other academic leaders can find themselves leading change with existing policies and processes that were designed for a very different time and circumstances. Campus procedures for revising policy may make it impractical to secure approval for a policy change before leading a pressing change initiative. Department chairs, however, can augment existing policy by adding steps and levels of review to the existing policy and practice. For example, should faculty members be concerned that revising the curriculum to require an internship would hurt enrollment, the department chair can augment the procedure for curriculum revision by gathering student feedback about the proposed requirement so the student perspective can help inform department deliberations. In other words, existing policy need not limit or hinder informed departmental deliberations.

RECOMMEND TRYING THE CHANGE ON A PILOT BASIS Should all else fail and a needed change is at risk of being voted down, department chairs can recommend that the change be tried on a trial basis. Even those who are opposed are likely to agree to a trial when a better solution to an existing problem cannot be imagined. When recommending that a change be tried out temporarily, it is imperative that department chairs establish the date and criteria to be used to evaluate it. The criteria should incorporate the concerns that faculty hold about the proposed change. For example, if faculty members are reticent to support a change because they fear it could reduce the number of students who graduate in 4 years, then examining graduation rates will be important to reviewing the pilot. The date established for review should correspond with the nature of the change. For example, if the change impacts the full academic year, the review would not need to be conducted before the completion of at least one academic year. When asking others to support trying a change on a pilot basis, it is imperative that the review be done on schedule using the agreed upon criteria. Failure to do this will damage the department chair's leadership credibility. Conversely, holding fast to the criteria and date for review can enhance a department chair's leadership credibility for leading change in the future.

Putting Theory into Practice

Consider how these leadership communication strategies might be used in a specific situation. In Case 4.1, a relatively new department chair hired from outside the institution faces the difficult task of deciding whether to take the initiative to develop a new academic program that will be unpopular with the faculty. Place yourself in the role of department chair as you read.

Case 4.1: Time to Take Initiative?

Beth Eyer was hired 2 years ago from outside the institution to chair the Department of Health and Wellness. Although the faculty supported her hire, Beth recognizes that some faculty members are concerned that her vision for the department is to completely overhaul and transform the curriculum. The bulk of Beth's professional experience is in health care. She began her career as a registered nurse, and when she discovered that she enjoyed supervising nursing students doing clinical rotations she returned to school. Upon the completion of her doctorate, Beth accepted a faculty position in a large nursing school at a research university. Once tenured and promoted to full professor, Beth found herself more engaged in administrative work that went well beyond the management of nursing education.

Beth was motivated to apply for her current position for several reasons. First, the position announcement described work that Beth enjoys and wants to do. She looks forward to using her experience to enhance and further build the reputation of a solid program. Second, the position duties listed in the position announcement are a good fit with Beth's experience and leadership skill. She especially enjoys developing new programs and improving program quality, and the position announcement mentions seeking a department chair with the vision, experience, and leadership skill necessary to lead the program into the future. Third, the position would enable Beth to live closer to her aging parents.

For the most part, Beth believes that things have gone well. The department is endowed with many strong faculty members who are passionate about teaching and take pride in student success. Everyone is collegial and appears to respect the others in the group. Beth senses that the apparent mutual respect might be characterized as an unwritten covenant that promises support in return for receiving support. She has observed that several of the faculty members resist change on principle. Although Beth possesses expertise and experience that could help the department grow and evolve, she is painfully aware that her ideas are sometimes rejected without consideration. The change-resistant faculty members are fond of asserting that this or that new idea would never work in this department or at this institution. When Beth attempts to learn the basis for their thinking, the change-resistant faculty members fail to supply any substantive rationale for their belief. Instead, they counsel Beth that it will take time for her to learn the department and campus culture.

The Department

The department houses baccalaureate degree programs in nutrition, sports management, exercise science, prephysical therapy, and health and physical education, and each program is managed separately. The designated program coordinator for each program brings curriculum revisions to the full department for consideration and vote. Without exception, the faculty vote to support the recommendation after a very brief presentation of the proposed change. There is virtually no internal impetus for holding each other accountable for program quality or for assuring that every program is relevant in meeting the current educational needs of students. Consequently, the department offers essentially the same five programs that it offered 2 decades ago. Given some remarkable changes in the health and wellness industry nationally, Beth realizes that she needs to encourage the faculty to consider some substantial curriculum revisions in all five academic programs for them to remain viable.

The Immediate Challenge

The university failed to reach its enrollment goal for the current academic year. The entering class is significantly smaller than projected, and attrition of current students is greater than expected. At a minimum, the budget shortfall means another year of no salary increases for faculty and staff. The central administration warns that the institution will soon need to cut faculty and staff positions if enrollment is not quickly restored at least to the level of the preceding year. The central administration is careful to add that this is not the time to expand existing programs. Instead, the institution needs to be strategic in adding programs, activities, or support services that will recruit new markets of students to the institution. The administration stresses that curriculum revision, which merely gives enrolled students more choice, will not address the immediate challenge. In other words, curriculum change that entices currently enrolled students to transfer from one existing program to another existing program will not generate new revenue for the institution.

The Department Chair's Perspective

Beth perceives the immediate challenge facing the institution as a golden opportunity for the Department of Health and Wellness. In particular, adding a nursing program would enable the institution to recruit a new market of students. Moreover, the regional shortage of nurses would likely make nursing a popular program with career-focused prospective students. The Department of Health and Wellness could benefit the institution financially and enhance its position on the campus by developing a program in nursing. Beth recognizes that the existing department faculty lack expertise in nursing. However, she possesses professional expertise and contacts that could compensate for the lack of existing faculty expertise. Beth believes that an accelerated program in nursing that is restricted to students who already hold a baccalaureate degree could be staffed with adjunct professors from the internationally recognized medical systems that are located within the region. In addition, she is familiar with the accreditation requirements for nursing programs, so she feels confident in being able to guide program development and implementation.

The Department Chair's Dilemma

Beth is certain that the health and wellness faculty do not envision how the department might help the institution meet the immediate challenge of growing enrollment. She also recognizes that at least two of the existing five department programs are vulnerable to losing faculty positions should the institution be unable to restore enrollment. In Beth's view, the addition of an accelerated program in nursing would benefit both the institution and the department.

At the same time, Beth is sensitive to the fact that she has not yet earned the full support of all department faculty members. She is painfully aware that some view every suggestion she makes as evidence that she does not understand the existing culture. Suggesting that the department consider the development of the nursing program could provide her detractors with ammunition that could be used to undermine the support that she does have. Beth finds herself between the proverbial rock and a hard place as she contemplates what to do.

Let's Analyze the Case

One inevitable challenge that department chairs hired from outside the institution face is using expertise acquired elsewhere within a new culture and with faculty and staff who are familiar and comfortable with the status quo. It is ironic that new hires often discover that the very expertise the search committee considered desirable in a candidate is not welcomed by faculty members after the new hire is in the position. In the case, Beth has an idea that could help the institution recruit a new market of students: to add an accelerated program in nursing. If it is successful, it would generate new revenue for the institution and subsequently elevate the viability and status of the health and wellness department on campus. Should Beth be able to gain support for a new program in nursing and oversee the program's successful implementation, the process and outcome would also enhance Beth's leadership credibility with both the faculty and the administration.

There is, however, a huge risk in moving forward. As a relatively new department chair hired from outside the institution, Beth does not enjoy the level of leadership credibility needed to secure faculty trust and support that is essential to developing a new program, especially one that will likely be viewed by some as the department chair's effort to transform the department into something more like what the chair knew and managed at her previous institution. Beth realizes that the mere mention of her idea would likely hurt her leadership credibility with several of the faculty members. Without the full support of the department faculty, Beth fears that it would be difficult to secure support from the faculty senate, which is needed before the proposal can be considered by the administration. Indeed, Beth has good reason to conclude that broaching the department faculty with her idea is too great a risk to her leadership credibility and future at the institution.

Case 4.1 reveals that the institution's budget shortfall is serious. The most recent enrollment decline means another year of no salary increases for faculty and staff. Moreover, the central administration warns that faculty and staff positions will be cut if enrollment is not quickly restored at least to the level of the preceding year. Although the scenario does not reveal which academic departments are vulnerable to administratively imposed downsizing, we know that Beth believes that at least two of the five department programs are vulnerable to losing faculty positions. (The case scenario does not reveal the basis for Beth's thinking.) Furthermore, Beth believes that all five of the department programs would benefit from substantial curriculum revision, and there exists no internal impetus for undertaking serious curriculum review. Should the administration cut health and wellness faculty positions or programs, Beth would find herself defending programs that she recognizes are in need improvement. Should Beth be unsuccessful in preventing the loss of health and wellness faculty positions or programs, she would quickly lose leadership credibility with the department faculty. At the same time, Beth would likely lose leadership credibility with the central administration by championing the need to preserve academic programs that are in need of substantial revision unless the faculty members become willing to engage in serious curriculum review and revision. Consequently, Beth is truly between the proverbial rock and hard place.

It's Your Turn

Assume the position of department chair in this case as you consider the following questions:

1. List the pros and cons of moving forward with the idea to secure faculty support for the development of a nursing program. Distinguish between *probable* and *possible* risks and benefits. For example, is the demand for an accelerated nursing program sufficient to provide fiscal relief if added? What evidence would you gather to make this termination?

2. List the pros and cons of *not* moving forward with the idea to develop a nursing program. Distinguish between *probable* and *possible* risks and benefits. For example, how likely is it that the department would lose faculty positions? What factors and data would you consider in assessing the department's vulnerability?

3. Should you decide to move forward, what steps would you take to minimize the risk to your leadership credibility? Would you, for example, discuss the fiscal challenge facing the institution with the faculty and involve them in thinking through the probable and possible consequences of a budget shortfall?

4. Should you decide to not move forward, what steps would you take to strengthen the department against the possibility of position cuts? Would you involve the faculty? If so, how would you involve faculty? How would you frame the issue for faculty consideration?

Please Consider

Whenever department chairs or academic leaders find themselves between the proverbial rock and hard place, it is a good idea to take stock of the context. By assessing the context, it is easier to distinguish between outcomes that are probable and outcomes that are possible. This will help to determine the best course of action. If the department chair in the scenario determines that the health and wellness department is definitely vulnerable to position cuts, the chair will have more reason to confer with the faculty regarding the department's status given the immediate fiscal challenge facing the institution. Assessing the context enables the department chair to more credibly frame the issue for faculty consideration. This permits the faculty to understand the nature and scope of the immediate challenge before generating and considering the various courses of action that the department might take.

Let's Recap

Take a moment to review your response to the previous questions. Did you consider the context before listing the pros and cons of moving forward? What factual information would you gather to learn more about the departmental and institutional contexts? Are there specific perspectives you would assume to inform your understanding of the departmental and institutional contexts?

Putting Theory into Practice

In Case 4.2, the department chair decides to pursue the addition of a nursing program. Consider how the department chair's decision resonates with your own thinking regarding the situation as you read.

Case 4.2: Full Steam Ahead

After much thought and a few sleepless nights, Beth Eyer decides to pursue consideration of developing a nursing program with the department faculty. She recognizes that the idea will be unpopular with several of the department faculty members. At the same time, she believes that if she sits back and does nothing she will be forced to manage the department downsizing. Beth decides that it would be more painful to manage the downsizing of the department than to manage the anticipated negative reaction to an idea that could enhance the department's position on campus and provide some fiscal relief for the institution.

In reaching this decision, Beth reviewed enrollment and retention data for every program at the institution. Unfortunately, two of the five health and wellness department programs experienced noteworthy enrollment declines that would make it difficult to document the need for the current number of full-time faculty teaching in these programs. With three tenured faculty members nearing retirement, Beth knows that it is unlikely that the department would be approved to hire replacements for the retirees. As part of the department program review conducted 4 years earlier, the administration charged the department with revising the curriculum in all five department programs for the express purpose of making all five programs more viable and attractive to prospective students. The faculty failed to follow through on the requested curriculum revisions. Faculty members are convinced that extensive curriculum revision would require additional funding support from the central administration. Consequently, the faculty believe that revising the curriculum would be a waste of time because the administration would not support the resource needs of an expanded program.

Beth hopes that the process of considering an unpopular idea will ultimately improve her working relationship with the department faculty. She hopes that the process used to consider the addition of an accelerated program in nursing will evidence her commitment to strengthening the department and serve as a model for future department deliberations. At a minimum, Beth believes that the process will enable faculty to better understand the expertise and collaborative leadership style that she brings to the department if they will trust her to do the job she was hired to do.

Let's Analyze the Case

After reviewing enrollment and retention data for all academic programs at the institution, the department chair concludes that the health and wellness department is vulnerable to losing faculty positions should the institution be unable to grow its enrollment. The previous program review finding weakens any argument that the department chair might make to replace the three tenured faculty members upon their upcoming retirements. Rather than devoting time and energy to determining how best to rearrange the deck chairs on a sinking ship, the department chair decides to move forward to discuss the possibility of adding an accelerated program in nursing with the department faculty.

The department chair recognizes that the idea will be met with resistance. However, she hopes to frame the issue in a way that garners enough faculty support that the department faculty will give the idea fair consideration. Beth believes that the data she reviewed regarding the department's vulnerability to losing faculty positions make a compelling case for taking action. Case 4.2 does not offer any information on how the department chair plans to move forward. Yet *how* the chair frames and presents the idea will inevitably influence the outcome. Should the chair present the idea in a way that makes faculty defensive of the status quo, faculty resistance will increase and the chair's task will become more challenging. Moreover, should the idea heighten faculty resistance, the chair will lose leadership credibility with the faculty. The stakes are high so the department chair needs to give careful consideration to *how* she will proceed.

It's Your Turn

Assume the position of department chair, and develop a plan for how you would move forward.

1. What would you do first, second, third, and so on? Be specific is choreographing the steps you would take.

2. Are there data and perspectives that you would gather beyond what the chair examined to inform the decision to move forward? If yes, be specific in listing what information you would use to reach a decision.

3. Assuming you reach the same decision about moving forward, what department and campus policies would you review to inform how to proceed? For example, campus policy may stipulate criteria for dismissing tenured faculty or program elimination. Existing policy may also stipulate a provision for appealing such decisions. Written guidelines on faculty workloads, class size, and productivity might be used to document the need for faculty replacements.

4. Think ahead to your discussion with the faculty, and outline the points that the chair should make. How much would you share about your assessment of the department's vulnerability to losing faculty positions and programs? What evidence would you present to substantiate your assessment?

Please Consider

It can be dangerous to use fear of dire consequences to motivate faculty and staff to embrace change. In some instances, a department chair's description of possible and even probable dire consequences can heighten fear to the point of paralyzing others. Overworked and underpaid faculty members are less likely to expend energy and effort slaying dragons or tilting at windmills. If the anticipated dire consequence does not appear manageable or reversible, faculty and staff are likely to perceive the proposed change as an exercise in futility. Similarly, a department chair's description of the dire consequence must be credible to those being persuaded of the need to take action. Should faculty perceive the department chair as crying wolf or being an alarmist, resistance to the proposed change can increase. Using fear of some possible or probable dire consequence will serve only to motivate others if those being persuaded find the department chair's description of the likely dire consequence believable. For this reason, the anticipated dire consequence should never be exaggerated beyond what factual data and sound reasoning will support. As important, the factual data and analysis used to describe the anticipated dire consequence must be believable to those being motivated to take action. For example, the central administration's warning about the need to cut faculty positions will not be perceived as a credible dire consequence unless the faculty members believe the administration will follow through and cut faculty positions. Here again, campus context is important. Has the administration ever cut faculty positions? Do the faculty believe that tenure protects faculty from position elimination? Department chairs must assess both the probability and the believability of a dire consequence before using it to motivate others to take action.

Department chairs and other academic leaders damage their leadership credibility when they describe dire consequences that are not credible to others. Even when relating concrete facts that paint a clear picture of a probable dire consequence, department chairs risk losing leadership credibility if the facts presented are not believable to others. Department chairs must consider the perspective held by others when presenting this kind of information. For example, tenured full professors who have lived through previous enrollment declines and budget shortfalls without witnessing program elimination at the institution will be less likely to believe that program elimination is a probable consequence than untenured faculty who have no experience with how budget shortfalls are managed at the institution. For dire consequences to motivate others to take initiative, they must link to what faculty members know and have experienced.

Fear of a dire consequence can be a platform for change. When faculty have common concerns, department chairs can motivate people to take action by linking the need to change to concerns held by the faculty. For example, when faculty fear that the administration seeks to downsize the number of faculty positions at the institution, they will be generally more supportive of taking action that they are persuaded will help retain faculty positions. To the extent that department chairs and other academic leaders can credibly link change initiatives to existing faculty and staff concerns, the easier it will be to garner support for a change.

Let's Recap

Take a moment to review the points you would make when presenting this issue to the faculty. How would you present the dire consequence so it is believable for faculty members? What might you do to reduce the risk of heightening fear to the point of paralysis and damaging your leadership credibility? Does your plan

- Take stock of the context?
- Link the change initiative to existing concerns?
- Take the temperature early and often?
- Reduce the risk to leadership credibility?

Putting Theory into Practice

In Case 4.3, we learn Beth Eyer's plan for moving forward. As you read, note how the department chair's approach differs from the plan you would use.

Case 4.3: The Department Chair's Approach

Beth decides that there are a few things she must do before proposing the addition of the nursing program to the department faculty. She plots the steps as follows:

1. Talk with the dean.
2. Review relevant policy.
3. Validate thinking.
4. Anticipate sources and nature of resistance.
5. Gather evidence and relevant testimony.
6. Identify sources of support.
7. Frame the issue for faculty consideration.

Talk with the Dean

Beth decides that the logical starting point is to discuss her idea of proposing the development of an accelerated nursing program with the dean. She decides it would be futile to spend time and energy discussing the idea within the department if the dean does not perceive the idea as feasible. In talking with the dean, Beth seeks to learn the level of commitment that the department might expect from the institution should the department develop a proposal to add a nursing program.

Review Relevant Policy

Beth reviews campus policy regarding curriculum development and approval. She also reviews campus policy regarding the termination of tenured faculty in instances of fiscal exigency, program elimination, and enrollment decline.

Validate Thinking

Beth decides that she needs to validate her assessment of the health and wellness department's vulnerability should enrollment not be restored at the institution. Certainly, Beth wants to learn the dean's perspective on this matter. In addition, she decides to consult some long-term department chairs on the campus to learn their thoughts about how the institution is likely to manage the loss of revenue from declining enrollment.

Anticipate Sources and Nature of Resistance

Beth develops a chart listing those individuals on the campus who would be required to consider a proposal to develop a nursing program. Her list includes individual department faculty members, the dean, the faculty senate, and the provost. Beth then lists the response she anticipates that each will have to the proposed addition of a nursing program. In a third column, Beth makes a note as to when and how the reaction must be addressed. For example, Beth anticipates that the dean and provost will be concerned about cost, so she makes a note to include cost projections in the initial proposal. Beth anticipates that some on the faculty senate will fear that a nursing program would drain scarce resources away from existing programs, so she makes a note to include in the proposal an explanation of how a new nursing program would recruit students who otherwise would not enroll at the institution and thereby help the institution grow revenue through increased enrollment.

Gather Evidence and Relevant Testimony

Beth reviews the list of newly accredited nursing programs to identify comparable institutions that added nursing programs. She plans to contact individuals at these institutions to learn more about their experience. She hopes that their experience might yield some positive testimony that she can use to persuade the skeptics at her institution. Beth also hopes to learn from the experience of others so she can more effectively lead the development of a proposal to add an accelerated nursing program.

Identify Sources of Support

Beth realizes that she will not garner department faculty support to develop a nursing program if she is the sole advocate for the idea. She hopes to identify tangible sources of support in the spadework she will do before taking the idea to the department faculty. Beth plans to talk with the dean because the dean's support will evidence that the dean perceives the idea as a feasible and desirable response to the institution's need to recruit new markets of students to generate new revenue. Finally, Beth hopes to identify other sources of support through the testimony of faculty at other institutions where nursing programs have been added to increase campus enrollment.

Frame the Issue for Faculty Consideration

Beth plans to allow her work to inform how she frames the issue for faculty consideration. Initially, Beth senses that she might present the idea as an opportunity to help the institution and the department. She might also present the idea as a way to prevent dire consequences that could befall the department. Beth decides not to share her idea with any in the department until she has completed the other steps in her plan for moving forward.

Let's Analyze the Case

The department chair developed a plan for moving forward that delineates what the chair will do but does not speculate what the chair will learn in each step of the process. For example, although the chair plans to begin by learning the dean's reaction to the initial idea, she does not assume that the dean will be supportive. The department chair's plan is designed to uncover factual information and existing perspectives that will inform whether the idea is worth pursuing with the department faculty. Framing the issue for faculty consideration is the last step in the department chair's plan because it will be informed by the information obtained through all the previous steps.

Certainly the department chair's seven-step process will take time and effort. Department chairs feeling pressed for time might view the chair's expanded process as a potential waste of time and effort should the faculty remain resistant to the idea. There are times when it may make sense to assess and use initial perspectives to determine whether or not to move forward to consider a new program or some other change initiative. This can be an efficient way to proceed when the risk of not taking action is negligible. For example, department chairs would not need to do much, if any, spadework on changes that need to reflect only department preference. An idea for how the department might change the way students are assigned to faculty advisers, for example, might be discussed first with the faculty to learn their initial interest in the idea before doing anything further. In the scenario presented in this chapter, the department chair fears that an idea that could be beneficial to both the department and institution would likely be resisted without careful consideration should she take the idea first to the faculty.

It's Your Turn

Compare your plan to the one developed by the department chair in the case.

1. What, if any, changes would you make to the department chair's plan? Consider, for example, if you would review relevant policy before talking with the dean. Are there steps you would add or delete from the chair's plan? Are there other perspectives you would solicit to determine the feasibility and desirability of moving forward?

2. Is there other information you would obtain before talking with the department faculty? If yes, delineate the information you would seek and the source for that information.

3. Assume that your preliminary work yields information that makes a strong case for developing a program in nursing. How would you frame the issue for the faculty? Be specific. How would you word this issue on the meeting agenda? Would you have preliminary discussions with any in the department? Would you disseminate any information in advance for faculty to consider before the meeting?

4. What would be your goal for the first faculty discussion? Would you consider it sufficient to raise the issue and invite all to give the matter

more thought? Or would you hope to take a preliminary vote as to whether the faculty members believe it is a good idea to explore the feasibility of adding an accelerated program in nursing? What factors would help determine a reasonable goal for the first faculty discussion?

Please Consider

There are times when taking a preliminary vote can help build consensus for the change initiative and help inform next steps in the process. Informal votes can be used to confirm that the majority of those involved agree with some specific component of a larger initiative. For example, when leading core curriculum revision, it can be helpful to take a vote on individual requirements such as the number of credit hours to be reserved for a common core. An informal vote can also be used to seek clarity on a group's preferences for how to manage some aspect of process or change initiative. For example, an informal vote might be taken to determine if the department wishes to divide the work associated with the change initiative or complete all work in a group of the whole. Used in these ways, an informal vote helps to inform the process and provides valuable feedback for the leader. When an informal vote affirms the existence of a split among the faculty, the department chair knows that more discussion is needed on that particular issue before reaching closure on the change initiative. When an academic leader uses informal votes strategically to take the pulse of those involved in the change initiative, the process can help enhance leadership credibility because doing so demonstrates the leader's interest in learning what the group thinks and wishes to do.

It is not prudent, however, to take a preliminary informal vote on an issue when the department chair or academic leader seeks to engage the faculty and staff in discussing an issue that is initially misunderstood or unpopular. In such instances, department chairs will want to educate faculty and staff about the issue and the context before polling their preferences about what should be done. In the case presented in this chapter, the department chair would be ill advised to take a preliminary faculty vote on whether the department should move forward to develop an accelerated program in nursing because the faculty would likely vote against moving forward. Although that may be the best decision for the department in the long run, soliciting a likely negative faculty vote at a preliminary stage denies the department opportunity to reach an informed decision. To lead effectively in the situation, the department chair must first educate the faculty regarding the problem facing the institution and the pros and cons of developing an accelerated program in nursing.

Putting Theory into Practice

In Case 4.4, we learn the outcome of the department chair's conversation with the dean. Please consider the perspectives of both the department chair and the dean as you read.

Case 4.4: Factoring in the Dean's Perspective

Beth quickly discovers that the dean perceives the addition of a nursing program as a reasoned response to the institution's need to recruit new markets of students. The dean, however, has concerns about the feasibility and cost of moving forward.

The Dean's Initial Concerns

The dean raises two initial concerns. First, the dean fears that the department faculty's reaction to Beth's idea could affirm the suspicion voiced by a few during the search process that Beth hopes to transform the department into something it is not. In particular, with much of Beth's experience being in nursing education, a few faculty members prophesized that Beth would push for the creation of professionally oriented health-care programs. Consequently, the dean believes that Beth could very well jeopardize her leadership credibility and future at the institution by pursuing the idea of adding a nursing program with the department faculty. Second, the dean recognizes that even a successful proposal would require the central administration to commit the funds needed to develop and implement a nursing program. Although the proposal would project costs and anticipated revenues, it would require the administration to invest scarce resources now on the promise of revenue to be generated in the future. Because current policy requires that new programs be approved by the department, college, and faculty senate before being forwarded to the provost for review and approval, the department chair would be doing a lot of time-consuming work to develop a proposal and secure multiple levels of support for a new program before learning if the central administration is willing to make the initial investment.

The dean asks Beth to contact some institutions that have added nursing programs to learn their experience and to delineate more precisely the hurdles that would need to be cleared to have a new nursing program accredited within a reasonable timeframe. The dean offers to give his second concern more thought, and the department chair and dean agree to meet again to discuss the idea further after each has time to consider the idea further.

Second Meeting with the Dean

Beth shares with the dean that she identified two institutions that successfully added nursing programs when seeking to grow enrollment and revenue. Representatives at both institutions report that they filled their entering class and have a waiting list for next year's class. These conversations also provided Beth with some insight regarding likely faculty concerns including, the fear that a new nursing program would siphon funding support from existing academic programs. Beth learned that the biggest hurdle to accreditation is securing a sufficient number of clinical placement opportunities for students enrolled in the nursing program. This information propelled Beth to look more closely at existing nursing programs in the region to get a better sense of the competition for, and the availability of, clinical placements. Beth identified three medical facilities that are interested in being considered as a site for clinical placements should the nursing program be developed.

The dean is encouraged by Beth's report. He recognizes that the information obtained from faculty and staff at other institutions and letters of support from medical facilities interested in offering clinical placements will strengthen the proposal and quiet some likely resistance. It does not, however, guarantee that the central administration will invest the resources needed to develop and implement a nursing program. Nor does it protect Beth's leadership credibility with faculty who might use the very suggestion of adding a nursing program as ammunition to criticize Beth's leadership and fit with the department and campus culture. At the same time, the dean has no better solution for generating new markets of students among the academic programs in the college, so Beth and the dean agree to pursue the matter further.

Reducing the Risk

The dean suggests an approach that he hopes will reduce the risk of wasting time and damaging the department chair's leadership credibility. The dean it is not authorized to alter the current policy and procedure for securing program approval, but he believes that the unique circumstances warrant a modified approach. Current policy calls for new programs to be developed within an academic department by faculty with the requisite expertise. The full department must endorse the program proposal before it is forwarded to the college dean and faculty senate for review and approval. Because the health and wellness department does not have a faculty members with expertise in nursing education, the dean believes this circumstance warrants the involvement of individuals who process the specific expertise and experience needed to assess the feasibility of adding a program in nursing.

The dean envisions constituting a task force comprised of individuals from outside the institution who are knowledgeable of nursing education and other professionals who are expert in market research and cost analysis. The dean explains his plan to fill the task force with experienced professionals who could more accurately assess the feasibility of adding a nursing program at the institution than faculty and staff who lack training and experience in nursing. Should the task force finding be encouraging, the dean would seek a reaction from the central administration to the general feasibility and desirability of developing a nursing program. An important part of this discussion would be to learn whether the central administration believes adding a nursing program would enable the institution to recruit a new market of students and, if so, whether the central administration is willing to commit the startup funds needed to develop and implement a nursing program. Should the central administration commit to funding program development, then the customary program proposal would be developed within the health and wellness department for faculty review and approval before being forwarded through the approval levels prescribed in current policy. Should the task force finding be discouraging, the department chair and dean agree that the idea would be abandoned.

The dean believes that augmenting current policy and procedure reduces the risk of investing time and effort to develop and secure approval of a new program proposal that may not be supported by the central administration. Should the task force find that the idea lacks merit, the dean and chair can abandon the idea without damaging leadership credibility with either the faculty for the central administration. Should the task force find that the idea has merit, the task force testimony would lend credibility to the idea when Beth discusses the development of a nursing program with the department faculty. Beth would be able to reference the task force finding and quote professionals serving on the task force in addressing faculty concerns. Beth realizes that having this ammunition from the task force will spare her from needing to be the sole champion of the proposal. Similarly, having the central administration's commitment to provide the startup funds needed to develop and implement the nursing program will go a long way in addressing concerns about the futility of developing a program that will not be funded.

Let's Analyze the Case

Although the dean has concerns, he believes the idea for developing a nursing program warrants further consideration, so the dean partners with the department chair to explore the matter further. Notice the division of labor assigned by the dean. The dean asks the department chair to solicit information from other institutions that have added the nursing program and offers to give more thought how they might reduce the risk of moving forward. The dean is supportive of the department chair's idea to develop a nursing program but wishes to move forward in a way that reduces the risk to the chair's leadership credibility with the faculty. The dean suggests an approach that would augment but not require a formal revision of the current policy and procedures for program development. The dean suggests striking a special task force composed of professionals who can help assess the feasibility of developing an accelerated program in nursing. Although this would add to the work required by policy to develop a new program, the task force finding, if negative, could prevent the department chair and dean from pursuing an unrealistic initiative that could be costly to the department chair's leadership credibility. If positive, the task force finding would equip the department chair with expert testimony as to feasibility of developing a nursing program. Moreover, the task force finding would provide a platform for seeking the central administration's commitment to invest the initial funds needed to develop the program in advance of seeking faculty support. Taking these steps will enable the department chair to address two important issues that the faculty members are likely to raise: the feasibility and desirability of developing a nursing program.

There is some risk in appending the current policy and procedure for developing new programs. Some faculty may perceive the creation of a task force as an effort to circumvent current policy. Similarly, the administration might take exception to having a task force of professionals from outside the institution issue a finding that essentially directs the use of scarce fiscal resources. Moreover, faculty and administrative staff who perceive the addition of a nursing program to be beyond the scope of the institution's mission could view the creation of the task force as inviting professionals outside the institution to alter the institution's mission. The case does not offer any information on whether or not the department chair and dean plan to communicate the creation of the task force to the department faculty and the central administration.

The scenario does not mention who the dean would have chair the task force. Certainly, there needs to be some institutional presence on the task force. Someone from the institution should chair the group to ensure that discussion remains on point and the outcome serves the institution. It will be important to give the task force a very clear charge that frames precisely the issue under consideration.

It's Your Turn

Consider the role responsibility of both department chair and dean in answering the following questions:

1. As department chair, would you welcome the dean's proposed involvement in, and plan for, moving forward? Why or why not?

2. Is the dean's plan to create a task force of health-care professionals likely to serve its intended purpose? Why or why not?

3. What, if anything, would you change about the dean's plan to create a task force of professionals? What types of professional expertise would you invite to serve on the task force? For example, would you consider inviting practicing nurses, directors of nursing education, hospital administrators, marketing professionals, entrepreneurs, or financial analysts?

4. Draft the specific charge you would give to task force. Would you, as dean, chair the task force? If not, whom would you appoint to chair the task force? Does it matter that the department faculty and the central administration perceive the task force composition, leadership, and finding credible? If yes, what measures would you take to ensure that this occurs?

5. Would you seek permission from the central administration before creating the task force? Why or why not? If not, would you alert the central administration to the creation of the task force? If yes, how would you communicate the creation of the task force to the central administration (e.g., email, meeting request)?

6. Would you inform the department faculty of the creation of the task force? If yes, how would you communicate this to the department faculty? Would you send an email from the dean, the department chair, or both? Would you call a department faculty meeting?

7. Are there others you would inform about the creation of the task force? For example, would it be helpful to brief the faculty senate on the augmented procedure being used to assess the feasibility and desirability of a possible new program before expending faculty time and other scarce resources to consider the proposal?

Please Consider

In certain situations, involving industry professionals can greatly inform the development of the new academic program and the revision of existing curriculum. In the case presented in this chapter, health-care professionals can provide a perspective that will help inform campus decision making. As prospective employers of future graduates of the new program, health-care professionals have a perspective worth considering. The task force can offer insight regarding employment opportunities for the graduates of the program and can comment on the education and skills training graduates need. Consequently, the task force professionals can equip the department chair and dean with credible testimony regarding the need and learning objectives for the program. Depending on the specific expertise of the task force members, the group may also provide information regarding student demand for the program, ideas for marketing the program, and information on the cost of nursing education.

There are other tangible benefits of involving professionals in the development of a new program. Department chairs and deans enable industry professionals to become vested in the program. This insider's view can lead to the creation of internships for students and can also serve to cultivate a pool of professional mentors for students, classroom speakers, and student project jurors. The more professionals become involved with students and the academic program, the greater the opportunity to persuade them about the quality of the program and caliber of program's graduates. These professionals can supply important testimony of program quality for accreditation and other program reviews. They also hire graduates and may contribute to the program by guest lecturing in classes, gifting equipment, and creating student internships.

Hindsight Is 20/20

It is typically important to signal relevant constituencies when augmenting current policy and procedure. Although department chairs and other academic leaders may prefer to augment policy and procedure without a lot of fanfare as the dean in the case scenario plans to do, it is typically preferable to share information about the planned approach in advance. It is extremely difficult to augment process without others learning about it. Others are more likely to question the process and the academic leader's motives if the plan to amend existing practice is not shared in advance. When this happens, the adverse reaction to a suspect process can taint the reaction to the issue under consideration.

Instead, department chairs, deans, and other academic leaders should inform others of the additional steps to be taken in advance so everyone is aware of the intended purpose for the atypical approach. Done well, the process of notifying others can enhance leadership credibility. For example, the dean in the case could enhance his credibility with both the department faculty and the central administration by explaining that the task force is being formed to reach a preliminary determination about feasibility of a new program before taking faculty time or spending scarce resources to develop a program that may not help grow revenue by generating a new market students for the institution. It is important for the dean to stress that this work merely proceeds and does not replace the approval process outlined in campus policy. Similarly, by widely sharing a copy of the charge to the task force, the dean has an opportunity to evidence the parameters in place that will guide the work done by the task force. This can help silence resident pot stirrers who might otherwise create uninformed and unnecessary angst about the process and the possibility of developing a program in nursing.

Let's Recap

In the face of increasing competition for students, department chairs and other academic leaders can find themselves needing to develop new academic programs, activities, and support services that lack initial faculty and staff support. Leading change in this circumstance can be exceedingly challenging and potentially damaging to one's leadership credibility. Even department chairs with positive leadership credibility can find that championing the development of a new program that lacks initial faculty support can quickly damage their rapport and leadership credibility with faculty because the situation places them at odds with existing faculty perspectives when most faculty expect their department chair to represent and champion their views. Department chairs must proceed carefully when leading the development of a new program, activity, or support service that lacks initial faculty support.

This chapter presented four leadership communication strategies that department chairs and other academic leaders can use to more successfully lead the development of a new program without damaging credibility. First, it is important to take stock of the context. The context encompasses both the actual condition as evidenced by data and other factual information and perspectives held by others about the condition. In addition, department chairs must take stock of their leadership credibility while recognizing that one's leadership credibility is an assigned attribute that is specific to the issue and situation.

Second, department chairs will find it easier to lead the development of a new program that lacks initial faculty support by linking consideration of the new program to existing faculty concerns. Department chairs can melt resistance by helping faculty understand how the development of a new program addresses their concerns. This strategy, however, will be helpful only when department chairs have an accurate sense of existing faculty concerns and can make the connection between those concerns and new program development in a way that is credible for the faculty.

Third, department chairs will find it helpful to take temperatures early and often throughout the process of leading program development that lacks initial support. This strategy enables department chairs to identify and address remaining concerns. The strategy also provides valuable feedback on how faculty perspectives are evolving regarding the change initiative, thereby supplying department chairs and other academic leaders with information that informs their continued leadership of the change initiative.

Fourth, department chairs should take every opportunity to reduce the risk of damaging their leadership credibility. In the scenario presented in this chapter, the dean suggests augmenting existing policies and procedures in an effort to reduce the risk of damaging the department chair's leadership credibility with the faculty. This technique builds on existing policy and procedure in a way that lends credibility to the total process. Other techniques such as offering testimony and using data that the skeptics find credible will reduce the risk to one's leadership credibility. Finally, the tactic of recommending that the change be tried temporarily can be useful in persuading resistant faculty and staff to embrace a new program, activity, or support service. The pilot approach can help enhance leadership credibility when department chairs follow through in evaluating the new program according to criteria and the timetable established for review at the time faculty agreed to the trial.

The task of developing a new program that lacks initial support is an especially challenging leadership responsibility. At the same time, effectively managing this leadership challenge can enhance department chairs leadership credibility with those who were initially resistant to program development. As with most change initiatives, the more challenging initiative, the greater the potential benefits.

MANAGING RESISTANCE WHEN HIRED TO LEAD CHANGE

CHANGE IS THE ONE constant in higher education. Department chairs are often on the front line of change because chairs have leadership responsibility over academic programs and faculty performance. Search committees typically assess department chair candidates in terms of how successful each might be in leading the department to address specific challenges that inevitably involve leading change. Consequently, position announcements advertising department chair positions frequently carry an expectation for change leadership.

The goal of this chapter is to help department chairs understand the unique dynamic that exists when they are hired to lead change. A second goal of this chapter is to equip department chairs with leadership communication strategies for avoiding and minimizing the destructive conflict that can develop with and among faculty and others when department chairs are hired to lead change. While the case scenarios presented in this chapter focus on department chairs, the leadership communication strategies presented in this chapter can be used by all academic leaders to prevent unnecessary conflict when hired to lead change.

Defining the Task

When institutions search for a new department chair, the position announcement typically includes a list of required and desirable qualifications. The qualifications are position specific in that those drafting the position announcement have expectations for the work that the new department chair will do. More often than not, the new department chair will be expected to lead change. The nature of the change to be led is typically reflected in the specific qualifications described in the position announcement. For example, if the institution seeks a department chair who will lead faculty in building a strong research program, the position announcement will likely include *record of funded research* and *strong record of published research* among the required qualifications. However, these same qualifications will not likely appear in a position announcement when the institution seeks a department chair who will lead the development of new academic programs.

New department chairs must discern the change agenda that others hold for them. This can be difficult if constituencies do not agree on what or whether change is needed. It is entirely possible that the hiring administrator supports the need for some specific change that the department faculty believe is unnecessary. New department chairs must also discern existing perceptions regarding faculty and administrative role responsibilities. It is possible for the administration and department faculty to agree that some specific change is needed and disagree on who has role responsibility for leading that change. Finally, new department chairs must learn the department and campus culture such that they are able to lead change in a way that does not violate existing policy and practice.

New department chairs—hired because of the specific expertise and experience they bring to position—will be more successful in leading change if they first learn the existing department and campus culture. This does not mean that new department chairs must accept and operate within the confines of the status quo. However, to lead change, new department chairs must demonstrate an understanding of, and respect for, their new department and institution. When new department chairs are not savvy about using relevant leadership communication strategies to navigate within their new culture, they can quickly find themselves under attack for leading the very change that they were hired to lead.

Relevant Leadership Communication Strategies

Because change is uncomfortable for many people, department chairs can quickly lose their leadership credibility even when working to lead the change agenda shared at the time of their hire. Fortunately, there are leadership communication strategies that department chairs can use to enhance their leadership effectiveness when hired to lead change. Beginning with the search process, department chair candidates need to be proactive in exercising specific leadership communication strategies to accurately assess and implement the change agenda.

Things to Do Before Taking the Job

Department chairs and other academic leaders should use the search process to assess the feasibility of carrying out the change agenda *before* accepting a position for which there is an expectation of change leadership. This can be difficult because it is likely that individuals hold different perspectives on what change, if any, is needed. For example, a dean may offer a summary of the change that is needed within a particular department that differs from what the department faculty believe is needed. It is also possible that faculty within the same department do not agree on what, if any, change is needed. It is important to identify and understand the different perspectives as much as possible or to help inform the decision about accepting the position. The following two strategies help department chair candidates assess their fit with the institution and the change leadership expectation for the position they would hold.

LEARN THE EXPECTATIONS FOR LEADING CHANGE Ask the faculty and the supervising administrator what change is needed and why. It is also important to learn the time frame that each constituency has for change implementation. Be ready to ask follow-up questions when expectations for department chair leadership are not clear or the language used allows for multiple interpretations. For example, the hiring dean might tell a chair candidate that he will be expected to lead the department faculty in changes needed for an upcoming reaccreditation site visit. In this situation, the chair candidate should learn more about the specific changes that the hiring dean believes are necessary and whether the department faculty share the dean's view. Only by learning existing perceptions about what needs done and the timetable for doing that work can a chair candidate appropriately assess the performance expectations that others will have of him should he accept the position.

ASSESS THE CAPACITY FOR CHANGE The search process is an opportune time for a department chair candidate to test the waters. In particular, a chair candidate will want to assess the support and cooperation he would have for leading change should he accept the position. Faculty, for example, may agree that a specific change is needed until they understand how that change might alter their life or work in the department. Similarly, a dean may support the need for new program development to grow enrollment until that dean learns that the new program will require the addition of two full-time faculty positions. To the extent possible, a department chair candidate should assess the capacity for change by learning the response to the cost and other specific elements inherent in implementing the desired change. A chair candidate can do this by sharing his insights regarding how he would proceed when leading change and offering some sense of what investment the desired change would require from faculty and the administration. Although it would be difficult to hold individuals accountable for what they might say during the search process, being clear about such change implementation details during the search process will provide a department chair candidate with some sense of the existing capacity for change. It also offers faculty and the administration a glimpse of what will be required for change implementation and how a chair candidate would proceed to lead the change.

Practice Active Listening

Active listening involves understanding what is being said from the perspective of the person speaking. This involves more than hearing the words being spoken. It requires the listener to consider the speaker's perspective and understand the speaker's intent. Active listening requires department chairs to listen for the purpose of comprehending another's point to view. Active listening also implies an open mind on the issue and a genuine desire to understand another's perspective. Active listening does not obligate the listener to agree with what is being said. It merely evidences a commitment to understand what is being said.

Department chairs can enhance their leadership credibility by practicing active listening. By listening to understand another's point of view, department chairs demonstrate their regard for perspectives that may differ from their own and their commitment to collaborative problem solving. To reap this benefit from active listening, department chairs must evidence their desire to truly understand others' perspectives even when they disagree with their own. Department chairs can do this by parroting back the viewpoint expressed or by asking follow-up questions that evidence their desire to understand the viewpoint being expressed. Chairs can also demonstrate that they are listening actively by describing what they plan to do with the information. For example, a department chair might suggest that a concern raised be given more thought and discussed further at the next department meeting.

Clarify Leadership Expectations

Faculty and administrators have expectations for department chair leadership that derive from previous experience and their notions about how department chairs should work with faculty and the administration to accomplish a shared agenda. Expectations for department chair leadership encompass both *what* the department chair should do and *how* the department chair should work. By discerning existing expectations for department chair leadership, new department chairs can determine when differences in the expectations for chair leadership held among various constituencies place the department chair in a no-win situation. Consider, for example, the situation in which the dean expects a department chair to lead a particular change despite faculty opposition when the faculty expect that same department chair to protect status quo. The different expectations for department chair leadership place the department chair in an impossible situation. There is little point in addressing the change initiative before working through the differing expectations for department chair leadership.

It is especially important to clarify leadership expectations before leading change or tackling any significant task when there exists differing expectations for department chair leadership. Ideally, a department chair candidate can make good progress toward clarifying leadership expectations during the search process by clearly describing how he would carry out assigned role responsibilities. By striving to clarify leadership expectations during the search process, a department chair candidate is less likely to find himself in a new position working with faculty and administrators who do not support the chair's leadership agenda or approach.

The process of clarifying leadership expectations can be straightforward. It involves reaching agreement on what the department chair will and will not be responsible for doing and how the department chair will work with others to fulfill department chair responsibilities. For example, all may agree that the department chair will confer with the faculty about certain issues but act independently on other matters. Similarly, the dean and department chair may agree that it is the chair's responsibility to lead the department through curriculum revision but that the process used must incorporate existing policy and practice. By clarifying leadership expectations in advance of leading change, department chairs can reduce the risk of derailing the change initiative because the process being used does not fit with existing expectations for department chair leadership.

Manage Upward to Protect Leadership Credibility

New department chairs hired to lead change may believe that pursuing the change initiative is the best way to satisfy expectations for their leadership. However, should leading change create conflict or other problems, department chairs can quickly lose the leadership credibility that they need to be successful. Especially when faculty resist the needed change, department chairs should be careful to keep the dean informed so that the dean has a context for interpreting any complaints that the faculty might raise about the chair's leadership. Whenever possible, it can be prudent to secure the dean's insight on the planned approach for leading change. For example, a department chair might share with the dean an idea to have a department committee work on a particular change initiative and ask if the dean believes this is a wise approach. By seeking the dean's opinion on such procedural matters, a department chair makes the dean an accomplice in deciding on the process to be used.

Most deans will appreciate a new department chair who seeks their counsel before taking action that might create angst among the faculty. Seeking the dean's perspective on such matters paves the way for the department chair to keep the dean apprised of faculty resistance to the change initiative. The department chair, for example, might explain that using a department committee seems to be the best process given that many of the department faculty members resist and resent spending time in meetings. This brief exchange will give the dean some context should faculty later complain that the department chair worked only with a few favored faculty members.

It can seem counterintuitive for department chairs to share with their immediate supervisor that they are experiencing conflict or formidable resistance to change. Most of us prefer to keep quiet and work hard to resolve contentious situations rather than disclose them to others. Nonetheless, it is preferable for department chairs to alert their immediate supervisor and possibly others to an escalating conflict before others report the conflict in effort to discredit the department chair's leadership. When department chairs disclose the conflict to their immediate supervisor, they have an opportunity to present their perspective on the situation. The information shared provides the supervisor with a context should that individual hear about the conflict from other sources. Disclosing the conflict also enables department chairs to describe their efforts to date and to solicit the supervisor suggestions for what else might be tried. This allows the department chair's supervisor to be familiar with the situation and all that is being done to address the conflict. Should faculty attempt to discredit the department chair by reporting the conflict to the department chair's supervisor, that supervisor will have a context for interpreting the disparaging report.

Putting Theory into Practice

Now that these strategies are fresh in your mind, let's apply them to a specific situation. In Case 5.1, David Lee must weigh the pros and cons of accepting a position offer to serve as department chair of political science at his undergraduate alma mater. Place yourself in his shoes as you read.

Case 5.1: When to Accept the Challenge

Dr. David Lee has a decision to make. He is being offered the opportunity to return to his alma mater to serve as chair of the Department of Political Science. He has dreamed about the possibility of returning to the institution where he earned his bachelor's. He gives full credit for his professional success to the faculty who took him under their wings when he was a struggling undergraduate. These very special faculty members perceived and nurtured David's aptitude for doing academic work. It was their confidence in him that persuaded David to pursue graduate study in the discipline.

David's Current Position

Now a tenured full professor, David serves as department chair at a major research university. In this role, he is on a 12-month contract. In addition to chairing the department, David is required to teach one 3-credit graduate seminar each academic year. David directs three or so doctoral students even though he has no contractual responsibility for advising graduate or undergraduate students. He enjoys the leadership opportunities and challenges that accompany his role as department chair, particularly promoting the department's reputation on and off campus. He also assumes an active role in the ongoing development of every faculty member. Chairing a large, productive department is a full-time job. The lighter teaching load enables David to sustain an active research program, and he especially enjoys involving doctoral students in his research.

On campus, David is recognized as a skilled and effective department chair, and his department is recognized as one of the strongest on campus. The department faculty members are committed to effective teaching, active scholarship, and significant service to the institution and the discipline. David both enjoys and values his faculty colleagues. He believes the strong national reputation of the department's graduate program is directly attributable to the quality of the faculty. As important, faculty members respect each other and David's leadership. David recognizes that the positive department climate is helpful when he must lead the Department in addressing challenges. David wishes that faculty members had time for more direct contact with undergraduate students. However, undergraduate students are not likely to have a class with a full-time faculty member before their junior or senior year. Given the size of the graduate program, doctoral teaching assistants staff most of the 100- and 200-level courses. Despite David's wish that the department provide undergraduate students with the mentored learning experience he experienced as an undergraduate, above-average retention and graduation rates suggest that the department's undergraduate students do not feel slighted.

The Enticing Job Offer

David was not contemplating a move before he received a call from his undergraduate faculty adviser informing him that his alma mater was searching for a department chair of political science. David was flattered by the call and seized the opportunity to submit his application. In a matter of weeks, he was invited to interview on campus and now finds himself with an offer in hand. David recognizes that the offer is a generous one given the pay scale at small, private, liberal arts colleges. Well below David's current salary at a large research university, it is for a 9-month tenured faculty position at the rank of full professor and department chair of political science. As chair, David would be required to teach only two 3-credit classes each semester. There is an option for additional pay during the summer should he wish to represent his and other departments in the social sciences at all student recruitment events and the five 2-day orientation programs offered for incoming students.

Weighing the Pros and Cons

David thoroughly enjoyed his campus interview. It was a special thrill to be on the campus as a candidate for department chair of his old department. He appreciated the warm reception he received from the seven department faculty, three of whom taught David as an undergraduate. It is clear to him that they are proud of his success in the discipline and anxious for his return. Any reservations David had about their willingness to embrace him as their department chair quickly melted during the campus interview. Indeed, several of the faculty members described an urgent need for the type of experienced leadership that David would bring to the department. The campus interview unleashed many positive memories of David's days as an undergraduate student at the institution and also affirmed his attitude about the importance and value of the type of undergraduate mentored learning experience that can be offered at a small, private, liberal arts college. Despite the cut in salary, David finds the prospect of returning to his baccalaureate alma mater very appealing. He believes it would be rewarding to work side by side with his former faculty members to enhance the learning experience for undergraduates.

David's reservations about making the move derive from leaving his current institution and from his conversation with the college dean of his alma mater. He would be leaving an enviable position at a prestigious research university. Although his current leadership responsibilities are time-consuming, he operates with the full support of department faculty and the administration. David believes he would have the support of the faculty in the new position, but he is less certain about the support he might have from the administration even though the college dean articulated an urgent need to hire a capable department chair who would lead the department through some much-needed change.

The college dean was very forthcoming about his expectations for the new chair leadership. Specifically, the dean identified the following three concerns that the new department chair should address and remedy:

1. Curriculum revision: The dean believes the major in political science lacks a common core and depth in the major. A student can earn a bachelor's in political science by completing any 10 political science courses. Therefore, graduates in political science leave the institution without a common understanding of the discipline. The dean believes there is no depth to the major in political science because roughly 80% of the political science courses have been approved for elective credit at the 100- and 200-level within the institution's core curriculum. The dean showed David the transcripts of several graduates to illustrate that students can and do graduate with a major in political science composed of 10 courses at the 100- and 200- levels.

2. Department vision: The dean is concerned that the Department of Political Science lacks discipline focus. Faculty members were encouraged by the former chair to do their own thing rather than contribute to a shared departmental vision. Consequently, they collaborate with faculty colleagues in other disciplines. For example, one political science faculty member collaborates with a faculty member in business on ethical leadership. Another collaborates with a faculty member in history on governmental structures. Another collaborates with faculty members in communication studies and sociology on political communication. Still another faculty member

collaborates with faculty members in foreign languages and sociology on international politics. Although these collaborations have merit, the college dean is concerned that the political science faculty members lack departmental focus or vision.

3. Service on campus: The dean perceives the political science faculty as being uniformly disinterested in service to the College. According to the dean, political science faculty members are routinely missing from campus recruitment events, faculty governance, and other service initiatives. When appointed to a campus-wide committee, political science faculty members are typically lax about contributing time or effort to the committee's work.

When David asked the political science faculty about the department's rapport with the college dean, the more senior members dismissed the issue, saying that the dean is new and slow to learn the culture. One faculty member added that the department is anxious to find a strong department chair who can help him understand and value political science.

David has no real reason to leave his current position. Yet he relishes the idea of returning to his alma mater and is intrigued by the challenges he would face in the new position. Moreover, he believes he has the leadership experience and skill to address these challenges and would enjoy helping the faculty who did so much for him. David is not concerned about the loss of salary or the heavier teaching load. Nor is he concerned about the work involved in righting the political science department with the college dean and enhancing the department's reputation on and off campus. He is, however, worried about assuming leadership responsibility for a troubled situation that cannot be improved. To remedy the strained relationship between the college dean and the department faculty, David will need the cooperation of both parties in implementing curriculum revision and other change.

Let's Analyze the Case

David's emotional attachment to his alma mater is making his decision more difficult. Case 5.1 mentions that he has no reason to leave his current position where he and the department he chairs enjoy support from the administration and a favorable reputation on and off campus. If the job offer were from any other institution, David's decision would be easier to make. The decision is difficult because David feels indebted to the political science faculty and institution where he earned his bachelor's.

The faculty members who once helped him are now asking him to return and help them.

David is confident in his understanding of the discipline and in his leadership ability. Moreover, he enjoys departmental leadership and believes he possesses the experience and skill that could be helpful to both the college dean and the political science faculty at his alma mater. The college dean's change agenda for the political science department encompasses matters that David is comfortable managing. He is experienced in leading curriculum revision, developing a shared department vision, and cultivating faculty interest in service to the institution and discipline. David understands how this work can enhance the reputation all the department. The apparent disconnect between the college dean and the political science faculty is more puzzling. Even so, David is confident that he can bridge the existing gap between the college dean and political science faculty perspectives.

David is not concerned about taking a position that offers less pay or requires more teaching. Case 5.1 is silent on other personal issues such as whether the move would be good for his family or would enable him to live in a preferred geographic location. Absent these issues, we can focus on his professional reasons for accepting or declining the new position.

It's Your Turn

Assume the position of David Lee in this scenario, and think through how you would reach a decision about the job offer.

1. Would you discount the emotional aspect in making this professional decision? If yes, how would you go about detaching from the emotional component of David's decision? When, if ever, should emotion influence decision making?

2. Make a two-column list of the pros and cons—including those not listed in the case—you would consider in making this decision. Then prioritize the items in each column. Do all the pros and cons have equal weight? Why or why not?

3. Would you accept the position? Why or why not?

Please Consider

In making personal decisions, it is possible for two individuals to reach different decisions with the different outcomes being the best decision for each individual. In this case scenario, David needs to weigh the professional and personal reward of accepting the position against the professional and personal reward of retaining his current position. There is inevitably an element of subjectivity involved in making such a decision. For this reason, it may not be possible, or prudent, for David to completely disregard the emotional component in making his decision. Instead, he must acknowledge how the emotional component influences his view of factual information. For example, is David's desire to help the faculty who once helped him prompting David to inflate his assessment of his leadership experience and skill for handling the challenges he must address in the new position? If yes, then the emotional element is inappropriately influencing David's decision. In Case 5.1, David needs to examine the strained relationship between the college dean and the political science faculty objectively in order to more accurately assess his ability to manage the situation. David should not make the decision without objectively analyzing the situation because doing so will leave David less informed about the reality of the challenges he must address should he accept the position.

When a difficult decision seems impossible to make, it is likely that more information is needed. Additional information can include, for example, factual information and data, the subjective perspectives held by key individuals, available resources, and a better understanding of potential hurdles and available support. Much of this information can and should be obtained before accepting a leadership position. In the scenario, the college dean tells David that the new department chair needs to address three specific issues. The political science faculty members quickly dismiss the dean's agenda, explaining that the dean is new and slow to learn the campus culture. For any new department chair to be effective in mending the rapport between the college dean and the political science department, he or she needs the cooperation of both constituencies. Simultaneously, the department chair needs to satisfy, and perhaps modify, the performance expectations that each constituency holds for chair leadership.

Again, put yourself in David Lee's position as you answer the following questions:

1. What might you do before reaching a decision about the job offer to get a better understanding of the college dean's perspective of the political science department and the dean's change agenda for the new department chair?

2. What might you do before reaching a decision about the job offer to get a better understanding of the political science faculty members'

perspective of the college dean and the dean's change agenda for the department?

3. How might you assess the willingness of the college dean and the political science faculty to consider perspectives that differ from their own?

4. What else might David do to assess the likelihood draft he can be successful in the new position?

Putting Theory into Practice

David Lee believes he needs more information to make a sound decision, so he decides to talk by phone with the college dean and a few of the senior faculty members. In Case 5.2, we eavesdrop on his conversation with both constituencies. Put yourself in his position as you learn more about the perspectives of the college dean and political science faculty.

Case 5.2: Separating Fact from Fiction

David decides to talk first with the college dean and finds the dean embraces the opportunity to talk candidly about the challenges facing the next department chair.

Conversation with the College Dean

David: Thanks for making time to talk with me.

College dean: No problem. I hope you are calling to accept our offer.

David: Actually, I'm calling to follow up on our conversation during my campus interview.

College dean: I'm pleased to oblige because the political science department is at an important crossroads. Without the changes I outlined, the department cannot survive.

David: The situation seems very dire in your mind.

College dean: It is. To be honest, I was not initially in favor of conducting a national search for a new department chair. My inclination is to eliminate the department.

David: Why?

College dean: Why not? Political science is a weak major. Students majoring in the discipline can earn a bachelor's by completing courses designed for nonmajor freshmen and sophomores.

David: I shared with you the life-changing experience I had as a student majoring in political science at the institution.

College dean: "I remember, and I am glad for that. I also realize that some of faculty members who mentored you still teach at the institution, and I believe these faculty members truly care about students. A sound curriculum, however, involves much more than caring faculty. Had you completed a major in political science with only 100- and 200-level courses, I doubt you would have been admitted to a reputable graduate school.

David: I understand the point you are making. Still, it is a big leap from documenting the need for curriculum revision to eliminating the department.

College dean: Eliminating the department is, for me, the only logical outcome should the political science faculty continue to resist substantive curriculum revision that derives from a relevant department vision. Virtually every political science faculty member is aligned with another discipline on the campus. If the next department chair is unable to build consensus around a department vision that clearly defines the department's academic scope and purpose that leads to a substantive curriculum revision, my best option will be to dismantle the political science department and transfer individual faculty members to the disciplines with which they currently collaborate.

David: You seem persuaded that the political science faculty will not embrace curriculum revision.

College dean: I am. This is my third year at the institution. I spend more time talking with the political science faculty than with any other department faculty at the institution. I share data and discuss the challenges facing higher education generally and this institution specifically. The political science faculty ignore the information and data I present with a naïve "This too shall pass" mind-set. They also reject offers of professional development support and additional resources. For example, I offered to cover the cost of bringing political science faculty from other institutions to campus to conduct a review of our political science program. The faculty members rejected this offer is a waste of resources because faculty from other institutions could not possibly grasp the unique nuances of our political science program. I am out of ideas for how to help them.

David: Given your experience, why did you conduct a national search for the next department chair?

College dean: Honestly, I believe that I am too new to the institution to dismantle the department without giving a new department chair hired from outside institution a chance to remedy the situation.

David: Should I accept the position, is there a clock running for when these things we need to be done?

College dean: I expect to work closely with the new chair such that I will know if genuine progress is being made. I recognize that he or she will need some time to gain faculty trust and persuade the faculty that it is a new day. I know that the faculty perceive me as being too new to understand the political science department or the campus culture. If only the situation were that simple. I hope you will accept the position because the more change-resistant faculty members know and trust you. I remain hopeful that the brick wall I encounter will crumble when the problems we discussed are presented to the political science faculty by a trusted department chair.

David: I appreciate your candor and your time. You have given me much to think about.

College dean: No thanks necessary. I am pleased to talk further with you if it would be helpful. Again, I truly hope you will accept our offer.

Conference Call with Three Faculty Members

David: Thanks for taking the time to talk to me.

Charley: No problem, although we were hoping to hear that you accepted the offer.

David: I want to talk more with you and the college dean to make certain that I am the best person for the job.

Charley: We are glad to help, but I'm surprised you would want to talk to the college dean. I believe we told you that he is new and very slow to learn the campus culture.

David: I remember. Still, the political science department deserves a department chair who can work effectively with the college dean.

Derek: We understand. Now, how can we get you to agree to take the job?

Tim: Seriously David, we need a strong department chair who understands us and can represent us well to the college dean.

David: The college dean has an unfavorable perception of the political science department.

Charley: No kidding! That's why we need a strong department chair. I did my best chairing this department for some 25 years, but I am worn out from trying to help college deans understand this department. I resigned as chair when I realized that we now have a college dean who seeks change for the sake of change when I believe you don't fix what isn't broken. We have two very different philosophies.

David: The college dean shared his concerns about the curriculum. Having graduated from this program, I was surprised to learn that 100- and 200-level courses that count for elective credit in the institution's core curriculum also count toward a major in political science. When and why was this change was made?

Charley: We've always been a department that lives by its wits. When declining enrollment threatened our ability to justify replacing retiring faculty members, we realized that we can document the need for faculty if overall course enrollment remains strong. Political science courses are popular with students completing the core curriculum, so we removed the prerequisites on our major courses and got them approved for core curriculum credit. Our quick thinking rescued this department from downsizing at a time when we were losing political science majors.

Tim: We don't see this as a problem, but it is clearly a serious issue for the college dean. Political science majors can still take these courses and have them count toward graduation, so what is the harm?

Charley: The dean's needle gets stuck on things he believes justify change.

David: I am only beginning to look into this issue, but I wonder what political science majors think about being in classes that count toward their major with nonmajors who are less serious about studying political science?

Derek: We haven't heard any complaints.

Charley: To the contrary, the number of political science majors is increasing. We pick up a lot of students who discover that degree completion in other academic programs will require them to stay at the institution another year or more. By switching their major to political science, the political science courses they took for core credit count toward their major. It is a tangible benefit of our quick thinking that we didn't anticipate.

Tim: The college dean refuses to understand that the current curriculum works for us. This is why we need a strong department chair who understands and values this department.

David: I will always be grateful for the educational experience I had under your mentorship, and I do value you and the study of political science. Should I accept the offer, would you be willing to work with me to conduct our own assessment of the political science curriculum to identify its strengths and possible needs for improvement?

Charley: Sure.

David: What about the faculty not on this phone conversation. Can I count on their support as well?

Charley: Without a doubt.

David: If I take the job, I will hold you to that. Thanks for taking the time to talk to me. I value your perspective and candor.

Charley: We are glad to help. We cannot stress enough how much everyone in this department hopes you will take the job.

Let's Analyze the Case

In deciding whether to accept the position, David must assess several things. First, he needs to assess the leadership challenges he would face if he assumes the position of department chair. Only after he understands the leadership challenges can David determine if his experience and leadership skill are well suited to the task and whether these are leadership challenges he would enjoy doing. Second, David needs to determine if his experience and leadership skill are a good fit with the performance expectations others have for the department chair. This is difficult because the college dean and department faculty hold different performance expectations for the new department chair. The college dean seeks a department chair who can successfully move the department faculty to address three specific concerns. The department faculty seek a strong department chair who can educate and manage the college dean. Third, David must assess if he would have sufficient support from all relevant constituencies to successfully handle the leadership challenges and meet performance expectations. This is also tricky because the college dean will measure David's success through changes such as curriculum revision, whereas the department faculty members are inclined to measure David's success through preservation of the status quo.

David realizes that the campus interview did not provide enough information for him to make an informed decision. David makes two phone calls: one to the college dean and the other to three of the department faculty members. These conversations help to fill in more information about the perspectives held by the college dean and a few department faculty members and the differences between the two constituencies. The college dean is adamant that the political science faculty must revise the curriculum, and he discloses that without curriculum revision he plans to dismantle the political science department. Whether or not campus policy will afford the college dean this opportunity, his disclosure evidences the level of his frustration with the political science faculty. The department faculty perceive the current curriculum as prudent and necessary response to declining enrollment. Charley, the former department chair, sees the curriculum as evidence of how the department lives by its wits. The faculty realize that the college dean wants curriculum revision but do not agree that curriculum revision is necessary. The preferred faculty outcome would be to have a strong department chair who can improve the college dean's view of the department and keep him out of the department's business.

Both the college dean and the department faculty emphasize how much they hope David will accept the offer. Both constituencies perceive David as having the requisite leadership experience and skill necessary to do the job well. Yet each constituency expects the new department chair to work toward a particular outcome, and the preferred outcomes are different for each constituency. The phone conversations provide David with more information even though the additional information may not make it easier for him to decide whether to accept the position.

It's Your Turn

1. Review David's phone conversation with the college dean, and note where you would use a different approach or language. For example, in talking with the dean, David challenges his thinking when he points out that there is a big difference between requesting curriculum revision and eliminating the department. Is this wise? If yes, why? If no, how would you rewrite David's portion of the conversation?

2. Review David's phone conversation with the three faculty members, and note where are you would use different language. For example, does David risk losing faculty support when he asks if they would be willing to conduct their own review of the curriculum to identify strengths and areas for improvement? If no, why not? If yes, how would you rewrite David's portion of the conversation?

3. What, if any, additional issues would you raise in these phone conversations that David does not mention? For example, would

share more of the college dean's perspective when talking with the faculty? In talking with the college dean, would you discuss all three of the concerns raised by the dean during the campus interview?

4. What does David learn from the phone conversation about the support he would have from the college dean?

5. What does David learn from the phone conversation with the faculty about the support he would have from the faculty for reviewing and revising the curriculum?

6. Do the phone conversations help inform how David should proceed with each constituency should he accept the position? If yes, how? If no, how might David have approached the phone conversations to obtain more insight for how to work with each constituency?

7. Would you advise David to accept the position? Why or why not?

Please Consider

Every conversation communicates more than the literal message conveyed. For example, the college dean never says he is frustrated with the political science faculty, but it is apparent in his comments about the amount of time he spends with the political science faculty, their naïve perspective, and their practice of ignoring all he says and the data he shares. Often, the message embedded in the words spoken can offer important insight on the issue being discussed and about the individuals in the conversation. To put it another way, much of the message can be lost if department chairs and other academic leaders fail to practice active listening. Active listening requires paying attention to an individual's tone and nonverbal expression that provide context and meaning to the words being spoken. Consider how many different ways an individual can say, "It's a great day!" It is possible for a person to speak this sentence in a way that suggests he or she has had either a wonderful day or as a sarcastic comment that suggests it was a horrible day. It is impossible to know what is meant by the sentence without listening to the person's tone and expression when speaking the words.

Review the phone conversations again and highlight the phrases that provide some insight as to how collaborative the college dean and department faculty would be in working with David. Granted, you would be better able to discern these things if you heard an audio recording of the phone conversations. Nonetheless, there exist some clues in the transcript of the phone conversations. For example, the way the college dean quickly discloses his thinking suggests he seeks to hire a department chair with whom he can collaborate and resolve problems. The college dean did not need to disclose his thoughts about dismantling the political science department. In fact, disclosing this to a chair candidate who is also a graduate of the program could be risky. The fact that he is candid suggests his leadership style is more open and collaborative.

Let's Recap

Take a moment to review your answers to the previous questions. Does your approach to the phone conversations make use of active listening and help to clarify leadership expectations with each constituency? If not, give some thought to how you might use these leadership communication strategies to modify your approach. For example, you might describe for the faculty how you would lead department consideration of the dean's concerns. Similarly, you might inform the college dean of your intent to engage department faculty in an honest review of his concerns without committing to a particular outcome. In other words, as department chair, you would be responsible for leading the department faculty to make informed decisions without persuading the faculty to reach any particular conclusion. Sharing that this would be your approach will likely help you learn if he perceives value in having the department faculty undertake a serious review of the curriculum or would rather have a department chair who will take action to implement what he believes should be done. Is this an opportunity for David to manage upward before accepting the position?

Putting Theory into Practice

In Case 5.3, we learn that David decides to accept the position of department chair at his alma mater. Two years into the job, he is finding change leadership more challenging than he anticipated.

Case 5.3: Going Home

David Lee accepted the position at his alma mater and believes he did so for all the right reasons. He decided that the new position would afford him the opportunity to work on new leadership challenges while serving an institution and faculty he values. He took the post with full confidence that he has the leadership experience and skill needed to remedy a troubling situation that will likely grow worse without the unique intervention he can provide as a graduate of the program. David felt called to serve his alma mater, an institution committed to the undergraduate learning experience.

Now 2 years later, David finds that he has not made much progress. The department faculty meet regularly to discuss the curriculum. Although they are collegial in discussing suggested curriculum revisions, their rhetoric is directed at informing David why the curriculum is the way it is. For a year, David listened patiently to stories of why and how the current curriculum came into existence. David recognizes that the faculty members are proud of the curriculum because it evidences their ability to be strategic at a time when declining enrollment put other departments in jeopardy of losing faculty positions. Not once has David heard a faculty member defend the academic integrity of the current curriculum. A year in the position, he decided that it was time to move the conversation forward to consider specific curriculum revisions that would be responsive to the current learning needs of students. David began interrupting the history lessons and directing faculty attention toward concrete facts and data that define the current situation. When it became clear to the faculty that David was serious about curriculum revision, they responded in a number of different ways. The tenured faculty, who remember David as an undergraduate student, adopted a stern tone when informing him of matters he did not know and needed to understand. The untenured faculty, who are newer to the department, became silent. The untenured faculty members are unwilling to suggest or consider revisions to the curriculum when the tenured faculty members are obviously opposed to any revision of the curriculum.

During the same period, David came to value and appreciate the college dean's leadership. David finds the college dean willing to listen and offer suggestions for how he might manage specific leadership challenges. Because David shares his leadership struggles with the college dean, the dean has been patient in waiting for the curriculum revision that he believes is essential to the future of the political science department. The dean has helped David understand that a year was sufficient time for him to learn the history of the department and how the practice of informing David of why and how curriculum was developed may be a tactic to resist change. The department faculty recognize that David enjoys a productive working relationship with the college dean. Although all are relieved to be out from under the college dean's demand for immediate change, the tenured faculty members find David's positive rapport with him worrisome.

Faculty Expectations for Department Chair Leadership

Faculty expectations for department chair leadership developed during Charley's 25-year tenure as department chair. Charley chaired the department through five different college deans. He likes to say that each one arrived bright-eyed and bushy-tailed, ready to make changes that would build the Dean's resume to earn the next promotion. Charley believes that all administrators have no understanding of faculty perspective. In fact, he perceives the difference between administrators and faculty members to be inherent, so he believes it is dangerous to trust any administrator. As department chair, Charley worked hard to protect the department from ill-meaning and uninformed college deans who could not possibly care about the department's welfare. Consequently, faculty suspicions are heightened when David shares information that evidences how he and the college dean are working together to benefit the department.

David's Dilemma

Before accepting the position, David failed to recognize that the tenured faculty members believe no administrators can be trusted. If the untenured faculty believe differently, they are unwilling to challenge the views of the tenured faculty. David realizes that he must evidence doing battle with the college dean to protect his leadership credibility with these faculty members. He also recognizes that perpetuating the leadership style Charley used will not benefit the political science department. Although the college dean has been patient through 2 years, David realizes that time is running out for securing faculty support for a substantive curriculum revision. At the same time, David fears that should he push for curriculum revision without tending to faculty expectations for department chair leadership, he will quickly lose leadership credibility with the faculty from whom he needs support to effectively lead the department.

Let's Analyze the Case

The new position has not worked out as David anticipated. The faculty members are as resistant to curriculum revision as they were two years earlier. Worse yet, David fears he is losing credibility with faculty members who expect him to protect the department from the college dean. Sadly, David now realizes that the very leadership behaviors he embraces such as working collaboratively with the college dean are the source of growing faculty distrust for his leadership. Consequently, David is not providing the helpful and effective leadership he hoped to offer the political science department that he seeks to repay for investing in him as an undergraduate student.

David is truly between the proverbial rock and hard place. The faculty assess David's leadership in relationship to how Charley chaired the Department. Charley exercised a fortress mentality in protecting the department from college deans who could not possibly understand faculty perspective and who only cared about acquiring the experience necessary to secure their next promotion. This model assumes that college deans (and all other administrators) cannot possibly help inform department discussion and decision making. Indeed, the fortress model measures department chair leadership effectiveness by the chair's ability to keep the college dean away from and out of department business. David's experience, however, derives from a model of collaborative leadership. At David's previous institution, his department flourished because he had the respect of the administration and was able to work collaboratively with the Dean to enhance the Department's work and reputation.

David realizes that he is in a no-win situation unless he can help faculty revise their perception of department chair leadership. This will not be easy because he must also lead the department faculty in addressing circumstances they had previously ignored. Moreover, Charley's leadership allowed the faculty to believe they were right in ignoring the changing circumstances that now threaten the viability of the political science department. Because curriculum revision is essential to the future of the department, David championed change before fully discerning and addressing faculty perceptions of department chair leadership. Now he risks losing leadership credibility with the faculty and has made no progress in revising the curriculum.

It's Your Turn

Assume the position of department chair in this case scenario and think through how you would manage David's dilemma.

1. Would you interrupt work on curriculum revision to address faculty perceptions and expectations for department chair leadership? If yes, think through how you would address faculty perceptions and expectations for chair leadership. Would you, for example, discuss the issue directly or indirectly?

2. Charley and others might interpret a discussion of the characteristics of effective department chair leadership as an indictment of Charley's leadership. What might you do to minimize a defensive

reaction from Charley and other faculty members? For example, would you spend time educating the faculty on how changing conditions warrant different department chair leadership? Would you reference and describe the leadership styles of department chairs on campus who have been successful despite changing conditions? Are there credible sources who might be asked to talk with the faculty about changing times and the need for a different chair leadership? For example, faculty from a department that successfully grew enrollment through curriculum revision might be asked to share their experience with the political science faculty.

3. Would you seek the college dean's reaction to your plan for addressing faculty perceptions of department chair leadership? Why or why not?

4. What might you do to safeguard your leadership credibility with the college dean in moving forward? For example, he may perceive a plan to address faculty perceptions of chair leadership as a justification to halt efforts to secure curriculum revision.

Please Consider

Department chairs occupy a difficult leadership position. While many department chairs hold faculty status, they also hold front-line administrative positions. To be effective, department chairs must lead in a way that benefits the department faculty and the institution. To represent the department well, department chairs must be about the business of educating the college dean and other administrators about the department's achievements and resource needs. To serve the institution well, department chairs must keep faculty informed about institutional priorities and challenges. When department chairs fail to serve well both the department and the institution, the department can quickly fall on hard times. While tilting at windmills to safeguard the status quo can be a popular stance with some faculty, this leadership approach will inevitably hurt the department's status on campus. College deans, for example, are less likely to invest finite resources in departments that seek to operate outside the scope of institutional priorities and challenges.

It is imperative to assess and clarify leadership expectations before addressing any change initiative. This can often be done effectively during a search process and before accepting the new position. In this case scenario, David might have a candid discussion with the faculty regarding his view that the curriculum needs revision before accepting the position. Similarly, he might share during the search process how he plans to proceed in managing the college dean's agenda for the political science department. At a minimum, this would prevent the faculty from supporting David's candidacy because they mistakenly believe he would chair the department as Charley did. It is prudent for a department chair candidate to make every effort during the search process to help others understand how he or she would carry out assigned leadership responsibilities.

Putting Theory into Practice

In Case 5.4, a new business school director hired from outside the institution must protect her leadership credibility with her supervisor when faculty attempt an end run in order to derail a change initiative that the new director must lead.

Case 5.4: A New Day

Many were impressed that April McAuliffe began work immediately after accepting the position of director of the School of Business. Before April moved her family to their new home, she was in daily communication with faculty and staff on the campus. She requested data and reports, conferred with folks, sent emails, and scheduled conference calls. Even the business school secretary and office manager observed how the new director seemed to be working full-time 3 months ahead of her official starting date. Once on campus, April's pace quickened. She approached every task with an undeniable sense of urgency.

The New Director's Agenda

April McAuliffe brings a lot of know-how and energy to everything she does. April likes to hit the ground running, and she is anxious to assume her new duties as director of the School of Business at Suburban University. April accepted the position because the leadership tasks described by the faculty and the administration are precisely what April enjoys doing. The most pressing objective is to make the school's curriculum more relevant and attractive to students in order to arrest a precipitous decline in enrollment. April recognizes that the best approach will be some blend of new program development and curriculum revision. Her experience with an entrepreneurship program at her previous institution will be invaluable in developing a new program in entrepreneurship at Suburban University, where the business faculty have no expertise in entrepreneurship. April plans to lead the faculty in overhauling the curriculum while she tackles the development of an entrepreneurship program. April's vision is clear, and she plans for this work to be done during her first year so the School of Business can begin to reverse the downward enrollment trend by her second year at university.

The Administration's Perspective

The administration was pleased when the business faculty recommended the hire of April McAuliffe. The dean is confident that April possesses the leadership experience and skill to know precisely what is needed to grow enrollment in business programs. The administration believes that April can help a talented business faculty address the need to make the business programs more attractive to students. Although the administration respects the teaching of the business faculty, they perceive the business faculty as being stuck defending the status quo because their experience does not enable them to consider program development or curriculum revision beyond the scope of their current practice. The dean believes that April's experience and skill will enable an otherwise talented Business faculty to think outside the box on issues of curriculum development and revision.

The Faculty's Perspective

The business faculty members were immediately taken with April during search process. She has experience chairing a business program that enjoys robust enrollment and a strong reputation. Moreover, April impressed the faculty as being genuine in her desire to build a strong School of Business at Suburban University. The faculty recognize that April's experience and expertise is different from theirs, and they truly believe that her perspective would be a valuable addition to the school.

Some faculty members were put off by April's insistence on working before her official start date of July 1. By doing so, she kept faculty and staff busy after the spring semester ended, when many faculty are on vacation. By the close of fall semester, the faculty were already tired of her intensity for tackling program development and curriculum revision. Rushing major curriculum change seems reckless to the business faculty. The faculty believe that April is ignoring other school priorities to focus on her agenda. Some suspect that her ambitious nature is focused on early success to help her secure a dean position elsewhere. Most agree that regardless of her motivation, April is not listening to them. She appears more concerned about staying on schedule than hearing faculty perspectives for how the change she is championing will not work for the school or university.

In particular, the faculty are troubled by the development of a new program in entrepreneurship without faculty input and support. When faculty members ask for information about the entrepreneurship program, April reminds them that they have enough work on their plates revising the existing curriculum. April routinely offers updates on her work in developing the new program in entrepreneurship that summarize the meetings April has had with area businesses, administrators, and prospective donors. She dismisses faculty requests to review the curriculum being developed for the entrepreneurship program adding that professionals with relevant expertise in entrepreneurial studies will be asked to review the program before it brought before the school. The faculty worry that they will not have an opportunity for meaningful input on a new program that might drain resources away from existing programs. Although April is always professional and polite, her leadership style has many of the faculty feeling discarded or run over. The easygoing and collegial climate that once characterized the School of Business is being replaced with an intense, deadline-driven pace and top-down leadership. The harder April works, the greater faculty concern.

The End Run

The break between fall and spring semesters did little to quiet faculty concerns. April continued to send the faculty positive updates of her progress in developing the new program in entrepreneurship. She expects the faculty to be pleased that she is working through the break to develop a new program that will likely attract new students to the school. The updates, however, affirm faculty fears that their director has little time or regard for faculty perspectives. April's updates persuade a sufficient number of faculty that they must take action to protect themselves and the School of Business from their autocratic director.

As soon as spring semester begins, the faculty meet privately to devise a plan to regain faculty authority over the curriculum. After much consideration and debate, they decide to apprise the dean of the situation. The business faculty believe the dean respects their teaching, scholarship, and service to the institution. They also know that he values collaborative leadership and embraces the important role of faculty in curriculum development. A few faculty members are concerned that running to the dean will put them at odds with the director. At the same time, they need help because their efforts to have April involve them in new program development proved unsuccessful. They decide that the tenured full professors will request a meeting with the dean to speak on behalf of the entire business faculty. In requesting the meeting, they respectfully ask him to not inform April of their request to share with him their grave concerns for the future of the School of Business. They explain that the opportunity for amicable resolution would likely be lost should April learn of the meeting before they have an opportunity to brief the dean.

Meeting with the Dean

Dean: I was surprised to receive your request for a meeting.

Amy Lynn: We're not surprised. We are confident that you don't know how April McAuliffe's autocratic leadership is hurting faculty morale and the School of Business.

Guy: We're coming to you for help and appreciate that you are willing to hear us out without involving our director.

Dean: To be honest, I am uncomfortable having this meeting without letting your director know that we are meeting.

Amy Lynn: I understand, but we believe you will be better able to remedy a harmful situation if we brief you on the problem privately.

Dean: I'm listening.

Amy Lynn: The director is not a collaborative leader. In fact, she operates more like a drill sergeant. She unilaterally sets the agenda, assigns tasks, and establishes deadlines. She has no regard for faculty perspective and regularly usurps faculty authority and responsibility.

Dean: That's quite an accusation! What is the basis for your assessment?

Amy Lynn: Virtually every action April McAuliffe takes affirms our view of her.

Guy: At the first faculty meeting of the new academic year, *she* informed us that *our* agenda for the year is curriculum development and revision. We had no input in developing the school's agenda for the year.

Dean: You have to know that I believe curriculum development and revision are essential to growing enrollment in business.

Guy: Yes, but April not only announced what our agenda would be but also told us that *she* would develop a new program in entrepreneurship while *she* directs our work in overhauling the current curriculum.

Amy Lynn: April does not understand that program development is a faculty responsibility.

Dean: Granted, except none of the current business faculty have the expertise to develop a new program in entrepreneurship. You might consider it fortunate that the new director has this expertise.

Amy Lynn: That assumes that entrepreneurship is a program that should be offered at this institution. We are not certain that this School of Business should offer a program in entrepreneurship. If the program content is so far removed from current faculty expertise that it must be developed by a full-time administrator, how will we staff the courses?

Dean: I see your point.

Guy: We are willing to consider a program in entrepreneurship, but the director dismisses us every time we ask to be involved.

Amy Lynn: The director likes to remind us that only she has the expertise needed to develop the new program. It's insulting!

Kenneth: This brings us to another serious concern. The director's autocratic leadership style is demoralizing to the business faculty. She tightly controls our work in revising the existing curriculum while usurping faculty responsibility to pursue new program development.

Amy Lynn: The director makes all decisions without seeking faculty perspectives or learning about the school's history and mission.

Kenneth: She believes she has all the right answers so everything must be done her way. Some of the newer faculty are talking about leaving the institution. They know the school is changing into something that is very different from the school they joined.

Dean: I would be sorry to see any of the business faculty leave the institution.

Amy Lynn: Then you must help us. April McAuliffe is not a good fit for the School of Business. She needs to be replaced before she does irreparable harm.

Let's Analyze the Case

There is no bad guy in Case 5.4, but there is an escalating conflict between the new director and the business faculty. The new director is working hard to address the declining enrollment in business. The agenda derives from information learned during the search process, and the new director has good reason to believe that both the administration and faculty believe growing student enrollment is the school's top priority.

The conflict between the new director and the business faculty is about process and differing expectations for director leadership and faculty responsibility. The director believes she is charged with leading change that will reverse a precipitous enrollment decline. The director perceives a sense of urgency that has her so focused on this task that she does not tune into other variables that will ultimately determine her effectiveness in leading change with the business faculty. In particular, the director fails to take into account faculty expectations for her leadership and faculty responsibility for program development and curriculum revision. The business faculty may agree that program development and curriculum revision are essential to growing enrollment, but they disagree with the process that April is using. Faculty are sufficiently concerned about a process that they believe undermines faculty authority and responsibility that they decide to seek the dean's help and ask that April be replaced. In one semester, the new director lost leadership credibility with the faculty. Now, she will need to explain and perhaps defend her leadership to the dean.

It's Your Turn

Review the sequence of events in Case 5.4, and put yourself in the new director's position as you answer the following questions:

1. When and how did the new director get sideways with the business faculty? Identify the specific instances when she acted in a way that contributed to the conflict with the faculty.

2. Is the new director's conflict with the faculty inevitable? If not, how might she avoid creating the described faculty conflict?

3. What might the director do now to ease the conflict with the faculty?

4. What, if anything, can the director do to build leadership credibility with the faculty?

5. Has the new director lost leadership credibility with the dean?

6. What will it take for the director to rebuild leadership credibility with the dean?

Please Consider

In Case 5.4, the new director takes immediate and decisive action to lead an essential change initiative without regard for faculty expectations for director leadership and faculty role responsibility. This approach causes her to lose the initial support that existed for the change initiative. Information shared during the search process made clear that the administration believes program development and curriculum revision are the remedy for enrollment decline and faculty are aware of the administration's view. The new director had a platform for making program development and curriculum revision the top priority for the School of Business. The new director could credibly make program development and curriculum revision the agenda focus without surprising faculty or giving the faculty reason to believe the new director is acting unilaterally. She, however, sacrifices the initial support she had for leading program development and curriculum revision by failing to use active listening to clarify leadership expectations before addressing a pressing task in which the faculty are vested. Moving fast is not always the quickest way to successful change implementation. When hired to lead change, it is especially important to not allow expectations for leadership and process to distract from the task at hand.

Hindsight Is 20/20

When hired to lead change, it is easy to believe that those who supported your hire also support the change you are to lead. This may be true initially, but the new director or department chair must lead change in a way that encourages others to support the change. Directors and department chairs cannot work in a vacuum because successful change implementation inevitably requires the support and cooperation of many throughout the process. Moreover, it is possible for folks to support the change generally while possessing very different expectations for how that change should be implemented and what the final outcome will look like. For this reason, department chairs cannot assume that views expressed during the search process represent unqualified support for change.

Both David Lee and April McAuliffe made assumptions about the support they had to lead change that jeopardized their success. In Case 5.3, David realizes that the faculty supported his hire on the belief that he would protect them from the dean. In Case 5.4, April learns that knowing what is needed is not sufficient to successfully lead change. Both David and April fail to clarify leadership expectations before leading change. In doing so, both jeopardize their ability to be successful in implementing the change that they were hired to lead.

Let's Recap

Institutions sometimes seek to hire department chairs or other academic leaders to lead change. In these instances, department chair candidates can exercise specific leadership communication strategies to help inform their thinking about how to lead the desired change should they accept the position. To the extent possible, it is important to use the search process to understand the specific change expectations for department chair leadership and assess the existing capacity for change before accepting the position. Only by understanding the expectations for department chair leadership can chair candidates appropriately assess their preparation and ability to meet the leadership performance expectations of the position. This assessment becomes more complicated and the leadership demands become more challenging when others hold differing expectations for department chair leadership. Expectations for department chair leadership may differ on *what* the department chair should do or *how* the department chair should work. Understanding these differences is essential to knowing how to proceed in the position in order to successfully lead the desired change.

Department chairs must practice active listening in order to discern existing expectations for department chair leadership. Active listening is also an essential leadership communication strategy throughout the process of leading change. Only through active listening can department chairs evidence their genuine desire to understand perspectives that may differ from their own and their commitment to collaborative problem solving. Active listening can enhance a department chair's leadership credibility with both faculty and the administration. This is hugely important to leading change successfully because department chairs with high or positive leadership credibility will experience less resistance to change than department chairs with low or poor leadership credibility. The higher one's leadership credibility, the more others trust that leader's decisions and actions.

It is important to clarify leadership expectations before leading change or tackling any significant task when faculty and administrative staff hold differing expectations for department chair leadership. When department chairs fail to clarify the leadership expectations for their performance, they place themselves in a no-win and sometimes risky situation. It is impossible to satisfy the expectations of others have for department chair leadership unless there is a shared understanding of *what* the department chair will address and *how* the department chair will work with others. The process of clarifying involves reaching agreement on the department chair's role and responsibility in relation to the roles and responsibilities held by others. For this reason, the process is as important as the task. When faculty perceive the process is usurping faculty authority or responsibility, they will likely resist work on the task. Department chairs will find it easier to lead change if they take the time to clarify expectations for their leadership; it is time-consuming but well worth the effort.

New department chairs cannot assume that those who supported their hire also support the change they are expected to lead. By managing up, department chairs can protect their leadership credibility with their immediate supervisor should department faculty run end to complain about chair leadership. Managing up involves keeping one's administrative supervisor informed of the approach being taken to lead the desired change. Adding this additional step enables department chairs to share their perspective of the change process and their efforts to be respectful of faculty perspective while addressing institutional priorities. By taking this action, department chairs equip their administrative supervisor with the context for hearing complaints forwarded by those who may be resistant to the change or unhappy with the process and the chair's leadership.

Leading change can be challenging for new department chairs. The leadership communication strategies presented in this chapter help new department chairs navigate possible potholes that might undermine their leadership effectiveness. Veteran department chairs and other academic leaders will find these leadership communication strategies helpful when required to lead a change initiative that is beyond the scope of what they have previously been expected to manage.

PART TWO

MANAGING CONFLICT WHEN ADDRESSING PROBLEM FACULTY PERFORMANCE

THIS SECTION DISCUSSES leadership communication strategies for managing conflict when addressing problem faculty performance. Department chairs with responsibility for program quality and department productivity need to be skilled in leadership communication strategies that enable them to manage problem faculty performance. Each chapter in this section addresses a specific scenario in which the department chair must address problem faculty performance while managing the conflict associated with the situation.

6

MANAGING AN UNSUCCESSFUL
PROMOTION APPLICATION

FEW SITUATIONS CAUSE GREATER angst than an unsuccessful application for promotion or tenure. The faculty member whose application is denied can experience reactions that range from embarrassment to anger. Chairs must be prepared to manage both the applicant's reaction and resulting collateral damage. At a minimum, there will be damage to the failed applicant's psyche that can impact that person's attitude, communication, and productivity. At the same time, an unsuccessful promotion or tenure application can be stressful on the applicant's faculty colleagues. Voting on promotion or tenure is always easier and less stressful when the application merits a positive vote. Should the unsuccessful promotion or tenure application be shrouded in controversy, the scope of the collateral damage can extend to the chair's leadership credibility and the department's productivity and reputation. Department chairs who have experienced contentious, unsuccessful promotion or tenure applications will attest that it can take years to manage the collateral damage.

The goal of this chapter is to help department chairs understand how a faculty member's reaction to a negative promotion and tenure decision is shaped and the range of collateral damage that can result from a failed bid for promotion or tenure. A second goal of this chapter is to equip department chairs with leadership communication strategies for minimizing the destructive conflict and damage that can accompany an unsuccessful promotion or tenure application. Although the case presented in this chapter focuses on managing an unsuccessful promotion application, the leadership communication strategies presented can be used in managing an unsuccessful tenure application.

Defining the Task

Promotion review is an emotionally charged process during which a faculty member's professional work is presented for multiple levels of scrutiny and judgment. Being judged and found wanting is never a pleasant outcome for the faculty applicant. The failed faculty applicant can experience a range of emotions, and the applicant's emotional response will likely dictate that person's behavioral response to the negative decision. If, for example, the failed applicant is embarrassed by the outcome, the applicant may withdraw from department work. If, however, the failed applicant is outraged by the promotion denial, he or she may lash out in a number of ways toward those individuals who the applicant blames or holds responsible for the negative outcome. Typically, there is a direct correlation between a faculty member's surprise by the promotion denial and the rage that follows. In other words, a faculty member who expects the promotion to be granted will be more upset when the promotion is denied than the faculty member who submits the application with full recognition that the promotion may be denied. Ideally, a faculty applicant is not surprised by the promotion review outcome because he or she has benefitted from ongoing performance counseling that offers the constructive feedback and professional development support needed to successfully meet all performance expectations. For information on conducting effective performance counseling, see Higgerson (1996, pp. 106–138) and Higgerson and Joyce (2007, pp. 115–130). For this reason, the chair's influence on how a faculty applicant reacts to promotion denial is greatly influenced by how that chair has engaged in ongoing performance counseling. Although a department chair does not have complete control over how a faculty member reacts to promotion denial, the chair's professional rapport with that faculty member and the department chair's ongoing performance counseling will influence how the faculty applicant perceives and reacts to a negative promotion decision.

The chair must also manage the impact of the disappointed faculty member's reaction on the department. A failed promotion application can strain working relationships between the failed faculty applicant and others in the department. It might create a strained or even hostile working relationship between the faculty applicant and department chair. The unsuccessful promotion application can leave a bruised psyche that may act out in an infinite number of ways. The faculty applicant may, for example, withdraw from department activity or blossom into an in-your-face combative personality. Regardless, it is the department chair's responsibility to manage the outcome scenarios. Should the faculty applicant decide to badmouth department colleagues or grieve the negative decision, the chair will need to manage a host of subsequent situations and meetings in a manner that preserves the chair's leadership credibility and the department's reputation.

Managing the conflict and collateral damage associated with an unsuccessful promotion application takes time and leadership skill. The ease with which a chair can effectively handle this situation will depend, in part, on the department chair's leadership credibility. For example, a chair with strong for positive leadership credibility on the campus will have an easier time responding to the charges filed by the unsuccessful faculty applicant than a chair with poor leadership credibility because the actions of department chairs with positive leadership credibility are trusted more than the actions of department chairs with poor leadership credibility. Consequently, how a chair employs leadership communication strategies in managing the conflict and collateral damage associated with an unsuccessful promotion application will depend, in part, on the department chair's leadership credibility. Please consider the strength of your leadership credibility as you learn more about the leadership communication strategies presented in the following section. For information on building leadership credibility, see Higgerson and Joyce (2007, pp. 50–63).

Relevant Leadership Communication Strategies

Department chairs can use specific leadership communication strategies to facilitate successful promotion application and to manage the conflict and minimize collateral damage that can accompany an unsuccessful promotion application.

Engage in Ongoing Performance Counseling

In preparing faculty for promotion review, the best defense is a strong offense. Department chairs can minimize the possibility of unreal expectations by providing individual faculty with constructive feedback about their performance and accomplishments in light of established standards for promotion and expectations for faculty performance. When performance counseling is limited to an annual performance review required by policy, many of the benefits of conducting ongoing performance counseling are lost. Instead, department chairs should cultivate a department climate in which sharing constructive feedback informally and formally about what went well and what might be tried differently is a routine practice. This will reduce the anxiety sometimes associated with the policy-mandated annual performance review and help individual faculty obtain a more accurate and operational understanding of performance expectations. When faculty are permitted to work without such ongoing feedback, they have no objective basis for knowing when they have met the established standards for promotion. Individual faculty members will know only how hard they have worked and what they have done. They will be less able to measure their performance against departmental and institutional expectations for faculty work and the standards established for promotion or tenure. For example, it is possible for a faculty member to notice that 20% of the students enrolled in a core course he teaches drop the class before the end of the first week and not realize that this is not the norm for faculty colleagues who teach the same core course. Discussing this data in relation to institutional expectations for faculty performance and helping the faculty member devise strategies to address the higher than normal attrition is an effective way to help the faculty member operationally understand performance expectations. When faculty possess an operational understanding of the standards for promotion, they are better able to self assess their readiness for promotion.

By offering constructive performance counseling year-round, department chairs can enhance their leadership credibility and establish a productive working relationship with individual faculty members. Think about it. Is there any better way for a department chair to build trust than by demonstrating a sincere commitment to faculty success? Department chairs enhance their overall leadership credibility when they cultivate trust and more effective working relationships with individual faculty members. Moreover, a strong working relationship with individual faculty is an enormous advantage in helping individual faculty members accept and constructively process negative outcomes such as a failed promotion application.

Depersonalize Negative Decisions

It will be easier for a faculty member to accept and respond constructively to a negative promotion decision if the decision is not taken personally. It is one thing for a faculty member to conclude that more work needs to be done before being granted promotion and quite another to believe that promotion denial is an indictment of one's professional achievements to date or, worse yet, an indication that the failed faculty applicant is not a valued member of the department or institution. When communicating a negative department vote to a faculty member, department chairs should avoid language that might be viewed as labeling the individual faculty member with some permanent deficiency. Consider the situation in which faculty colleagues vote against promotion because the applicant's work in service is limited to highly visible roles in the national discipline association. A department chair will want to discuss this one reason for the negative vote in a way that does not suggest a value judgment. For example, a department chair might discuss the department's expectation for the same leadership skill being shared with the national discipline association to be invested on initiatives within the department. This framing allows the faculty applicant to view the deficiency as work yet to be done. However, should the department chair explain that colleagues perceive the faculty applicant as only interested in performing service when it accrues individual recognition within the discipline, the faculty applicant is likely to hear the comment as a personal attack rather than work to be done and a promotion standard that can be satisfied by investing one's recognized leadership skills within the department.

Be Clear about What Is Needed for Success

It is important for department chairs to clearly communicate what behaviors and achievements are needed to successfully earn promotion. The to-do list for individual faculty must be both explicit and manageable for the faculty applicant. It will likely be different for each faculty member even though the standards for promotion remain the same across all faculty members because each faculty member possesses unique training and skills that will determine the best way for each to satisfy the common criteria for promotion. The underlying message for all faculty members is that promotion is within reach, but there may remain a few more things to do. With to-do lists established for individual faculty, it is less likely that faculty will seek to apply for promotion prematurely. Department chairs might involve the faculty applicant in estimating what time is needed to meet the remaining performance expectations. This affirms that promotion is within reach and feasible and helps the faculty applicant to more objectively assess progress. This can help to prevent the faculty member from submitting a second premature application for promotion.

Demonstrate Commitment to Helping the Faculty Applicant Achieve Success

Department chairs can help soothe the pain of a failed promotion application and enhance their leadership credibility and rapport with the faculty applicant by lending support to the work that the faculty applicant needs to complete to earn promotion. In fact, this can and should be done with all faculty as a part of ongoing performance counseling and not just a service reserved for faculty who have been denied promotion.

Department chair support can encompass commitments of expertise, time, and fiscal resources. For example, support might be the commitment of travel funds, the purchase of webinar that would be useful to the faculty member or the assignment of a graduate student assistant to help a faculty member perform a time-consuming service assignment for the department. Department chairs can also demonstrate their commitment to a faculty member's success by serving as a sounding board in discussing everything from how to revise a syllabus or work with a difficult student to brainstorming ideas for developing a timely research program or deciding where an article might be submitted for publication. Department chairs can demonstrate their commitment to individual faculty member's success by introducing them to respected colleagues in the discipline or to people on campus who can be helpful resources to them. Again, the specific ways in which department chairs can best demonstrate commitment to individual faculty success will vary with the faculty member and the institution. Support offered, however, should correlate with ongoing performance counseling. For example, if ongoing performance counseling is focused on teaching improvement, the support offered should be consistent with this goal. In this instance, the department chair would not want to offer support for extended travel that would require missing several classes when teaching improvement is the key to securing promotion.

If support from the department chair is not specific to the individual faculty member and anchored in ongoing performance counseling, it will not be perceived as sincere. If the effort to be supportive is not perceived as sincere by the individual faculty member, the department chair's effort will likely lower that chair's leadership credibility with that faculty member. The lower the department chair's leadership credibility, the more difficult it will be for that department chair to manage an unsuccessful promotion application.

Demonstrate Respect for the Faculty Applicant's Perspective

When working with the faculty member whose promotion has been denied, it is important for department chairs to consider that faculty member's perspective. Only by considering the failed faculty applicant's perspective can a chair hope to select language and frame conversations without adding insult to injury. For example, the words that a chair should use and the approach a chair might take will be different if the failed faculty applicant is embarrassed by the outcome or raging with hostility because others dared to recommend against promotion. Unless the chair's communication takes into account the perspective of the failed faculty applicant, the chair's message will not be heard as intended and could even make the situation worse. For example, if the failed applicant feels embarrassed and is having a hard time facing colleagues, it will do little good for the chair to begin by listing the work that needs to be accomplished before promotion can be granted. Instead, the department chair in this situation needs to begin by assuring the failed faculty applicant that a vote against promotion does not mean that the faculty applicant or his or her work is not valued by department colleagues or that promotion is out of reach. Similarly, if the failed faculty applicant is openly hostile, it will do little good for the department chair to begin with a pep talk about how promotion is within reach. Instead, the department chair will need to address and manage the faculty member's anger before that faculty member will be able to hear and accept any advice on how to succeed in earning promotion. By using words and an approach appropriate to the failed applicant's perspective, department chairs can demonstrate their respect for the failed faculty applicant. This not only aids a chair's management of an unsuccessful promotion but also can increase a chair's leadership credibility with the failed faculty applicant.

Putting Theory into Practice

Although these strategies will make good intuitive sense to most department chairs, they can be difficult to implement. In Case 6.1, the department chair must manage a meeting of the tenured full professors in the department as they pass judgment on a colleague's application for promotion to full professor. Place yourself in the role of the department chair as you read.

Case 6.1: The Premature Promotion Application

Jeremy Wilson, longtime department chair of sociology, was surprised when Dr. Lin Yang submitted her application for promotion to full professor. It was just 5 years ago when, after long debate, the department voted to support her application for tenure and promotion to the rank of associate professor. Even though Jeremy never shared with Dr. Yang that the vote on her application for tenure and the previous promotion was close, applying for promotion to full professor in the first year of being eligible seems like a bold move. But then, making bold moves from inflated self-confidence is typical for Dr. Yang.

By nature, Dr. Yang is a very pleasant, soft-spoken person, but she also demonstrates great persistence in pursuing the outcome she wants.

When asked to do something she does not wish to do, Dr. Yang offers countless excuses as to why she should not accept the assignment. She frequently reminds others that English is her second language, which limits her ability to accept assignments for which there are significant oral or written communication expectations. After extended discussion, the task being debated is typically passed to someone else. Only once in the 11 years that Dr. Yang has been in the department did Jeremy succeed in getting Dr. Yang to accept an assignment she did not want. Jeremy persisted after hours of listening to excuses and, finally, Dr. Yang half-heartedly agreed to serve as the department's assessment coordinator for one academic year while a colleague was on leave. Dr. Yang was not diligent or effective in carrying out the duties of assessment coordinator so much of the work was left undone. When the faculty member returned from leave, she complained that it would have been easier to keep the assignment while on leave than to clean up the mess created by Dr. Yang.

Although Lin Yang submitted her application for promotion to full professor without conferring with him, Jeremy believes he has no choice but to move forward and subject Dr. Yang's promotion application to the review process detailed in the department guidelines. In keeping with department policy, Jeremy requested the five tenured full professors in the department to read Dr. Yang's promotion materials and be ready to vote on her application at a meeting he scheduled expressly for this purpose.

Jeremy is doubtful that the five tenured full professors will support Dr. Yang's application. He also finds it hard to support her application, but he dreads having to break negative news to Dr. Yang. As Jeremy enters the meeting with the tenured full professors, he is immediately hit with a question from Tom, who believes that Dr. Yang should not have been promoted to associate professor. Five years earlier, Tom and several others supported Dr. Yang's application for tenure, but not her application for promotion to associate professor. When a majority of the faculty and Jeremy, however, pointed that the criteria for tenure and promotion to the rank of associate professor were identical, Dr. Yang received department support for both tenure and promotion to associate professor.

Meeting Discussion

Tom: Did you know Lin planned to apply for promotion this year?
Department chair: No. I was caught by surprise, too.
Debra: I can't believe this. Lin was just tenured and promoted to associate professor 5 years ago. We all waited longer than that before coming up for promotion to full.

Tom: Right, and we all worked a lot harder than Lin does.

Sally: The time in rank doesn't bother me as much as Lin's view that she is worthy of promotion. Granted she teaches well, but what else has she done? She is still writing articles on the same research project she completed before her last promotion. That one study is the only research project she has done since her dissertation. How does that make her eligible for full professor?

Tom: Exactly, I had completed and published on at least half a dozen research projects before applying for promotion to full professor.

Luis: What I find most troubling about Lin is that she never pitches in on department work. Lin's claims of service to the department are greatly embellished.

Tom: I served as president of the faculty senate before applying for promotion to full professor. Lin has never served on a single faculty senate committee.

Renee: Lin says that she cannot participate in faculty senate or committee work because English is her second language.

Tom: That's a convenient excuse. Lin never worries about English being her second language when she wants to do something. Remember how she petitioned Jeremy to be included in the teaching rotation for the graduate seminar.

Department chair: It doesn't sound like any of you are inclined to support Lin's application for promotion to full professor. Is this the case?

Tom: She is several years away from promotion, and that assumes she begins to give more effort to departmental and institutional service.

Debra: I agree.

Sally: I think she might be ready in 2 years if she will heed the advice we give her about meeting performance expectations in research and service.

Luis: What makes you think she will do anything differently now? We voted to tenure and promote Lin to associate professor, and her service was insufficient then.

Renee: I thought supporting her for tenure would enhance her commitment to the department.

Tom: Well, it didn't work, and I do not favor making the same mistake.

Department chair: Even though Lin surprised us by seeking promotion, I am confident she will not take kindly to learning that her colleagues recommend against promotion at this time.

Tom: That's not our problem.

Renee: She has a lot of pride and will likely be embarrassed and
angered by our decision.

Tom: Good. Maybe this will be the wake-up call she needs.

Department chair: With your support, I could talk with Lin informally
about all of this and encourage her to withdraw her application.
It might be a way for her to save face on campus.

Sally: That's a great idea.

Luis: I like it.

Debra: I agree. By withdrawing her application, she would avoid
getting a letter from you that is copied to the dean and the
university tenure and promotion review board indicating that we
are unanimous in recommending against her promotion.

Tom: If Lin is smart, she will thank us for the opportunity to withdraw
her application.

Department chair: Renee, you haven't said anything.

Renee: Well, I'm fine with what you propose doing, but I doubt Lin
will go along with it. In all honesty, I expect her anger to
overshadow any embarrassment.

Department chair: I hope I can get her to hear me.

Let's Analyze the Case

Jeremy Wilson is not surprised by the unanimous vote of the tenured full
professors to recommend against Dr. Yang's application for promotion to
full professor. He recognizes that this is the right decision. Jeremy must
decide how to make this clear to Dr. Yang and he knows this will not be
easy. There is a serious disconnect between Dr. Yang's perception of her
own achievements and the perception her colleagues hold of her work.
Jeremy hopes he can persuade Dr. Lin Yang to withdraw her application,
but realizes this will not be easy.

It's Your Turn

Assume the position of department chair in this case scenario and think
through how you would approach Dr. Yang.

1. How would you deliver the news? Would you communicate in writing? If so, would you send a letter or opt for a less formal communication channel such as email? If you decide to talk with Dr. Yang,
   would you schedule a meeting or wait for a chance meeting to
   discuss the issue. If you opt for a formally scheduled meeting, please

think through how you would call the meeting. Would you, for example, indicate the purpose for the meeting and, if so, consider the precise language you would use. Would you, for example, indicate that you wish to talk with Dr. Yang about her colleagues' assessment of her promotion application? If not, why not?

2. Assume you decide to meet with Dr. Yang and schedule a meeting to discuss her promotion application. How would you frame and present the news that all of the tenured full professors of the department are unanimous in believing that her application for promotion to full professor is premature? Consider specifically what language you would use. Anticipate Dr. Yang's reply and consider what you might say in response. Give some thought to what you might do should Dr. Yang burst into tears or storm out of the office.

Please Consider

Dr. Yang is unaware of how close the vote was on her tenure and promotion to associate professor. Clearly, the discussion around Dr. Yang's application for tenure and promotion to associate professor contributes to the negative reaction to her application to full professor. Believing she has the support of her department colleagues and chair, Dr. Yang sees no reason to wait in applying for promotion to full professor. Her colleagues, however, perceive Dr. Yang's application for promotion to full professor as bold and premature. As chair, Jeremy saw no reason to share how close the vote on tenure and the earlier promotion were with Dr. Yang. Again, put yourself in the chair's role as you answer the following questions:

1. Would you share anything about the discussion surrounding Dr. Yang's application for tenure and promotion to associate professor with Dr. Yang at this point in time? If so, specifically what information would you share? When and how would you present this information during the meeting?

2. The previous question is difficult to answer without knowing more about Dr. Yang's personality and the existing rapport between Dr. Yang and the department chair. What factors would you consider to determine the advisability of sharing information about the previous promotion application with Dr. Yang beyond taking stock of Dr. Yang's personality and your existing rapport with Dr. Yang? For example, would your approach be different if Dr. Yang consistently seeks your counsel on professional matters?

Let's Recap

Take a moment to finalize your notes for the meeting with Dr. Yang. Highlight your main objectives and be certain that the strategy you outline will serve the purpose that you have set for the meeting. Does your approach

- o Make use of previous performance counseling?
- o Depersonalize the negative recommendation?
- o Make clear what is needed for success?
- o Demonstrate your commitment to Dr. Yang's success?
- o Demonstrate respect for Dr. Yang's perspective?

Putting Theory into Practice

Once you are prepared for the meeting with Dr. Yang, you are ready to read Case 6.2. Does the department chair manage the meeting as you would?

Case 6.2: Please Hear Me

The department chair took some time to prepare for his meeting with Lin Yang. He hated to disappoint her even though he believes that Dr. Yang's application for promotion to full professor is premature. The department searched for 2 years before hiring Dr. Yang, whose expertise is in an area that is difficult to staff and teach. With some trepidation, the department chair requests a meeting with Dr. Yang to discuss her promotion application and is relieved when the meeting request does not appear to raise any angst. The chair is tentatively optimistic that Dr. Yang knew the promotion application was a long shot and that she will not be terribly surprised to learn her colleagues' reaction.

The Meeting

Department chair: Thanks for meeting with me.
Dr. Yang: I am pleased to meet with you. You said it was about my promotion application, and that is very important to me.
Department chair: Your success at the university is important to me also.
Dr. Yang: I worked a long time on the application.
Department chair: I am certain you did, and I believe the materials do a good job of presenting all you have done to date in the most positive light possible.

Dr. Yang: Thank you.

Department chair: Unfortunately, you submitted the application before you had sufficient time to meet performance expectations for full professor.

Dr. Yang: What are you saying?

Department chair: As you know, department policy requires all tenured full professors to review application materials and determine whether the applicant has met the established standards for promotion to full professor.

Dr. Yang: Yes, so . . . ?

Department chair: Five tenured full professors in the department read your application materials and are unanimous in believing that your application is premature.

Dr. Yang: I don't understand. They all supported my application for tenure and promotion to associate professor.

Department chair: I know, but the performance standards for promotion to full professor are different from those for the rank of associate professor.

Dr. Yang: Yes, but in my annual review meetings, you have always said very positive things about my work. You led me to believe my work is good.

Department chair: Your work is good. You simply need more time to do more good work to meet all of the expectations established for promotion to the rank of full professor.

Dr. Yang: You led me to believe that promotion is based on the quality of one's work and not time in rank.

Department chair: Quality does matter. However, it often takes more time than you have allowed to accumulate the level of achievement needed to meet the standard set for the rank of full professor.

Dr. Yang: This feels like a new rule. According to policy, a faculty member is eligible for promotion to full professor after serving 5 years at the rank of an associate professor.

Department chair: Yes, that is the soonest one can apply for promotion, but few do.

Dr. Yang: This is not making any sense.

Department chair: I'm sorry. Perhaps it would help if we reviewed your accomplishments in light of the standards for full professor.

Dr. Yang: No, this is ridiculous. I am being held to a different standard. According to the policy, I am eligible for promotion now, and you have never led me to believe that my work is in any way inferior.

Department chair: You certainly have the right to advance your application to the university tenure and promotion review board. However, your colleagues and I want you to know that we cannot support your application at this time. We wish to give you an opportunity to withdraw your application rather than have it forwarded with a letter from the department recommending against promotion at this time.

Dr. Yang: I can understand why that would be easier for all of you, but why would I want to withdraw my application?

Department chair: Well, the university review board gives a lot of weight to the department recommendation, and it might be more comfortable for you to wait until you have the full support of the department.

Dr. Yang: You are asking me to put my professional future in your hands and wait until you decide I'm ready? That's not going to happen. Besides, it is you who will feel uncomfortable when the review board members learn how I am being treated.

Department chair: Please think about this. I'm happy to talk further with you at a later time. I am willing to share precisely what you must do to earn the support of your department colleagues.

Dr. Yang: There is nothing more to talk about. I am so sorry I ever trusted you. Clearly you do not have my best interests at heart.

Let's Analyze the Case

As Renee predicted, Lin Yang is outraged when her department chair suggests that she withdraw her application for promotion. She is shocked to learn that her tenured full professor colleagues are unanimous in believing that her application for promotion is premature. Dr. Yang contends that she has sustained the same excellent performance that earned her tenure and promotion to associate professor. The chair explains that performance expectations for the rank of full professor require more than what is required to earn tenure and promotion to associate professor, but Dr. Yang is defensive to the point where she can no longer comprehend what the department chair is saying. Dr. Yang demands that the department chair forward her application to the next level of review, which is the university tenure and promotion review board. Dr. Yang believes it is her chair and colleagues who will be embarrassed when they and the provost overturn their negative recommendation.

As soon as Dr. Yang learns of the negative recommendation, she stops listening. The chair's approach is not inherently wrong, but it is ineffective in this instance. When Dr. Yang mentions that she worked a long time on the application, the chair should have realized that she is vested in it and in her promotion to full professor. At this point in the conversation, the chair might redirect the conversation to more neutral issues before presenting the bad news that the department recommendation is against promotion at this time. For example, the chair might have interjected, "I am certain that you did. Sadly, you never mentioned your plan to apply for promotion. Typically, faculty members consult with me in compiling their application materials. By working together, I can help individual faculty know how their achievements stack up against the established criteria for promotion to full professor." Even though Dr. Yang believes her achievements are worthy of promotion, this sidestep in the conversation may have allowed the chair to first discuss how the documentation presented in Dr. Yang's application materials falls short of meeting the standards for promotion before sharing the negative department recommendation.

By sharing news of the department's negative recommendation early in the conversation, the chair allows Dr. Yang to personalize the negative decision because she knows only that her faculty colleagues refuse to support her application for promotion. Without understanding the basis for their decision, the negative recommendation is more likely to appear arbitrary and unfair to Dr. Yang. Until she can understand and accept the basis for the negative recommendation, Dr. Yang will likely take the outcome as a personal affront. Because Dr. Yang becomes defensive upon learning that her application for promotion does not have department support, the chair has virtually no opportunity to demonstrate his commitment to Dr. Yang's eventual success or to discuss what Dr. Yang must do to meet the established criteria for promotion to full professor.

Dr. Yang takes the chair to task, claiming that her annual performance reviews led her to believe that she was ready for promotion. Assuming the department chair does effective ongoing performance counseling, he might have interjected specific issues that were discussed and documented during the annual reviews or in other performance counseling conversations. For example, the annual review conducted after Dr. Yang's temporary assignment to serve as the department's assessment coordinator should include discussion and documentation regarding the quality of her work on this task. If, however, the department chair in this case did not discuss Dr. Yang's inadequate performance as the temporary assessment coordinator with her, then the chair's negligence in conducting effective performance counseling will contribute to the immediate problem.

It's Your Turn

1. In what ways would your approach to the meeting with Dr. Yang be different from the approach used by Jeremy Wilson in Case 6.2? Would your approach have netted a better outcome with a quickly defensive Dr. Yang? Why?

2. Would you attempt to talk further with Dr. Yang? If so, how would you approach her, and precisely what would you say? What would you hope to accomplish?

3. Your next task is to draft a letter that details the department's recommendation against promotion. Keep in mind that although your letter will be addressed to the university tenure and promotion review board, it will eventually reach the provost, and policy requires that you send a copy to Dr. Yang.

Please Consider

It is not clear from the information presented in Cases 6.1 and 6.2 that Dr. Yang benefited from effective performance counseling. The chair's decision to spare Dr. Yang learning about the reservations expressed when she applied for tenure and promotion to associate professor denied Dr. Yang feedback that might have been helpful to her. The conflict exists between the department and Dr. Yang because each holds different assessments of the scope and quality of Dr. Yang's work. Dr. Yang's self-perception is very different from the perceptions that her colleagues have of her contributions to the department. Effective ongoing performance counseling helps to bridge such disconnects because faculty members receive continual feedback that encompasses the perceptions held by others toward their work. Effective ongoing performance counseling enables a faculty member to receive information essential to improving performance before that faculty member has unfounded pride and psyche vested in a premature application for promotion.

The department chair is in a difficult position. The department chair needs Dr. Yang to understand and accept the negative recommendation without becoming combative, nonproductive, or resigning her position. At the same time, the chair must clearly detail the basis for the negative department recommendation in the letter forwarded with Dr. Yang's promotion materials, and reading the basis for the negative recommendation will likely further anger Dr. Yang. Moreover, if the chair did not previously discuss and document the shortcomings that now serve as the basis for recommending against Dr. Yang's promotion, the chair will have a difficult time responding to Dr. Yang's contention that she had every reason to believe her performance met expectations.

Putting Theory into Practice

The chair works hard to have his letter, presented in Case 6.3, both provide a basis for the department's recommendation against Lin Yang's promotion and stipulate the work she will need to do to receive favorable department support for promotion.

Case 6.3: Letter Recommending against Promotion

Since his meeting with Dr. Yang, Jeremy has noticed that Dr. Yang is cool and distant with everyone in the department. She speaks only when directly addressed and appears to be going out of her way to avoid contact with others. Any hope the chair had that he might talk further with Dr. Yang about withdrawing her application were quickly dashed by her persistent efforts to avoid talking with him. When Jeremy stops by Dr. Yang's office door to say good morning, she keeps working without looking up or responding. Others in the department are openly discussing Dr. Yang's newfound rudeness. Consequently, Jeremy backs off trying to talk further with Dr. Yang for fear of making matters worse. He spends hours drafting the letter recommending against promotion and hopes it will explain the basis for the negative department recommendation in a professional way that helps her recognize that the promotion to full professor is within reach even though she does not yet meet the criteria.

The Letter

Memo to: Members of the University Tenure and Promotion Review Board
From: Jeremy Wilson, Associate Professor and Chair, Department of Sociology
Subject: Recommendation against Dr. Lin Yang's application for promotion to full professor

After thorough review of Dr. Lin Yang's promotion application and supporting materials, the five tenured full professors in the department are unanimous in believing that Dr. Yang does not meet the minimum criteria established for the rank of full professor. As chair, I completed an independent review of Dr. Yang's application and must concur with the tenured faculty members' negative recommendation. Consequently, the five tenured professors in sociology and department chair are unanimous in recommending against Dr. Yang's promotion to full professor at this time.

With the support of the tenured full professors in the department, I met with Dr. Yang to explain the basis for our recommendation against her promotion at this time. I suggested that Dr. Yang withdraw her application for promotion and work with me to address our suggestions for improvement. Dr. Yang did not accept my counsel. Instead, she insisted that her application for promotion be forwarded with full understanding that her department chair colleagues would unanimously recommend against her promotion at this time.

According to department criteria for promotion from associate to full professor, the successful candidate must provide evidence of notable accomplishment in all three areas of faculty work: teaching, scholarship, and service. We value Dr. Yang as a colleague in the department and acknowledge her work to date, but we believe she has not achieved notable accomplishment in the areas of scholarship and service.

Teaching

The department values Dr. Yang's good work in the classroom. Student evaluations of her teaching suggest she is well prepared for class and is quick to mentor students when asked. She particularly enjoys involving undergraduate students in research. Dr. Yang is faithful about keeping office hours, and, as department chair, I have never received a student complaint about her teaching. I had hoped that once Dr. Yang was tenured and promoted to associate professor she would agree to direct more graduate students in completing their master's theses and dissertations. However, she has not been willing to accept this responsibility. She reminds us that English is her second language and believes such assignments require extraordinary time and work on her part. Dr. Yang typically directs no more than one graduate student at a time, whereas the department norm is for faculty to direct four to five graduate students at a time.

Scholarship

As evidence of scholarship, Dr. Yang cites two peer-reviewed publications. This is insufficient to meet the department standard for notable accomplishment in the area of scholarship. Furthermore, one of the two articles was published in a journal that is not peer reviewed. Nor is this publication the top journal in the field, as Dr. Yang asserts in her promotion materials. The second article is coauthored with three other colleagues, and Dr. Yang is listed as the fourth author. It is not clear what her contribution was to this jointly authored publication.

Dr. Yang also lists three articles that have been submitted for review and eventual publication. However, all three articles are based on research that began more than a decade ago as part of her dissertation research. This does not provide evidence of a timely, productive scholarly agenda. Further, there is no certainty that these articles, which are based on research conducted 11 years ago, will be accepted for publication.

Service

Even if Dr. Yang met the performance criteria in teaching and scholarship, we would recommend against promotion. Department criteria require that a successful candidate must, at a minimum, demonstrate active participation in department, college, and campus faculty governance through participation on formal and ad hoc committees. By our assessment, Dr. Yang falls well short of achieving this minimum standard.

Dr. Yang's service to the Department of Sociology is exceptionally thin. She lists only two contributions: participating in student recruitment activities and serving as the department's assessment coordinator. All faculty members are called upon to attend student recruitment events that require relatively minimal commitments of time. Dr. Yang's service as assessment coordinator was for only one academic year while a colleague was on leave. She accepted the temporary assessment assignment only after repeated urging, which was prompted by the fact that Dr. Yang is the only faculty member not involved in service to the department or at the university. Moreover, Dr. Yang's tenure as assessment coordinator did not go well in that new assessment methods approved by the department faculty were never implemented, data collected were never summarized, and the annual report was never written. The department faculty are unanimous in believing that Dr. Yang needs to commit to department service and become a more fully functioning member of the department.

In closing, we would like to again reiterate that Dr. Yang is a valued member of the sociology department. However, we believe that her application for promotion to full professor is premature because she has not yet met the performance criteria established for the work in the areas of scholarship and service.

Let's Analyze the Case

The department chair indicates that inadequate work in the areas of scholarship and service are the basis for the department's decision to recommend against Dr. Yang's promotion to full professor. Nonetheless, the chair mentions one seemingly important shortcoming in the area of teaching. Specifically, the chair mentions that Dr. Yang is willing to direct only one graduate student at a time, whereas her faculty colleagues each direct four to five students. If failing to direct more graduate students was part of the negative recommendation, the chair should identify this as one of the reasons for the negative recommendation. If, however, this was not part of the basis for the negative recommendation, then the chair's purpose for mentioning it in the letter is unclear.

The letter should detail the basis for department's negative recommendation. If no problems were identified in the area of teaching, that's all that need be said about the faculty applicant's teaching. Chairs may be tempted to include additional information that paints a broader picture of inadequate faculty performance even though these additional items did not contribute to the department's negative recommendation. This is a dangerous practice because, depending on the specific issues raised, it can give the appearance of picking on the failed faculty applicant. It can also create the perception that the chair believes the basis for the department's negative recommendation needs bolstering with information about additional issues not noted by the tenured full professors who voted against recommending the applicant for promotion. The basis for the department's negative recommendation should be explained clearly and stand on its own merit.

Conversely, chairs sometimes sense the need to offer positive feedback in an effort to appear fair or perhaps to ease the pain of a negative recommendation. This, too, is dangerous because it can undermine the basis for the negative recommendation. In this instance, the basis for the negative recommendation is read in the context of the total letter that includes all of the positive comments regarding the faculty member's performance. Consequently, this practice invites others at every subsequent review level to weigh the department's positive and negative comments. If the letter is limited to providing the basis for the department's negative recommendation, others at every subsequent review level will more likely confine their review to assessing whether the basis for the department's negative recommendation is sufficient.

The department chair discusses the basis for the recommendation against promotion in an objective manner in an effort to communicate that the negative recommendation is not personal. Never does the chair suggest that Dr. Yang is incapable of earning promotion to full professor. She needs only to improve her work in two areas to secure the support of her department colleagues. Precisely what Dr. Yang needs to do each of these areas, however, remains somewhat vague. For example, it is not clear how many publications would be needed or what type of service activity would be considered sufficient. Consequently, Dr. Yang still has little information regarding what she might do to attain promotion to full professor. Dr. Yang will need to sense that promotion is attainable and know precisely how to be successful for her anger to dissipate.

It's Your Turn

Consider the letter included in Case 6.3 in answering the following questions:

1. Did the chair provide sufficient documentation to justify the department's negative recommendation? If not, what would you add to the letter?

2. Anticipate Dr. Yang's reaction to the letter. Will it likely help Dr. Yang's understanding of the department's negative recommendation? If not, underline the statements in the letter that might be rewritten to promote better understanding of the department's negative recommendation.

3. Should Dr. Yang decide to grieve the decision, do portions of the letter offer ammunition for a grievance? If so, please identify the troubling statements, and indicate how each may license Dr. Yang to grieve the negative recommendation.

Please Consider

The basis for the department's negative recommendation should encompass performance issues that have been discussed with the faculty applicant. Although no faculty member likes to receive a negative recommendation from department colleagues and the department chair, the outcome is easier to understand and accept if the faculty applicant is not surprised by the negative recommendation and understands the basis for the decision. For example, if Jeremy Wilson had merely hoped that Dr. Yang would direct more graduate students after being tenured and never asked her to accept more graduate advisees, Dr. Yang will be surprised to read the statement in his letter about her work with graduate students. Such surprises work against helping a faculty member understand and accept a negative recommendation on promotion. Similarly, if no one asked Dr. Yang to serve on a faculty senate committee, then she is justified in feeling wronged by the department's negative recommendation because it was not clear to her that this was a performance expectation for promotion.

When faculty feel unfairly treated because a negative recommendation is based on issues that no one ever mentioned so that perceived deficiencies can be addressed, they are more likely to grieve the decision. Should a failed faculty applicant be able to document that they had no forewarning that their performance was insufficient, they are more likely to receive a receptive ear from a faculty grievance committee or review board. This helps to underscore how vitally important effective ongoing performance counseling is to managing the conflict and collateral damage that might derive from a negative recommendation on promotion. Department chairs who are not fully confident in the effectiveness of their ongoing performance counseling should consider reading the reference cited earlier in this chapter.

Putting Theory into Practice

In Case 6.4, we learn what Dr. Yang takes action to right the wrong she perceives has been done to her. As you read the case, give some thought to how you would manage the collateral damage to the chair's leadership credibility and the department's reputation.

Case 6.4: Dr. Yang's Rebuttal

Dr. Yang's anger grew when she read Jeremy Wilson's letter describing the basis for the department's negative recommendation, but she decides to do nothing. She is confident that the members of the university tenure and promotion review board will see through the lies and recommend in favor of her promotion.

Although Dr. Yang remains cool and distant with department colleagues, Jeremy Wilson is encouraged when she does not respond to his letter explaining the department's negative recommendation to the university tenure and promotion review board. Given the silent treatment he is receiving from Dr. Yang, he would not be surprised to receive a hostile letter challenging the department's negative recommendation.

Jeremy is even more encouraged when he receives a letter indicating that the review board recommends against promotion. Dr. Yang, however, is furious when she reads her copy of the review board's letter to the provost recommending against her promotion. She reasons that the conspiracy against her is growing without her having an opportunity for rebuttal. Dr. Yang is shocked by the outcome because she knows several faculty members serving on the university tenure and promotion review board and cannot believe they would vote against her. These people have always been friendly toward her. Although she cannot understand why they would turn on her, she decides that she cannot remain passive while the negative recommendations of her department and the university tenure and promotion review board are forwarded to the provost.

The provost helped to recruit Lin Yang to the university, and the provost has been especially supportive of her interest in involving undergraduate students in research. She trusts the provost to do the right thing, but she decides it is time to set the record straight. Armed with a lot of pride and fresh indignation, Dr. Yang schedules an appointment with the provost.

Meeting with the Provost

Provost: My secretary said you wanted to talk about your promotion application.

Dr. Yang: Yes, I believe it is very important that you hear the facts from me.

Provost: I must confess that I have not begun to read any of the applications. In fact, I have not yet had a chance to read the recommendations of the university tenure and promotion review board.

Dr. Yang: When you do, I believe you will be shocked to discover that my department and the review board members have turned against me.

Provost: Really? Why would they do that?

Dr. Yang: I don't know, but I need for you to understand that the assertions they make are lies.

Provost: How can that be when the review at every level is based on what you include in your application materials?

Dr. Yang: That's what I thought. To justify a negative recommendation, my department chair and colleagues made up facts that are not true, and the university tenure and promotion review board believed their lies.

Provost: I promise you that I will read all carefully and will give your application fair consideration. I will add that should you not be granted promotion at this time, you will learn precisely what you need to do to earn the promotion in the future.

Dr. Yang: I deserve promotion now, and I believe you will see that. You have always been so supportive of my work at the university.

You know how hard I work. Please remember that my department's negative recommendation is based on lies. All my annual reviews have been positive. I have no idea why my colleagues have turned on me.

Provost: Not having looked at your application, I can promise only to give it fair consideration.

Call to Department Chair

Any optimism the department chair felt when he read his copy of the review board's letter to the provost indicating that the review board recommends against Dr. Yang's promotion was dampened when he received a phone call a few days later from the provost, who called to inform him of his meeting with Dr. Yang.

Provost: I'm sorry to interrupt your day, but I thought you should know that Dr. Yang asked to meet with me.

Chair: I can guess that she wanted to discuss her promotion application.

Provost: Actually, she wanted to forewarn me that the department has turned against her.

Chair: That's not the case. In fact, I spent a lot of time trying to help her understand why her application for promotion was premature.

Provost: I promised Dr. Yang that I would read her application carefully and give it every serious consideration. Obviously, I could not discuss the details because I have not read the application.

Chair: That's fair.

Provost: I believe it is important that you know Dr. Yang believes she is a victim of discrimination. She told me that the case against her is based on lies and that, before learning of the department's negative recommendation, she had no idea that her performance was not meeting expectations. I recall that your letters documenting annual reviews of Dr. Yang's performance are quite positive. What happened?

Chair: The five tenured full professors in the department are unanimous in concluding that Dr. Yang does not meet the performance standard establish for the rank of full professor. In particular, they find her scholarship thin and her contribution in the area of service very weak. This is explained in greater detail in the department letter recommending against promotion at this time.

Provost: I look forward to reading it and Dr. Yang's promotion materials. I would add, however, that given your very positive annual reviews of Dr. Yang's work, I am not surprised that she believes she is qualified for promotion to full professor.

Jeremy Wilson was replaying his conversation with the provost in his mind when the department secretary interrupted to tell him that he had another phone call. Upon answering the call, Jeremy immediately recognized the familiar voice of Emmitt Jones, a well-known and highly regarded faculty member at the university.

Jeremy: I always enjoy hearing from you, but I am curious to learn what the chair of the religion department needs with the chair of sociology.

Emmitt: I'm afraid I'm not calling as the chair of the religion department.

Jeremy: That's good. I hope you are calling to schedule a time to play golf. It's been too long since we've taken an afternoon to critique each other's golf game.

Emmitt: I am afraid this is not a social call.

Jeremy: I am sorry to hear that. How can I help you?

Emmitt: I am calling in my capacity as chair of the faculty grievance review board. I'm obliged to tell you that one of your faculty, Dr. Lin Yang, has filed a formal grievance against you as department chair.

Jeremy: Against me?

Emmitt: That's right. She is grieving your decision to recommend against her application for promotion to full professor.

Jeremy: Apparently, Dr. Yang has decided to kill the messenger. I hope she mentioned that all five tenured full professors in the department voted against her promotion.

Emmitt: She did. However, she also maintains that, as chair, you can decide to accept or overturn the vote of the department faculty.

Jeremy: It is unlikely I would ever overturn the unanimous vote of the tenured full professors in this department. I may be chair, but I hold the rank of associate professor. Besides, I believe the tenured full professors reached the right conclusion regarding Dr. Yang's promotion application.

Emmitt: I understand. At the same time, I believe Dr. Yang's interpretation of policy is correct in that the policy charges the chair with taking a faculty vote, conducting an independent review of the applicant's materials, and rendering a final recommendation. She attached a copy of the letter you wrote, and I see only your signature on it.

Jeremy: My letter summarized the thinking of the five tenured full professors in the department.

Emmitt: Unfortunately, this may not be the biggest bone of contention between you and Dr. Yang.

Jeremy: What else?

Emmitt: She maintains that the arguments detailed in your letter justifying your negative recommendation are based on lies. Further, she says that you tried to strong-arm her into withdrawing her application for promotion.

Jeremy: I certainly did not try to strong-arm her into withdraw her application. I merely forewarned her of the unanimous negative recommendation and suggested that she may wish to withdraw her application to avoid advancing it without the support of the department.

Emmitt: Believe me, I understand the situation you are in. I will send you a copy of Dr. Yang's grievance. The grievance review board members must meet and decide whether to hear the case. If the board decides to hear the grievance, you will have ample opportunity to document the decision you made.

Let's Analyze the Case

The department chair must now manage collateral damage created as a result of Dr. Yang's response to learning that the university tenure and promotion review board also recommends against her promotion. When informing the chair of his meeting with Dr. Yang, the provost mentions her positive annual reviews. Even though the provost has not yet read Dr. Yang's application for promotion, the provost seems concerned that Dr. Yang may not have had sufficient counseling about how her performance needed to change or improve to meet the department criteria for promotion to full professor. In particular, the provost cannot recall previous mention of the specific issues that have now become the basis for the department's recommendation against Dr. Yang's promotion. The provost likely understands that although ineffective performance counseling does not warrant the granting of a promotion prematurely, it does open the door for the faculty applicant to grieve a negative outcome. The chair needs to address the issue the provost raises in a way that enhances the chair's leadership credibility. More specifically, the chair must establish that he is engaging in effective ongoing performance counseling with all faculty and that Dr. Yang had sufficient counsel about the issues now used to recommend against her promotion.

The chair must also manage collateral damage with the faculty grievance review board. Should the review board agree to hear Dr. Yang's complaint, the chair will need to document the basis for the department's negative recommendation thereby demonstrating that the decision is based on facts and not lies. The chair will also need to respond to Dr. Yang's charge that he strong-armed Dr. Yang in an attempt to have her withdraw her application for promotion. Grievance hearings can demand a lot of time and energy. Even if the faculty grievance review board decides not to hear Dr. Yang's complaint, the chair will likely have some collateral damage to manage with the members of the faculty grievance review board. As a result of Dr. Yang filing a grievance with the review board, the faculty serving on the review board could now have a less favorable perception of the chair and the sociology department.

The department chair should realize that collateral damage might extend beyond the provost and faculty grievance review board. In controlling the collateral damage, the chair will need to give careful thought to whom else might be privy to Dr. Yang's rants. There would be no way to generate a precise list, but it will be important for the chair to anticipate possible audiences that are relevant to the ultimate promotion decision or that have important bearing on future department business. For example, the department chair need not do much to address what Dr. Yang might say in her condo neighborhood. However, should her passion for bridge place her within earshot of an university board member, the chair needs to consider the possibility that she will inform the board of her plight. It would be inappropriate for the department chair to initiate contact with the board member who plays in the same bridge club with Dr. Yang but appropriate to anticipate how he might respond should he hear directly or indirectly from that board member.

It's Your Turn

Place yourself in the department chair's role in answering the following questions:

1. What information would you gather in preparing for the possibility of a grievance hearing? Would you plan to call witnesses, and, if so, who would you call to testify?

2. What documentation would you pull together to answer the provost's concern about Dr. Yang receiving sufficient notice of what she needed to do to meet the criteria for promotion to full professor? Would you request a meeting to review the matter with the provost or wait until contacted again by him?

3. What information, if any, would you share with the five tenured full professors in the department? How might they be helpful to you in safeguarding the department's reputation and your leadership credibility?

Please Consider

In managing collateral damage, department chairs are never starting from scratch. Instead, a department chair is managing from whatever happens to be the current perception of the chair's leadership credibility. Generally, the stronger or more positive the chair's leadership credibility—built on actions he or she takes in the department—the easier it is for him or her to manage the conflict associated with a negative promotion recommendation and the resulting collateral damage. The provost in Case 6.4, for example, will react differently to his conversation with Dr. Yang depending on his assessment of the chair's leadership credibility. If the provost perceives Jeremy Wilson to be a skilled and very effective department chair, he will put less stock in the accusations being made by Dr. Yang. However, if the provost doubts the chair's effectiveness in leading the Department of Sociology, he is likely to give her more initial credence. Similarly, if a department is perceived as giving junior faculty a difficult time when supporting promotion or tenure, the accusations of a failed faculty applicant will be heard in the context of that perception.

Hindsight Is 20/20

A department chair does not need to wait to manage potential conflict until the failed faculty applicant is upset. Rather than rely on faculty members to signal their plans for seeking promotion, department chairs can initiate discussion about the anticipated timeline through ongoing performance counseling. This can be done in a positive manner that demonstrates for the faculty member that the chair expects that faculty member to work toward promotion. Few faculty members will object to having a department chair that is forward looking regarding their promotion. By initiating discussion about a timetable, a department chair can establish a structure by which he or she can offer specific counsel regarding the faculty member's readiness for promotion. Such counsel need not be limited to the formal annual review required by college or university policy. For example, the following informal comment from the department chair will help the faculty member both know that he or she is on track toward promotion and what remains: "Congratulations on your recent publication in a top-tier journal. Two or three more of those publications, and you will satisfy the established scholarship criteria for promotion."

The more difficult a faculty member is to counsel, the more reason there is for a department chair to share the nature of these difficulties with others. By sharing that a difficult faculty member refuses to heed the chair's counsel with a few key individuals, the department chair is able to describe the effort made to effectively counsel the difficult faculty member to improved performance. A department chair in this situation may also solicit ideas for being more effective in counseling the performance of the difficult faculty member from the college dean by saying, "I have been unsuccessful in getting Professor X to understand the criteria for full professor. To date I have tried X, Y, and Z, but Professor X insists that I am making too much of the established criteria for promotion. Do you have ideas for what else I might try? I worry because Professor X seems determined to apply for promotion this fall, and I doubt he will have the support of his department colleagues." The college dean may have additional strategies that the department chair can try. If the strategies work, the department chair will be successful in getting through to a difficult faculty member. If the strategies do not work, the department chair can report back to the college dean about the failed effort and the college dean will have a sense of the department chair's efforts to help a difficult faculty member. Should the difficult faculty member insist on applying for promotion without heeding the performance counseling offered by the department chair and receive a negative recommendation from the department, the college dean will not be surprised by the outcome.

The nature of the problem will dictate who might be kept apprised of the problem. For example, if a faculty member resists performance counseling from the department chair because a few senior faculty members have persuaded the more junior faculty member that applications for promotion are routinely approved, the department chair will want to brief those senior faculty members. The department chair might approach the senior faculty members by soliciting their help in rescuing a more junior, but valued faculty member who has some misperceptions about the rigorous nature of the promotion review process. In making clear the current criteria for promotion, the department chair can make clear what the more junior faculty member needs help in recognizing and achieving.

Let's Recap

Department chairs can lay a foundation that is helpful to preventing and, if necessary, managing an unsuccessful promotion application by engaging in effective ongoing performance counseling. Through effective ongoing performance counseling department chairs can cultivate their leadership credibility and the working rapport needed to provide faculty members with constructive feedback about what is going well and what might be tried differently in order to meet established performance expectations. Effective performance counseling provides a structure through which department chairs can help faculty members assess their readiness to apply for promotion and thereby limit, if not eliminate, the premature application for promotion. When faculty members benefit from effective performance counseling, they possess a more accurate understanding of when their accomplishments warrant successful promotion. When faculty members lack this understanding, they are more inclined to submit a promotion application prematurely because it is the only certain way to discover if their accomplishments meet the established criteria for promotion. Through ongoing performance counseling, department chairs can guide faculty members toward a successful promotion and, in the process, enhance their leadership credibility with the faculty.

An unsuccessful promotion application can spawn destructive conflict. It is never pleasant for a faculty member to have an application for promotion judged by peers and found unworthy of promotion. The intensity of the failed faculty applicant's response will correlate directly with the faculty member's investment in the process and outcome. To manage the situation, department chairs should use communication that accomplishes the following purposes:

o Depersonalize the negative promotion decision.
o Make clear what action will lead to successful promotion.
o Demonstrate the department chair's commitment to the faculty member's success.
o Demonstrate respect for the failed applicant's perspective.

In doing so, department chairs can help redirect the failed faculty applicant's focus from feeling hurt or perhaps mistreated to what few things remain to realize success.

If the failed faculty applicant persists in feeling hurt or mistreated, there will likely be collateral damage for the department chair to manage. Collateral damage occurs when the aggrieved faculty member takes action to right the wrong of a denied promotion by recounting his version of what happened to others on and off campus, filing a grievance or taking legal action. In managing the resulting collateral damage, department chairs must use communication that protects and improves others' perception of the chair's leadership credibility and department reputation. Department chairs can help mitigate the potential collateral damage that might accrue by sharing with key individuals when a faculty member is resisting performance counseling. Doing so will provide key individuals with some context should the difficult faculty member lash out when the premature promotion application is denied.

7

MENTORING THE SEASONED PROFESSIONAL HIRED INTO AN UNTENURED FACULTY POSITION

INSTITUTIONS SOMETIMES HIRE faculty who are seasoned professionals from other institutions of higher education or from the private sector. Their interest in a faculty position may be motivated by a desire to try teaching late in their career or at a different type of institution or in a different part of the country. Some faculty members elect to retire from one institution and begin drawing retirement while accepting a part-time or full-time faculty position at another institution. These individuals have been successful elsewhere and typically possess significant professional experience. Nonetheless, the seasoned faculty hire is often employed without tenure and, unless his or her previous experience has been in higher education, at the rank of assistant professor. Despite the professional expertise that seasoned faculty hires possess, department chairs can discover that putting them in an untenured position can yield a variety of performance and conflict issues.

This chapter has two goals for department chairs regarding hiring seasoned professionals for faculty positions: (1) to help them anticipate and address potential problems; and (2) to equip them with the leadership communication strategies for managing performance and conflict issues that arise. Although the scenario presented in this chapter focuses on managing the seasoned professional with experience in higher education, these strategies also apply to professionals hired from other industries.

Defining the Task

Department chairs and search committee members are understandably impressed with applicants who possess professional experience. Seasoned professionals often bring with them a wealth of expertise. Department chairs may assume that seasoned professionals will require less help in learning how to be successful in the department and at the institution. In contrast, applicants fresh out of graduate school seeking their first full-time position will likely need help on everything from how to discuss a poor grade with a disgruntled student to how to manage their time effectively to successfully meet the performance expectations for tenure and promotion at the institution. Although the seasoned professional may not need the same mentoring that a new doctoral graduate might need, it is a mistake for department chairs to assume that the seasoned professional will not have a learning curve or need for mentoring.

In hiring a seasoned professional, department chairs should consider the person's background and use the search process to assess his or her preparedness to be successful in assimilating into the department culture and in meeting performance expectations. For example, a seasoned professional hired from the private sector may need help learning how to teach today's college students, whereas someone hired from another institution may need help learning a new department culture and how policy and practice differ from what they previously experienced. Department chairs will likely encounter problems when a seasoned professional hired from another institution of higher education does not understand how performance expectations differ between the new and old post. Similarly, department chairs will encounter performance problems when a seasoned professional hired from the private sector does not understand precisely what work is involved in achieving success, such as constructing a syllabus or class assignments.

Department chairs must help the seasoned professional acculturate into the work life of the department. Even a seasoned traveler can get lost in a new city without an accurate road map. Department chairs must provide the road map that will help the seasoned professional achieve success both in working with department colleagues and in meeting performance expectations. This does not mean that the department chair must become the seasoned professional's only mentor. However, he or she must assume responsibility for devising a comprehensive plan that ensures the seasoned professional receives the information and support needed to be successful. This plan can encompass a network of mentors and contacts within the discipline and at the institution. Leaving this to chance sets the seasoned professional up for failure. Likewise, it is not sufficient to hand the new seasoned professional a copy of the faculty handbook. Department chairs are responsible for interpreting policy for new seasoned professional hires, whether they come from the private sector or another institution. Without the department chair's operational interpretation of policy, seasoned professional hires will interpret policy language within the context of their previous employment, which increases the likelihood that they will be on a different page from other department faculty. By helping seasoned professional hires understand the culture and performance expectations of their new position and academic department, department chairs circumvent conflict that might derive from cultural differences or confusion about performance expectations.

Relevant Leadership Communication Strategies

It can be a mistake to assume that the seasoned professional needs less mentoring than a faculty member hired right out of graduate school. Often more mentoring is needed when hiring a seasoned professional because that individual's previous experience may not be relevant to a new campus or department policy and practice. The following leadership communication strategies will help department chairs ensure the success of seasoned professional hires and minimize the accompanying potential for conflict.

Begin Mentoring during the Search Process

Department chairs tend to be in recruitment mode during the search process. However, this is the perfect opportunity to begin mentoring the prospective hire. When hiring a seasoned professional, it is absolutely crucial to use the search process effectively to begin mentoring.

MAKE EXPECTATIONS CLEAR   When department chairs are in recruitment mode, they tend to focus conversations with the prospective hire on the strengths that the candidate will bring to the department. This can mislead the new hire into believing that existing areas of strength represent the sum total of performance expectations for success. For example, when hiring a professional broadcaster to teach in mass communication, the conversation may focus on how the individual's professional network and experience will enhance the department program. Department chairs do the candidate a disservice if conversations during the search process do not also include very clear explanations of all performance expectations.

It is very important that department chairs present prospective hires with a clear understanding of all performance expectations for success in the position. Department chairs should be explicit in discussing specific performance expectations that might be new to the prospective hire. For example, the professional broadcaster will likely know little about performance expectations for service to the department. Faculty members hired from the private sector may not know how to write a syllabus, craft a class exercise or assignment, grade student work, or engage in ongoing research and creative activity. The search process affords a perfect opportunity to find out what the prospective hire needs to learn to be successful.

ASSESS POTENTIAL PERFORMANCE CONCERNS   No matter how experienced, the seasoned professional being hired will have a learning curve. The seasoned professional coming from another institution will need to learn a new culture and how policy and practice may differ from that used at a previous institution. The seasoned professional hired from industry will need to learn and understand how higher education works which is vastly different from industry. All seasoned professional hires will need to come to grips with the fact that, for all practical purposes, they are newbies despite their substantial expertise and experience. It can be challenging for many seasoned professionals to comprehend and navigate their experienced yet novice role.

TEST THE PROSPECTIVE HIRE'S RECEPTIVITY TO MENTORING   The search process affords department chairs with an opportunity to test the prospective hire's receptiveness to mentoring. Suppose, for example, the candidate has never seen or written a course syllabus. The department chair might provide the candidate several sample syllabi and describe the support available for learning how to craft a syllabus. Should the candidate appear genuinely appreciative and interested in reviewing the sample syllabi and using the available resources to learn how to write a syllabus, the department chair has some indication that the individual will be receptive to ongoing mentoring. However, if the candidate seems disinterested and professes that samples are unnecessary because he or she plans to recount professional experience that students need to be successful, it is less likely that he or she will be receptive to ongoing mentoring. Should this be the case, department chairs should be very cautious in moving forward. Before extending an offer of employment, it will be important for the department chair to review with the prospective hire precisely what the department expectations are for ongoing mentoring and faculty performance.

It is a mistake to assume that senior faculty members hired from another institution do not need mentoring. Often, these individuals can be the most difficult to mentor because they may not perceive the need for, or benefit of, being coached. To the extent that policies and performance expectations differ from one institution to another, the senior faculty member hired from another institution may need more mentoring than a new doctorate hired straight from graduate school. When a senior faculty member retires from one institution to begin work at another, that senior faculty member often selects a very different type of institution that, for any number of reasons, holds personal appeal for the senior faculty seeking to relocate. In this instance, the senior faculty member will need mentoring to understand the performance expectations at their new institution.

MENTOR FOR A SUCCESSFUL START IN THE POSITION Department chairs can and should begin mentoring during the search process. In particular, department chairs should mentor new faculty hires on any aspect that will help them be more successful in starting the position. Depending on the previous experience of the new hire, prestart mentoring might include such basics as how to prepare a syllabus or how to successfully navigate the interpersonal dynamics within the department.

This initial mentoring helps to establish the department chair's leadership credibility with the new faculty hire. Mentoring enables the department chair to demonstrate both an understanding of how things work at the institution and an investment in the new faculty hire's success. Most new faculty will appreciate the help and think more highly of the department chair for extending such support. However, should the new hire dismiss such mentoring as unnecessary, it suggests that the new hire is not receptive to mentoring or ongoing performance counseling.

Facilitate the Integration of Nontraditional Hires

A seasoned professional is, for all practical purposes, a nontraditional hire. Consequently, department chairs should exercise the same care in integrating the seasoned professional hire that they would with other nontraditional hires. A nontraditional hire might be the first African American or international faculty member in a department of all Caucasian faculty. A nontraditional hire can be the first male hired on a nursing faculty composed only of females or the first female hired in a physics department of all males. A new hire is a nontraditional hire when he or she does not fit the department norm.

Seasoned professionals can be different from the department norm in both the nature and source of their professional experience. Seasoned professionals hired from industry typically possess strong credentials in the practice of the discipline. However, they will likely lack knowledge of academic life and work. Department chairs need to be very intentional about facilitating the integration of seasoned professionals hired from industry. The long-term success of seasoned professionals hired from industry depends on their ability to successfully navigate life and work at the institution. Department chairs must facilitate their success by guiding their acculturation into academic life and work. This can be done through ongoing mentoring, planned introductions to key individuals and offices on campus, a teaching schedule that most closely matches the seasoned professional's expertise and experience, and strategic committee and other service assignments. In sum, department chairs should mentor and guide the seasoned professional hired from industry with the same care they would exercise in advising a new freshman student.

Seasoned professionals hired from other institutions possess information about life and work in higher education, but they, too, need explicit mentoring. These seasoned professionals need help learning the policies and practices of their new institution that may be different from those used at their previous institution. They will need help understanding that although they may have been successful at another institution they are essentially starting from scratch in establishing professional relationships with new colleagues. The credibility or special license they may have earned at a previous institution does not automatically follow them to the new position. Similarly, it is unlikely that their new department chair's leadership style will mirror that with which they are familiar so these seasoned professionals will need help in cultivating a productive working relationship with their new department chair.

Assess the Reason for Observed Performance Concerns

Any effort to remedy problem performance will be effective only if the strategy used addresses the reason for the performance concern. For example, it will be of little use to try to motivate a seasoned professional hired from industry to work harder and spend more time grading student work if that individual does not know how to grade student work. The only way to effectively address student concerns about unfair grading practices in this situation would be to help the seasoned professional learn how to grade fairly and constructively to facilitate student learning.

Similarly, assigning a seasoned professional hired from a prestigious graduate program at another institution to teach undergraduate classes without first making clear that the department norm is for all faculty to teach undergraduate courses could spawn avoidable conflict that may result should the new hire take offense at being assigned to teach undergraduate courses.

Illustrate Performance Concerns with Specific Behavioral Examples

Performance counseling will be most effective if it does not cause the person being counseled to become defensive. When a person being counseled to improve performance becomes defensive, that person will be less able to hear and constructively act upon the department chair's counsel. Because seasoned professionals have already achieved professional success elsewhere, they may have a difficult time comprehending that their performance is not meeting expectations.

One effective strategy for minimizing defensiveness is to illustrate the performance concerns with specific behavioral examples. By illustrating performance concerns with behavioral examples instead of descriptive adjectives, department chairs lessen the likelihood that the seasoned professional will take the concern personally. Consider the difference in the following two statements:

Statement A: You are insensitive to students' need for helpful feedback on their work.

Statement B: Students appreciate faculty who provide constructive comment on each assignment that will help guide their improvement on the next assignment.

Both statements address the need to provide students with more helpful feedback on their work. However, statement A is more likely to increase defensiveness because it labels the faculty member as insensitive. Statement B merely describes the behavior that will be appreciated by students. Statement B provides a road map to success without labeling the individual faculty member in a negative way. Further, by telling the faculty member what to do to be successful, statement B implies that the department chair believes the faculty member can be successful in addressing the student concern. It should be obvious that the faculty member hearing statement A is more likely to become defensive than the faculty member hearing statement B.

Document Performance Concerns with Third-Person Clarity

Performance concerns should be written with third-person clarity. In other words, a person not hearing the conversation about poor performance should be able to read the letter documenting that conversation and know precisely what the issues are, what suggestions for improvement were offered, and what support was provided or promised to help the person be successful. When a conversation about poor performance is intense or emotional, department chairs may be tempted to soft pedal the written summary of the meeting. This is not helpful for several reasons. First, it denies the individual faculty member an accurate summary of the substance of the meeting. The more emotional an individual faculty member may be during a performance counseling session, the more important having an accurate summary of the issues and strategies discussed will be to successfully addressing concerns. Second, accurate summaries of performance counseling will be essential should the problem performance not be remedied and the concern escalates into a grievance or dismissal of the faculty member.

In writing with third-person clarity, department chairs want to make sure that the content of the documentation matches the content of the meeting in both the issues discussed and the weight given to each issue. For example, if 75% of the meeting was spent discussing specific student concerns about teaching, 75% of the letter should address this same issue. By including the specific recommendations suggested to enhance performance, department chairs document their efforts to help the individual faculty member succeed. By sharing the behavioral examples used to illustrate the problem performance, department chairs demonstrate their desire to help the higher be successful such that the chair's comments do not represent a personal attack on the individual faculty member.

Writing with third-person clarity need not be mean-spirited or confrontational. When department chairs fear that an individual faculty member may become upset or angry after reading a letter documenting performance counseling sessions, they are tempted to rely on mixed signals and between-us phrases. Mixed signals are statements that attempt to soften or mitigate the concern. In the situation of a faculty member who must address student concerns about unclear grading practices, the following would be an example of a mixed signal: "Many students believe you work hard at grading even though some find your grading practices to be unclear." A third person reading the statement could conclude that the person is making acceptable progress toward clarifying grading practices when this is not the case. Moreover, the faculty member could conclude that the current efforts are sufficient in addressing the student concern. Unless these are the reactions the department chair seeks, the mixed signal is not helpful. Similarly, between-us phrases do little to help address the performance concerns because they are used to keep the issue a private matter between the department chair and faculty member. The following is an example of a between-us phrase used by the department chair in documenting the unclear grading practice: "I am confident that you know precisely what to do to address the student concerns we discussed." Between-us phrases are not helpful to the individual faculty member who may not recall precisely what should be done to remedy a student concern, nor do they provide a third party with any helpful understanding of the performance concern or the recommended remedy for the performance concern.

Putting Theory into Practice

Although some reading this text may already employ all of these strategies, new insights for improving current practice can be discovered as the strategies are applied to a specific case. In Case 7.1, the director of a School of Music is pleased to have hired a seasoned professional from a nationally renowned conservatory into an untenured faculty position. Place yourself in the role of the director as you read.

Case 7.1: The Promising Hire

Dr. Harold Weiss, director of the School of Music at Southeast University, could not believe his good fortune. After a long and sometimes contentious search process, he managed to recruit Dr. Jonathan Albrecht to the voice department of the School of Music. Dr. Albrecht recently opted to retire early from a well-known music conservatory to relocate for personal reasons. Dr. Albrecht is an internationally renowned tenor whose professional stature far exceeds the credentials of faculty in Southeast's School of Music. Harold recognizes that Dr. Albrecht's interest in the position is because Southeast University is within commuting distance of where Dr. Albrecht wishes to live.

The School of Music

The School of Music is one of the largest academic units at Southeast University with some 30 full-time faculty members and a host of adjunct faculty. With a strong emphasis on music performance, the School of Music enjoys a very positive reputation at the university and in the region.

Students seeking admission to the School of Music must audition before faculty and, once admitted, must perform annual recitals that are open to the public. The faculty take great pride in admitting talented diamond-in-the-rough students who would not likely gain admission to a major conservatory and then helping them reach levels of achievement never thought possible. Graduates of the School of Music go on to wonderful careers in music performance and music education.

In addition, the School of Music faculty and students staff a rigorous concert schedule for the campus and the surrounding community. With rare exception, the concerts are free to the public and very well attended. The advancement office at Southeast University delights in using the music faculty and students at fundraising events, and music faculty perform regularly at all major campus events.

Harold is certain that Dr. Albrecht will be a big draw for the school's concert series. Several faculty members have already indicated an interest in being paired with Dr. Albrecht in concert, and Harold is looking forward to the coming academic year with a noted celebrity on the faculty.

Search Process

The search process was anything but smooth. A sizable contingency of the faculty believed strongly that Dr. Albrecht should not be offered the position. Their negative view surprised Harold Weiss. As the longtime director of the School of Music, Harold hired most of the faculty and knows that, by nature, they are very accepting individuals who are typically interested in hiring strong and capable faculty colleagues. Consequently, Harold was surprised when several faculty members voiced concerns about extending an offer to Dr. Albrecht when the faculty met to compare notes on the candidates interviewed.

It did not help that Dr. Albrecht missed some of the scheduled interview meetings. Because Dr. Albrecht was already living in the area, he commuted to the interview and Harold accommodated Dr. Albrecht's request that his interview schedule be compressed into one day. The daylong interview started with a 7:30 a.m. breakfast meeting with the search committee members. Following the breakfast meeting, Dr. Albrecht was scheduled to meet with several faculty representatives for a briefing on promotion and tenure policies before meeting with the provost at 11:00 a.m. Dr. Albrecht did not show up until the 11:00 a.m. meeting with the provost. Because Dr. Albrecht went directly to the provost office, he did so without the customary escort, thereby making introductions somewhat awkward and leaving the provost to doubt that the interview was well organized.

Later, Dr. Albrecht explained that, given the hour commute, the first two meetings were inconvenient and addressed issues that he already understood. Dr. Albrecht reminded Harold that he recently retired as a tenured full professor at a major conservatory. Harold took this opportunity to remind Dr. Albrecht of Southeast University's policy against hiring new faculty with tenure and was relieved when Dr. Albrecht appeared unconcerned about interviewing for an untenured position.

Those who voiced concerns about offering the position to Dr. Albrecht view the situation differently. They reason from this one experience that Dr. Albrecht will not be a collaborative colleague. They worry that his ego will upset the harmony that currently exists within the School of Music. Nonetheless, the faculty agree that Dr. Albrecht's credential would enhance the reputation of the School of Music. Sufficiently comfortable in their own accomplishments, the music faculty members are not in any way threatened by Dr. Albrecht's celebrity credential. After long and serious discussion, all of the faculty members were at least generally supportive of offering the position to him.

Harold noticed, however, that the enthusiasm expressed by some faculty members when he announced that Dr. Albrecht accepted the offer seemed disingenuous. Harold did not give their subdued reaction further thought. He knew these faculty members well enough to know they would be professional when meeting and working with Dr. Albrecht.

Let's Analyze the Case

Harold Weiss is relieved to have hired a strong seasoned professional in an untenured faculty position in vocal performance. Harold recognizes that Dr. Albrecht's behavior during the interview created ill will among some of the other faculty. The School of Music at Southeast University enjoys a collegial atmosphere among the faculty, so Harold is confident that things will work out once Dr. Albrecht joins the faculty despite the hiccup during the interview process. There is no mention in Case 7.1 of Harold doing anything to facilitate Dr. Albrecht's integration within the School of Music.

Harold used the search process to clarify that the Dr. Albrecht would not receive tenure when hired, but there is no indication that he used it to make specific performance expectations clear and to assess potential performance concerns. Nor is there any evidence that Harold used it to test Dr. Albrecht's receptivity to mentoring. When Dr. Albrecht requested that his interview be compressed into 1 day, Harold had an opportunity to point out the importance of interview and how a request to abbreviate the search process might be perceived by faculty. Although Case 7.1 does not explicitly mention that Harold failed to give this counsel to Dr. Albrecht, we can be certain that Dr. Albrecht pays little attention to how his actions might be perceived by his new faculty colleagues. In fact, there's little doubt that Dr. Albrecht is motivated by what is convenient for him. Dr. Albrecht's focus on his personal agenda increases the importance of testing his receptivity to mentoring and ongoing performance counseling because seasoned professionals who resist mentoring can quickly generate conflict with the academic department or school.

As the facts are presented in Case 7.1, Dr. Albrecht will begin work at Southeast University without a clear understanding of performance expectations. Further, director Weiss has no sense of whether Dr. Albrecht will be receptive to mentoring and ongoing performance counseling. In sum, there is no evidence in Case 7.1 that Harold Weiss has used the interview process strategically to assess Dr. Albrecht's learning curve for being successful in the untenured faculty position or Dr. Albrecht's receptivity to ongoing performance counseling.

It's Your Turn

Assume the position of director in this case scenario and think through what you would do to ensure a more successful start for Dr. Albrecht.

1. What, if anything, would you have done to use the search process more effectively? Would you have denied Dr. Albrecht's request to compress the interview schedule into 1 day? How would you have handled Dr. Albrecht's missing the first two interview sessions?

2. Would Dr. Albrecht's actions during the interview alter your interest in hiring him? Would the mixed faculty reaction to Dr. Albrecht alter your interest in hiring him? What, if anything, would you do post interview before extending an offer to Dr. Albrecht?

3. What, if anything, would you say to the faculty to improve their perception of Dr. Albrecht? Would you share Dr. Albrecht's reason for missing the first two meetings of the interview itinerary? Would you invite or ask any faculty member to assume a special role in helping Dr. Albrecht get acclimated to the School of Music? If so, what criteria would you use to select a peer mentor for Dr. Albrecht and what would you ask that person to do?

4. What, if anything, would you communicate to Dr. Albrecht prior to the start of school? Would you share with Dr. Albrecht, the faculty reaction to his missing the first two interview sessions? What

information would you share with Dr. Albrecht in advance of the start of the semester? Would you share with Dr. Albrecht the names of faculty colleagues who are willing to help him become acquainted with the School of Music and Southeast University?

Please Consider

Helping Dr. Albrecht get off to a good start within the School of Music will likely require the director to work both with Dr. Albrecht and the other faculty. It will help Dr. Albrecht to have a clear understanding of performance expectations, but his ultimate success in working with other faculty in the School of Music will depend on how he interacts with his new colleagues. Communication is the dynamic exchange between and among individuals. Dr. Albrecht's integration into the School of Music will be shaped by the communication he and the other faculty use in forging a new working relationship. The school director must work intentionally with both Dr. Albrecht and the other faculty to ensure that his acculturation is successful and these efforts can and should begin during the search process.

Let's Recap

Take a moment to review your plan for using the search process in a way that would help Dr. Albrecht get off to a good start in working with the other faculty. Does your plan for using the search process

- o Make performance expectations clear?
- o Allow you to assess potential performance concerns?
- o Test Dr. Albrecht's receptivity to mentoring?
- o Provide helpful mentoring to Dr. Albrecht and the other faculty?

Does your plan for working with Dr. Albrecht and the other faculty members facilitate the successful integration of this nontraditional hire into the School of Music? Have you helped to facilitate constructive communication between the new hire and the other faculty? If not, take a moment to determine what revisions you would make to your plan to aid the successful integration of the new nontraditional hire.

Putting Theory into Practice

Fast forward to the spring of Dr. Albrecht's second year in the School of Music at Southeast University. Harold Weiss has completed the required second annual performance review meeting with Dr. Albrecht, which he now must document. Put yourself in the director's position as you read Case 7.2.

Case 7.2: Second-Year Review

University policy requires the director of the School of Music to conduct a performance review with each untenured faculty member every spring. The review is to be culminated in a letter to the faculty member with a copy to the provost. Harold knows that the provost reads these letters with great care. On occasion, the provost has worked with individual school directors and department chairs to terminate untenured faculty members before they come up for tenure review. Believing things will work out, Harold opted to gloss over the concerns he discussed with Dr. Albrecht during his first-year review in the letter to avoid prejudicing the provost against him.

Now in Year 2, Harold finds himself with a more serious challenge. The concerns discussed with Dr. Albrecht during his first-year review remain. Moreover, Dr. Albrecht quickly dismisses any mention of these concerns. Harold cannot determine why Dr. Albrecht, who is always cordial when discussing such matters, does not understand that the concerns are serious and warrant immediate remedy if he wishes to earn tenure at Southeast University.

Harold has three concerns. First, university policy requires that all untenured faculty members solicit peer reviews and collect student ratings on their teaching effectiveness. To date, Dr. Albrecht has not collected any peer reviews or student ratings on his teaching. He is quick to point out that because his credentials are superior to those of his peers, it would be pointless to ask them to review his teaching. He also believes that the best proof of his teaching effectiveness is the work done by his students and finds survey instruments a complete waste of student and instructor time. Second, Dr. Albrecht routinely declines opportunities to engage in service to the school and university. Dr. Albrecht, for example, contends that it would be an inappropriate use of his time and talent to spend a Saturday helping to staff the School of Music display when the university hosts a recruitment fair on the campus. Third, tension has replaced harmony in the voice department since Dr. Albrecht's arrival. It seems that Dr. Albrecht believes his credentials and experience license him to have the final word on most department matters. The other faculty perceive Dr. Albrecht to be questioning their intelligence and the voice department chair's authority. Harold believes that this interpersonal conflict will work itself out in time, but is concerned that Dr. Albrecht is not the least bit worried about how his actions are alienating his colleagues.

Harold spent considerable time preparing for the second-year review meeting with Dr. Albrecht. Harold values having Dr. Albrecht's credential on the faculty, and realizes that Dr. Albrecht will not earn tenure if these concerns are not addressed. Now in Year 2, Harold senses a greater need to document the concerns since Dr. Albrecht seems unable or unwilling to hear and respond to them. At the same time, he does not wish to alienate Dr. Albrecht by writing a performance review letter that he might find offensive or insulting.

The Letter

After much anguish, Harold drafts the following letter to Dr. Albrecht with a copy to the provost.

Memo to: Dr. Jonathan Albrecht
From: Harold Weiss, Director
School of Music
Subject: Second-year performance review

With this letter, I wish to summarize the conversation that you and I had last week. We met to conduct your second-year performance review and materials forwarded by you in advance of the meeting served as the basis for our discussion.

We began by discussing your performance in the area of teaching. I explained that the university policy requires all untenured faculty members to solicit peer reviews and student ratings of their teaching. It concerns me that you are not soliciting peer reviews or collecting student ratings of your teaching. I must impress on you the importance of doing these things beginning immediately with the current semester.

As expected, your work in the area of scholarship and creative activity is superb. You sustain an ambitious performance schedule and many of your colleagues enjoy performing with you. Moreover, your professional network enables us to interest well known artists in accepting invitations to conduct master classes and perform at Southeast University.

We discussed your current service contribution to the School of Music and the university. To date, you have not been engaged in service to the university and have invested very little in service to the School of Music. I understand that you spend time reaching out to professional colleagues to entice them to conduct master classes and perform on our campus. However, the department secretary handles all of the related correspondence and arranges travel such that your task is limited to the phone conversation during which you extend the invitation. This work by itself is not sufficient to satisfy the performance expectation for service at the university.

Because collegiality can be a factor in tenure decisions at Southeast University, it is only fair that I share with you my concern for the growing tension among the faculty in the voice department. There now exists significant tension in a department that had been harmonious. You agree that the tension exists and attribute it to territorialism around courses. In particular, you believe you are squeezed out of teaching some courses in which you possess strong expertise. I shared with you that others comment on your practice of challenging voice department decisions that do not support your thinking about what should be done. They perceive you as acting as though your credential entitles you to have the final say on all voice department matters. I hope having this information will enable you to work with your colleagues in a way that demonstrates your respect of their professional credentials and perspectives.

Permit me to say again how very pleased I am that you accepted our offer for an untenured faculty position at Southeast University. Your talent and professional stature contribute much to the School of Music and the university. Please don't hesitate to talk with me if I can be helpful to you in meeting the performance expectations for tenure. It is my fervent hope that you will be successful in securing tenure at Southeast University.

Let's Analyze the Case

It's clear that Dr. Albrecht is not very receptive to mentoring. Through 2 years, Dr. Albrecht has been unresponsive to his director's efforts to discuss performance concerns that are serious and warrant remedy. Harold Weiss cannot determine why Dr. Albrecht seems intent to ignoring his counsel. Although Dr. Albrecht remains cordial, his behavior has introduced tension within a voice department that was previously collegial.

Harold Weiss is in a difficult position. He values the credential and expertise that Dr. Albrecht brings to the School of Music. At the same time, Dr. Albrecht's presence in the School of Music has produced tension among an otherwise collegial faculty. Further, unless Harold is able to get Dr. Albrecht to remedy some serious performance concerns, it is unlikely that Dr. Albrecht will be successful in earning tenure at Southeast University. When Dr. Albrecht fails to grasp the seriousness of the performance concerns in the second annual performance review meeting, Harold feels a greater sense of urgency to document the concerns in writing. Harold hopes to craft a performance review letter that will get Dr. Albrecht's attention without igniting defensiveness and possibly alienating him. Moreover, failure to signal the provost by documenting the performance concerns in writing could damage Harold's leadership credibility with the provost when Dr. Albrecht submits a tenure application that does not include the minimally required documentation on teaching effectiveness.

Review the second-year letter that Harold wrote. Although he mentions his three performance concerns, he stops short of stating explicitly what the performance expectation is with regard to teaching and service. For example, Harold writes that Dr. Albrecht has invested very little in service to the School of Music. Harold then briefly describes some service done by Dr. Albrecht and adds that this is not sufficient to satisfy the performance expectation for service at the university. Harold, however, fails to describe precisely what activities would enable Dr. Albrecht to satisfy performance expectations in the area of service. There is no mention of what service activities Harold believes Dr. Albrecht could and should perform that would satisfy the school's performance expectation for faculty service. A good performance review letter documents performance concerns in relation to established performance expectations. In doing so, the performance review letter serves as a guide for the faculty member on how to be successful while making clear that the director (or department chair) is providing appropriate counsel.

As written, the letter does not document Harold's efforts to mentor Dr. Albrecht. For example, Harold writes of his concern that Dr. Albrecht is not soliciting peer reviews or collecting student ratings of his teaching and stresses the importance of doing these things beginning immediately. Without some specific mention of previous conversations regarding this issue, a third-person reading the letter might conclude that Harold failed to advise Dr. Albrecht of the policy requirement for peer reviews and student ratings before Dr. Albrecht's second-year review. A good performance review letter not only will document performance concerns but also will detail efforts to assist the individual faculty member in meeting performance expectations. A good performance review letter will also document the specific suggestions made and support provided were promised to help the individual faculty member achieve the needed remedy.

In documenting the tension that exists in the voice department, Harold is careful to document both Dr. Albrecht's assessment and the perception held by other faculty. The inclusion of some specific behavioral examples would help to illustrate the practice being used by Dr. Albrecht that is contributing to the tension. Without the inclusion of behavioral examples to illustrate the performance concern, a third party reading the letter could conclude that the tension is the result of an interpersonal conflict rather than any inappropriate behavior on the part of Dr. Albrecht. Further, the inclusion of specific behavioral examples can help the individual faculty member understand better what actions are creating undesirable responses in others.

The final paragraph is likely to mislead or confuse anyone who reads the letter. By ending on a positive note, a reader is likely to conclude that Harold believes the performance concerns are minor and that, overall, Dr. Albrecht is making acceptable progress toward the eventual tenure review.

It's Your Turn

Spend some time editing the performance review letter presented in Case 7.2. When done, ask someone who has not read the case to read your edited letter and describe the personnel issue. If your invited third person draws the conclusion you would want them to draw, then you have drafted an effective letter. However, if your invited person describes a scenario that is different from what you would want, review your letter again, and determine how it might be revised to achieve third-person clarity.

Please Consider

There is a tendency to soften language in print especially following a very direct meeting about performance concerns. We are often moved to soften the language in the follow-up letter documenting a bumpy performance review meeting to avoid the sense that we may be pouring salt in an open wound. This is not a sound practice. Instead, the letter documenting performance review meetings should mirror the meeting both in terms of the issues discussed and the percent of time spent discussing each issue. If Harold spent 60% of the performance review meeting talking about the tension within the voice department, then 60% of the letter documenting the performance session should be on the issue of tension within the voice department. Similarly, if Harold suggested three ways in which Dr. Albrecht could meet the performance expectation for service during the meeting, those three avenues should be recounted in the letter. A good performance review letter is written with third-person clarity such that a person not in the meeting can obtain an accurate understanding of the issues discusses and the suggestions made during the performance counseling session.

Putting Theory into Practice

Fast forward to Dr. Albrecht's fourth-year performance review. Harold Weiss continues to struggle in helping Dr. Albrecht understand the performance concerns that warrant immediate remedy. Put yourself in the director's position as you read Case 7.3.

Case 7.3: Fourth-Year Review

Harold Weiss sits solemnly in his office as he contemplates how to draft a letter summarizing his fourth-year performance review meeting with Dr. Albrecht. It seems that performance review meetings with Dr. Albrecht have been pointless: The same concerns persist despite Harold's efforts to offer constructive counsel.

Harold went into the meeting with a heavy heart realizing that his mentoring has not motivated Dr. Albrecht to comply with performance expectations for earning tenure at Southeast University. Dr. Albrecht continues to resist gathering peer reviews or student ratings to document his teaching effectiveness. His service contributions remain minimal and Dr. Albrecht refuses all advice for how he might improve his relationship with colleagues. In fact, Dr. Albrecht appears to view the existing tension with colleagues as predictable given his superior professional credential. Consequently, the voice department, which was once collegial and productive, is now dysfunctional. Almost daily, Harold finds himself listening to individual faculty members who lament difficulties in working with Dr. Albrecht.

Harold is out of ideas for how he might help Dr. Albrecht understand that he needs to become part of the solution. Although Dr. Albrecht remains cordial, he has steadfastly ignored all of Harold's mentoring through 4 years at the university. Harold believes it is now necessary to inform Dr. Albrecht that his performance is not sufficient to meet the standards for tenure. Doing so, however, left Harold feeling very unsettled about the fourth-year performance review meeting with Dr. Albrecht. Although Harold succeeded in capturing Dr. Albrecht's attention, he was dumbfounded to learn that Dr. Albrecht blames Harold for all existing problems.

According to Dr. Albrecht, Harold created the current tension when he failed to counsel other faculty regarding the expertise that Dr. Albrecht would bring to the School of Music. Dr. Albrecht reasons that if Harold Weiss were an effective director of the School of Music, he would be able to help the administration understand why it is a complete waste of time to ask colleagues and students to supply documentation on Dr. Albrecht's teaching effectiveness. Similarly, Dr. Albrecht believes that if Harold had counseled the other faculty on how much they could and need to learn from him, the voice department would be light years ahead of where it is, and there would be no animosity. Dr. Albrecht believes he has been exceedingly patient with an ineffective director who persists in wasting his valuable time with unimportant committee assignments.

The Letter

Realizing that he has no choice but to register the ways Dr. Albrecht is failing to meet performance expectations for tenure, Harold drafts the following letter to Dr. Albrecht with a copy to the provost.

Memo to: Dr. Jonathan Albrecht
From: Harold Weiss, Director
School of Music
Subject: Fourth-year performance review

The purpose for this letter is to summarize the discussion we had during your fourth-year review. In particular, we discussed your performance in relation to the standards established for tenure in the School of Music at Southeast University.

In discussing your teaching effectiveness, I referenced previous performance review letters in which I described the university expectation for all untenured faculty members to solicit peer views and student ratings of their teaching. Given that this has been a persistent theme in all of our conversations, I was surprised when I again found no peer reviews or student ratings of your teaching included with the materials you submitted for the annual performance review. I understand that you believe your long tenure of service at a major conservatory of music should be ample and sufficient evidence of your teaching effectiveness. However, you accepted an untenured position at Southeast University, and I am not at liberty to alter the university's criteria for tenure. As I explained, your application for tenure will be subjected to review at several levels, and all will expect to find documentation of your current teaching effectiveness in the form of peer reviews and student ratings.

Your work in the area of scholarship and creative activity remains exceptional. You have amassed a substantial number of laudatory reviews of your performances that amply document the quality of your contribution in this important area of faculty work. I am disappointed, however, that this past year you declined many opportunities to perform with colleagues in the School of Music.

There have been modest improvements in your work in the area of service to the School of Music in that you now serve on one standing committee each academic year. Still, this level of service falls well below the average service contribution made by your colleagues. On several occasions, we have discussed your need to improve how you work with colleagues. The way you interject your professional opinion gives the impression that you do not value your colleagues' professional expertise. In the past 4 years, a collegial voice department has become very contentious, and you appear to be indifferent to working to improve the situation.

Finally, I must comment on the increased tension between you and your colleagues in the voice department. Despite repeated conversations about how colleagues perceive and reaction to your practice of challenging all department decisions, you have made no discernable effort to use this information to work more effectively with them. I would agree with your belief that your experience and expertise enable you to contribute much to the voice department. However, your manner for imposing what should be done has created tension that undermines the department's collegiality and productivity.

I would do you a disservice if I permitted you to believe that you are currently making acceptable progress in meeting the established performance criteria for tenure at Southeast University. As you move into your fifth and final year before tenure review, I strongly encourage you to give this matter serious thought. I sincerely wish I could be more positive, but regrettably the situation and the materials you submitted for your fourth-year review do not permit me to be very optimistic.

Let's Analyze the Case

In Year 4, Harold documents more directly that Dr. Albrecht is not meeting the performance expectations for tenure at the university. The letter essentially serves Dr. Albrecht with notice that failure to remedy the performance issues will result in tenure denial. The letter also serves to notify the provost that Dr. Albrecht is not making acceptable progress toward tenure. Harold Weiss can be fairly certain that this letter will capture Dr. Albrecht's attention.

Harold describes the three performance concerns and references previous conversations to document that Dr. Albrecht has received ongoing performance counseling regarding these issues. The letter, however, does not document the suggestions made or support provided to Dr. Albrecht for remedying the situation. For example, were specific service assignments offered to Dr. Albrecht that would satisfy the performance expectation for service? If yes, what were they? Did Dr. Albrecht refuse to accept them? Again, documenting such details will go a long way in affirming that the director (or department chair) offered appropriate performance counseling. These details also help to illustrate the nature of the performance concern.

In the fourth-year review meeting, Dr. Albrecht revealed that he blames Harold for the tension in the voice department. According to Dr. Albrecht, had Harold appropriately mentored the other voice faculty on how they could benefit from Dr. Albrecht's experience and expertise, the department would be light years ahead of where it is, and there would be no tension. Similarly, Dr. Albrecht believes that Harold is an ineffective director because he has not explained to the administration why it would be a waste of everyone's time for Dr. Albrecht to collect peer reviews and student ratings of his teaching. None of this is summarized in the letter documenting the fourth-year performance review meeting. Given the circumstances, the director might reference Dr. Albrecht's views and his response to them.

Harold Weiss is surprised by Dr. Albrecht's accusation that the problem is his poor leadership. Had Harold sought to learn why Dr. Albrecht ignores his counseling, he might have uncovered Dr. Albrecht's faulty reasoning in time to address it. It is helpful to determine the reason for the problematic performance. It appears that Harold tried to persuade Dr. Albrecht to do X and Y behaviors without ever understanding the basis for Dr. Albrecht's resistance. If Harold understood that Dr. Albrecht believes he did not need to collect peer reviews or student ratings of his teaching, he would have known that he needs to do more than simply repeat what Dr. Albrecht should do. Ongoing performance counseling can be effective only when the person doing the counseling understands the basis for the problem performance. Knowing the motivation or reason for the problem performance is essential to framing discussions about the need for improvement in a way that will make sense to the individual faculty member.

It's Your Turn

1. Given the circumstances, has Harold Weiss drafted an effective letter documenting the fourth-year performance review meeting? If not, please delineate what is wrong with the letter.

2. Edit the letter to correct for the deficiencies you noted. Be specific in crafting language to accomplish your purpose.

3. As director, would you mention in a letter that Dr. Albrecht blames you for the tension in the voice department? If yes, how would you introduce and describe this issue? Would you rebuke Dr. Albrecht's assertion in the letter? If so, how?

Please Consider

It can be uncomfortable for department chairs or directors to share that they are having a difficult time mentoring a faculty member. The temptation is to work hard to remedy problem performance without revealing to others that a problem exists. However, sharing the situation with key individuals is essential to managing a difficult personality or problem performance. For example, Harold Weiss might share with the provost the difficulty he is having in persuading Dr. Albrecht to collect and use peer reviews and student ratings of his teaching as feedback to improve his teaching effectiveness. By sharing the challenge with the provost in advance of the tenure decision, Harold has an opportunity to share what he has done thus far to address the problem performance, brainstorm other approaches, and make the difficulty generally known to the provost. This strategy will accomplish much. First, it illustrates that the director is taking responsible action in mentoring the individual faculty member. Second, it can uncover some new measures that might be tried in addressing the problem performance. Third, making other key individuals generally aware of the problem performance will provide them with a context for understanding conflict that might grow out of the situation. For example, it would be helpful to Harold to have shared the situation with the provost should Dr. Albrecht complain about his director's ineffective leadership. Should the provost hear first from Dr. Albrecht about the difficulty, he will not have context for hearing and understanding Dr. Albrecht's complaint.

Let's Recap

A solution is only as effective as the assessment of the problem is accurate. In addressing performance concerns, take time to assess the individual's motivation for the problem performance. Determine, for example, whether the performance concerns are attributable to a lack of knowledge, a desire to renegotiate one's job responsibilities, or something else altogether. If problem performance is attributable to a lack of knowledge, the solution will reside in helping the individual acquire the needed information or skills to be successful. If the problem performance derives from the nontraditional hire's difficulty in transitioning to a new campus community, the solution will reside in helping that individual understand the key differences in policy and practice. In sum, the motivation or basis for the problem performance must be considered when addressing the situation.

Putting Theory into Practice

A few days after receiving the director's memo, Dr. Albrecht replies in writing addressing his memo directly to the provost with a copy to Harold Weiss. Dr. Albrecht's missive is presented in Case 7.4. Assumed the position of director as you read.

Case 7.4: Dr. Albrecht's Perspective

Dr. Albrecht's reply
Memo to: Provost
From: Dr. Jonathan Albrecht
Subject: Objections to the fourth-year performance review summary

I must object to the fourth-year review submitted by director Harold Weiss. Dr. Weiss would have others believe that my performance is substandard, when in fact it is his leadership that is woefully lacking.

When Dr. Weiss recruited me to the university, he told me that the School of Music needed my credential and expertise. I accepted an untenured position believing that I could be helpful to the School of Music and that the unique expertise I can provide would be appreciated by Dr. Weiss. Dr. Weiss, however, insists on treating me like some junior faculty member who lacks both credential and experience. He acts as though all of my previously acquired expertise and experience was lost the minute I began working at Southeast University.

I have been exceedingly patient believing that Dr. Weiss would eventually realize and correct his mistake. However, I will not remain silent while Dr. Weiss blames me for what is not working. I recognize that Dr. Weiss is not accustomed to working with internationally renowned professional musicians so permit me to delineate the leadership mistakes he is making. First, Dr. Weiss is not taking full advantage of my credential and professional experience. He makes no effort to help others understand what might be gained from my credential and experience and how I can be helpful to the voice department if others will listen to what I have to say. Consequently, whenever I share what I know in an effort to help my colleagues, I encounter resistance and sometimes hostility. I do not blame my colleagues for their ignorance because they are professionals who have never worked within a major conservatory or on the international stage. I blame Dr. Weiss for shirking his leadership responsibility.

Second, Dr. Weiss insists on taking my valuable time with unnecessary busywork. For more than a decade, I have been teaching master classes around the globe. Students and professionals pay a sizable sum to take a lesson from me. Still, Dr. Weiss would have me taking colleagues' time and students' time from class to gather peer reviews and student ratings of my teaching effectiveness, which would be a complete waste of time. Similarly, Dr. Weiss seems more concerned with assigning me to pointless committee work than finding appropriate uses for my time and expertise. For example, this year I meet weekly with the school's faculty committee on student retention. I know absolutely nothing about student retention so serving on this committee is a complete waste of my time. In more than 25 years of teaching, I have rarely lost a student from my studio and, in those few instances, the student needed to withdraw for personal reasons. Surely Dr. Weiss can find better ways for me to contribute to the School of Music.

At this point, I do not know what, if anything, can be done to remedy the situation. My primary purpose for responding to Dr. Weiss's memo is to set the record straight. Although I would agree with Dr. Weiss that the situation is regrettable, none of it is my fault.

Let's Analyze the Case

Dr. Albrecht's response transforms this situation for Harold Weiss from one in which he is attempting to counsel a new faculty member on how to meet performance expectations to one in which his leadership is called into question. Up until this moment, Harold viewed his responsibility as one of needing to mentor Dr. Albrecht. Now, Harold finds that he must also protect and possibly defend his leadership credibility.

Dr. Albrecht wrote a letter to the provost. It is doubtful that the provost would accept all that Dr. Albrecht asserts at face value, but his letter will likely raise some red flags. The provost's interpretation of the letter will be based on his assessment of the director's leadership skill and experience, his perception of Dr. Albrecht, and any background information the provost might have on the director's efforts to mentor Dr. Albrecht for successful tenure review. If, for example, the provost is enamored with Dr. Albrecht's stature in the field of vocal performance and has no information about the director's ongoing efforts to have Dr. Albrecht address performance concerns, he will react differently than if he is aware of the director's ongoing efforts to help Dr. Albrecht be successful at Southeast University.

The provost's assessment of the director and Dr. Albrecht is based on all previous interactions and information. Even if the provost had only the one meeting with Dr. Albrecht during the interview and no other information, the provost would still have a perception of Dr. Albrecht. Similarly, the provost's perception of the director's leadership is based on his previous experience with that director. Leadership credibility is not an objective skill set, but rather an attribute assigned by others. This is why it is possible to for some faculty to perceive a department chair being highly credible while other faculty members in the same department perceive that same department chair as lacking credibility.

Credibility is hugely important to effective leadership. The more credible a person is, the easier it will be for that individual to lead change, manage conflict, and secure support for his or her decisions and actions. A department chair influences his or her leadership credibility with every decision and action. Literally every action a department chair takes is an opportunity to either enhance or lower his or her leadership credibility with others. While it is often impossible to make decisions and take action that pleases everyone, it is possible to manage disappointments in a way that enhances one's credibility. For example, the director in the case scenario might have gone beyond trying to persuade Dr. Albrecht to collect peer reviews and student ratings of his teaching and addressed Dr. Albrecht's perspective. Had the director acknowledged that the policy was designed for a less experienced hire, he might have prevented Dr. Albrecht from concluding that he was be asked to start over as an inexperienced faculty hire. By acknowledging the problem from Dr. Albrecht's perspective and offering to help him know how to satisfy the necessary requirements, the director might have earned Dr. Albrecht's respect.

It's Your Turn

Put yourself in the role of the director and think how you would manage the escalating conflict with Dr. Albrecht.

1. Would you respond to Dr. Albrecht? If yes, would you respond in writing or in person? What would you say and what would be your ultimate purpose for responding directly to Dr. Albrecht?
2. What, if anything, would you say to the provost?

3. What actions would you take, if any, to protect your leadership credibility with the provost?

4. What actions would you take come, if any, to build your leadership credibility with Dr. Albrecht?

Please Consider

Please consider how different the management of Dr. Albrecht's response would be had the director kept the provost apprised of his ongoing efforts to help Dr. Albrecht understand and satisfy performance expectations. Keeping key individuals informed of personnel problems and potential conflict can go along way in allowing others to manage complaints that they might receive.

Department chairs can share personnel problems with their supervisors without evidencing ineffective leadership. For example, had the director in the case talked with his provost about his three performance concerns regarding Dr. Albrecht, the director would also have the opportunity to share what all he had tried in an effort to mentor Dr. Albrecht. In doing so, he would have been able to illustrate his leadership regarding this matter before the provost received Dr. Albrecht's complaint.

Hindsight Is 20/20

Department chairs or directors facing performance concerns like the ones described in case in this chapter may be tempted to just keep working at the issue without sharing the difficulty being experienced with others. By keeping key individuals apprised of challenges in mentoring problem performance, department chairs provide those individuals with context that will help inform how they perceive and react to complaints from the problem individual. Although it may seem counterintuitive to share problems in managing personnel issues, it can be the best way to protect and sometimes enhance one's leadership credibility.

Let's Recap

To be successful in mentoring a seasoned professional hired as an untenured assistant professor, department chairs must understand that the process requires all of the skill and care associated with mentoring a nontraditional hire. Whether the seasoned professional comes from industry or another institution of higher education, they typically possess substantial experience and expertise. While their professional credential is typically an asset to the department, it can also be the source of a blind spot for the new hire. Seasoned professional hires have a learning curve. Department chairs should use the search process to

○ Make expectations clear.
○ Assess potential performance concerns.
○ Test the prospective hire's receptivity to mentoring.
○ Mentor for a successful start in the position.

It will be easier to mentor a seasoned professional hire to success if these clarifications are established during the search process. However, should new seasoned professionals begin work without these clarifications, the new hire will be left to navigate and interpret a new work culture and performance responsibilities from their previous experience. Should their previous experience not be identical to the new work culture and responsibilities, there will likely develop performance concerns that may have been avoided had the performance expectations been clear from the beginning.

Department chairs should be proactive in facilitating the integration of the seasoned professional hire. The specific faculty development plan should address the new hire's learning needs, which can involve everything from mentoring about how to handle assigned work to introducing the new hire to others on the campus. Ideally, department chairs will want to help new seasoned professionals establish a network that supports their work at the institution.

Should performance concerns surface, it is important to spend time assessing the reason for the observed concerns. Knowing the basis for the problem performance can help shape the best approach for remedy. More importantly, knowing the motivation for the problem performance will help determine how best to approach the individual faculty member without igniting unnecessary defensiveness.

Illustrating performance concerns with specific behavioral examples instead of descriptive adjectives can be helpful for two reasons. First, it allows the individual faculty member to understand precisely what needs remedied. Second, it demonstrates the department chair's belief that the individual can make the requested remedy. When concerns are discussed using descriptive adjectives instead of behavioral examples, individuals whose performance is being reviewed are more likely to become defensive. When individuals become defensive, it is more difficult for them to hear and comprehend understand what is being asked of them.

Department chairs should document performance concerns with third person clarity. In doing so, they provide an aid to memory for the individual faculty member needing to improve performance. Department chairs also provide a descriptive account of their efforts to mentor the individual faculty member for success. Well written letters documenting performance concerns provide invaluable context should the performance concern escalate into a grievance or lawsuit. Finally, effective letters documenting performance concerns evidence the department chair's leadership skill and experience. By writing with third person clarity, department chairs can enable others who may be drawn into the situation to understand precisely what the performance concerns are and what the chair has done to mentor the individual faculty member to success.

8

MANAGING THE DISMISSAL OF A FIRST-YEAR TENURE TRACK FACULTY MEMBER

INSTITUTIONS EXPEND CONSIDERABLE human and fiscal resources in the search for a new faculty member. Funds are needed to advertise the position and bring the top candidates to campus for interview. When a position might be difficult to fill, there can be additional expense traveling department members to conferences to help recruit applicants. In addition, the department chair and faculty spend hours crafting a position announcement, managing paperwork related to the search, recruiting a strong applicant pool, pouring over resumes, calling references, developing interview schedules, interviewing candidates, and reaching consensus on the best possible hire. By the time an offer is extended and accepted, typically everyone in the department wants the new hire to succeed in meeting performance expectations. Nonetheless, there are times when it becomes painfully obvious that the person hired is not a good fit for the department.

The goal of this chapter is to help department chairs address the issues that may ultimately require terminating a first-year faculty member. A second goal is to illustrate the value of helping a new faculty hire acculturate into the department. Even when the department has been diligent is assessing the credential and fit of the new hire during the search process, it is possible for a new hire to quickly and inadvertently become at odds with the department. The search process typically helps the new hire know *what* work the department needs to do, but it seldom clarifies *how* work is done in the department. While the case scenario presented in this chapter focuses on managing an unsuccessful faculty member hired into a tenure track appointment, the leadership communication strategies presented can be used in managing an individual hired into a term faculty appointment or staff position when that person is not meeting performance expectations.

Defining the Task

The first year is a critical time for any faculty hire. The way in which a new faculty hire works with colleagues during the first year sets the tone for ongoing working relationships and provides the basis for how others perceive the new faculty member. While everyone in the department holds expectations for the new faculty hire's performance, they may not hold the same expectations. The expectations that individuals have for the new hire will vary in accordance with their direct involvement in the search process and their role and work within the department. For example, a faculty member serving on the search committee may understand that the new hire is not perfectly experienced in all of the responsibilities mentioned in the position announcement even though the new hire is appropriately assessed to be the best candidate. This knowledge will influence that search committee member's performance expectations for the new faculty hire. Similarly, a faculty member whose training may be similar to the new hire's credential will likely have performance expectations for the new faculty member that are different from those held by faculty colleagues who know little or nothing about the new hire's area of expertise.

The new hire brings expectations to the position that will guide how that individual interacts and works with others in the department. The new hire's expectations are shaped by the search process and perceptions that the new hire may hold about the institution, the department, and faculty work. For example, should the new hire perceive faculty work as involving a high degree of autonomy, the new hire will be less prone to collaborate with others. It may not mean that the new hire prefers to work alone, but merely that he or she perceives this is the way things are done. Similarly, if much of the search process conversation with the new faculty hire centered around the need for the department to become competitive in securing externally funded grants, the new faculty member will likely begin with the belief that working on grants is valued more than efforts in the classroom or time spent on service activities.

While there is a honeymoon period for most new hires and everyone generally wants and expects the new hire to be successful, the existence of varied expectations for how the new faculty hire will integrate within and contribute to the work of the department leave room for failure. The most rigorous search process cannot possibly tell a search committee and hiring officer everything about how the new hire will work out. The department chair needs to be ready to correct inaccurate perceptions and expectations held by the new faculty hire and other members of the department. As warranted, the department chair also needs to clarify both performance expectations and misperceptions about how members of the department work together. When such constructive intervention is ignored or is ineffective, the department chair needs to take action to register and remedy the situation even should it result in terminating a new hire at the close of the first year.

Relevant Leadership Communication Strategies

Department chairs cannot afford to ignore signs that the new faculty hire is not working out as anticipated. The following leadership communication strategies will aid department chairs in managing a new faculty hire that is not meeting performance expectations.

Build Consensus around a Shared Vision

Unless all members of the department share the same vision, there will be inevitable confusion and potential conflict for any new hire. When members of the department do not share a common vision, each operates from their own vision for the department. When this is the case, a new hire cannot be expected to discern the core department values and priorities that should drive individual and collective actions. Nor can the new faculty hire be expected to understand fully their anticipated contribution to the department vision. Trying to learn and contribute to a new culture that does not have a shared vision is like trying to find one's way in a foreign country without a map or signposts.

The process of building consensus around a shared vision is a time-consuming exercise with many tangible benefits. First, building consensus around a shared vision helps to keep all department members on the same page, which eliminates the conflict that can result when members of the department possess different and sometimes competing goals for the department. Second, the consensus-building process helps to make the shared vision more operational for all department members. Whereas a printed vision statement relies on readers to interpret its meaning for each decision and action, the consensus-building process helps to cultivate a common operational understanding of the vision for the department. Consequently, the consensus-building process enables all department members to help orient and work with the new faculty hire from a common understanding of the vision of the department. This frees the new faculty hire from needing to please many different colleagues who may hold different expectations for the new hire. Third, the consensus-building process helps individual department members commit to a shared vision. For a shared vision to be realized, all department members must own the vision and commit their actions toward realizing the shared vision. This cannot happen without some consensus-building process that permits individual members to weigh the relative merits of the ideas and actions being considered and influence the final vision embraced by the collective department.

CREATE A LEVEL OF SHARED UNDERSTANDING   In building consensus around a shared vision, department chairs need to help each individual faculty and staff member understand his or her role in realizing the shared department vision. Doing this will be helpful when conducting the search for a new faculty member because there will be greater clarity about what the new faculty member is expected to contribute to the vision for the department. This clarity will help in identifying the best applicant for the position. It will also help in orienting the new faculty member to the shared department vision and the new hire's anticipated contribution to that vision.

HELP THE NEW HIRE BECOME ACCLIMATED   With a shared vision in place, there will be greater consistency in the guidance that a new faculty hire receives from individual faculty colleagues about the vision for the department and the new hire's contribution to that vision. It will also guide when and how each faculty and staff member will work with the new faculty hire. The new hire can become more quickly acclimated to the department when everyone understands and shares a common vision for the department.

Should the department faculty and staff not possess a shared vision for the department, the department chair will need to help the new hire navigate the individual perceptions that exist about what the department values and the new hire's contribution to the department's future. This can be challenging because it places the department chair in a role of interpreting others' views for the new hire, and, unless managed very carefully, the chair can give the impression of passing judgment on others in the department. In general, it is more difficult for a new hire to become acclimated to the department when individuals hold different perspectives about where the department is going.

Discern and Correct Misguided Motives and Faulty Perceptions

When a new faculty hire pursues a personal agenda that is inconsistent with the shared vision for the department, it can lower morale and spawn destructive conflict. Faculty members typically have personal professional goals and objectives and, unless these individual goals are developed with full understanding of the shared vision, the goals will inevitably serve personal interests and not necessarily departmental or institutional purposes. It is possible to have a shared department vision and still need to manage personal agendas that are inconsistent with the shared vision. Presuming that the department has a shared vision that all faculty understand and support, it is imperative that the department chair orient the new hire to the shared vision for the department. Ideally, this work begins during the interview and is reinforced after the new faculty hire begins work.

Chairs can discern misguided motives by assessing whether the behavior supports or threatens the advancement of the shared vision and the department's ability to satisfy agreed on priorities. If the action threatens desired progress, it is likely motivated by a personal agenda that is inconsistent with the shared vision. Chairs can reinforce the shared vision by requiring the new hire to demonstrate that his or her actions support the accepted direction and priorities. Such discussion should provide an opportunity to make clear what actions would better serve the department's shared vision.

Establish and Sustain Practices and Processes That Support the Shared Vision and Department Culture

In addition to building consensus around a shared department vision, it is important to establish clarity for how members of the department will conduct business. It can be hugely helpful to establish a code of conduct for the department that facilities working through differences in achieving the shared vision. Something as simple as an understanding that every perspective will be heard and understood before a department vote is taken can set the tone for how business is conducted. The simple practice of ensuring everyone's right to express their views on an issue can help to reduce defensiveness and build trust. When faculty members trust the chair and one another, they are less defensive and the department culture is generally more constructive in that department chairs are able to more easily lead the faculty when managing challenges and change initiatives. However, if the department climate is characterized by distrust and defensiveness, department chairs will find it difficult to lead change or build consensus on how best to navigate the challenges facing the department.

The dynamic within the department will determine whether such a conduct code needs to be printed or can be an informally agreed upon way of working with one another. Whether printed or not, department chairs should establish and maintain practices and processes that support the shared vision and department culture by guiding how faculty and staff work with one another. The code needs to be department specific. For example, the personalities in one department will require the code be focused on how to air disagreements whereas the code in another department may need to focus on the expectation that everyone takes an interest and is part of the solution.

Whatever the practices and processes, department chairs must ensure that the rules are equitably applied to all department members. If, for example, the conduct code preserves the importance of hearing all perspectives, department chairs must make certain that the practice is uniformly applied. This does not mean that department chairs must permit a cantankerous faculty member to filibuster in order to prevent a final vote on an issue. On the contrary, department chairs have responsibility for conducting an efficient and constructive meeting. There is a dramatic difference between ensuring that everyone's perspective is heard and allowing some to derail a constructive conversation. However, department chairs will sacrifice leadership credibility if any in the department believe that their perspective has not been heard. Should faculty members perceive that the conduct code is not being equitably applied to all members of the department, they will feel less bound to follow the conduct code.

FRAME DIFFICULT DISCUSSIONS CAREFULLY   Framing the discussion of contentious issues is the key to managing Conversations about difficult issues. For example, department chairs can minimize the influence of personal perceptions by providing all parties with common data and other factual information. The issue of conflict should be framed in a way that transcends personal identities or vested interests. For example, rather than discussing the need to update a particular course that is always taught by the same faculty member, it is preferable to discuss the need to keep curriculum current and relevant for today's students. When dealing with contentious issues, department chairs must frame the issue of conflict in a professional way.

CLARIFY GUIDELINES FOR HOW TO WORK WITH OTHERS   Department chairs can help preserve a constructive department climate by clarifying expectations for how department members will work with each other.

For example, if a department chair prefers that faculty attempt to talk through individual differences before seeking the chair's intervention, the chair will need to clarify this expectation for how faculty will work with each other. Such guidelines need not be printed and distributed as a missive from the department chair. Instead, the department chair can reinforce the expectation that faculty will attempt to resolve individual differences before involving the chair in an informal way by asking if the effort was made every time an individual faculty member brings a concern about a colleague to the chair.

SHARE DECISION-MAKING CRITERIA   Seldom does a decision please everyone. By sharing the decision-making criteria, department chairs can reduce conflict that might result when department members are disappointed with a decision. If, for example, all faculty members understand that seniority will be used to assign office space in the department some new location, there will be less grumbling about the chair exercising favoritism in assigning office space. This does not mean all faculty members will like the outcome, but they will at least understand the basis for the negative decision and will be less likely to take the decision personally or view it as evidence that the chair does not value them or their work. By sharing decision-making criteria, department chairs make the outcome predictable. When an outcome is consistent with expectations, the potential for outrage and indignation is dramatically decreased. When department chairs avoid creating unnecessary conflict or ill will, they help to keep the department climate constructive.

Consider Both the Immediate and Long-Range Ramifications

It is important to consider both immediate and long-range contexts when helping a new faculty hire acclimate into the department. It can take some time for a new hire to acclimate to the department, and the entire process requires chair leadership and guidance. Department chairs must continuously assess the effectiveness of ongoing efforts to help a new faculty hire acclimate into the department and revise the approach as warranted. For example, if the department chair becomes doubtful that the new hire will be successful, there is tremendous advantage to going the extra mile to afford the new faculty hire every possible support because having done so will remove the possibility that the new hire's failure to succeed is attributable to a lack of support from the department or the department chair's ineffective leadership.

INFORM OTHER KEY INDIVIDUALS OF ONGOING ISSUES It can be difficult to communicate with others that a new hire is not meeting performance expectations. Department chairs may worry that doing so will bias others against the new hire, give the impression that the department did not conduct a credible search, or cause others to think poorly of the chair's leadership. Nevertheless, it is important to keep key individuals informed of such ongoing issues, and this can be done in a way that enhances chair credibility. For example, telling the dean that, despite frequent conversations, the new hire seems intent on making substantive changes in the courses he or she is teaching without first securing appropriate approval forewarns the dean of the issue and apprises the dean of the chair's efforts to remedy the issue should students complain to the dean.

INVOLVE OTHERS IN SEEKING REMEDY Too often, the more difficult a personnel issue is to manage, the more guarded department chairs are in sharing the problem with others. Doing so can feel like admitting failure. If, however, the department chair also details what all has been tried to remedy the situation, then sharing the personnel issue can actually enhance department chair credibility. Moreover, in reviewing all efforts to date to remedy the problem, it is possible that the person learning of the personnel issue will be able to suggest new strategies that might be effective. Should the personnel issue persist after trying the strategies suggested by others, those alerted to the personnel problem will be more likely to agree with the department chair's conclusion that the best remedy is dismissal of the new hire. However, a recommendation to dismiss a new faculty hire will seem rash unless key individuals possess an accurate understanding of the performance problem and the efforts made to support the new faculty hire's success and address the problematic performance issue.

DOCUMENT EFFORTS TO ADDRESS PERFORMANCE ISSUES Even when the department chair believes the performance issue being addressed will not result in dismissal, there is an advantage to documenting the problem performance, the remedies suggested, and the support provided to help the new faculty hire make the requested remedy. Such documentation need not sound mean or be threatening. The documentation should record specific behaviors that are an issue and the specific suggestions made for remedy. If the documentation describes behaviors and avoids labels and adjectives that might be offensive to the individual, the documentation will serve as an aid to memory in attempting to make remedy. It can be difficult for a new faculty hire to hear all the advice being given and having a written summary of the issues to be address and the suggestions for realizing success can helpful. The documentation also helps to communicate that the problem performance is serious and warns remedy.

Putting Theory into Practice

Now that these strategies are fresh in your mind, let's apply them to a specific situation. In Case 8.1, the department of communications studies has successfully hired a new faculty member on a tenure track appointment. Place yourself in the role of the department chair as you read.

Case 8.1: The New Faculty Hire

The decision to hire Dr. Natasha Singh on a tenure track appointment was unanimous. Dr. Singh came highly recommended by faculty colleagues at her previous institution where she successfully earned tenure and promotion to associate professor before leaving to follow her husband, who accepted a position in the private sector near Midland University.

Dr. Singh exhibited a lot of energy throughout the interview. As part of the process, she taught a class. The students were on the edge of their seats throughout the class, and faculty colleagues observing the class were impressed with the way Dr. Singh commanded student attention. She proved to be a quick study with names and called on individual students in a manner that had all students fully engaged in the class discussion. The department faculty members were impressed with Dr. Singh's enthusiasm for teaching. Because she had worked in the film industry before her previous faculty appointment she would bring both teaching and professional experience to the program. Dr. Singh had done her homework before the interview and was able to suggest specific changes that would enhance the courses she would teach.

The Department

The Department of Communication Studies has 13 full-time faculty and roughly 25 part-time faculty who staff majors in communication studies, organizational communication, public relations, and mass communication. The public relations and mass communication programs boast large enrollments and enjoy a favorable status on campus. The administration relies on the tuition revenue generated by these academic programs and often showcases these programs to illustrate how students enrolled at Midland University receive an education that prepares them for success in the real world.

Midland University is located in a suburban community about 20 minutes from a major metropolitan area, and students majoring in public relations or mass communication have ample opportunity for a range of nearby internships in industry. The part-time faculty members teaching in these programs are practicing professionals from industry, who enjoy helping students network with professionals and find employment in the industry.

The Position

Dr. Singh was pleased to be offered a tenure track appointment at the rank of associate professor. As the trailing spouse, she was elated to find work doing what she loves. Although she would have preferred to be granted tenure at the time of hire, Dr. Singh was confident in her ability to earn tenure at her new institution. She was heartened because it is clear that the Department of Communication Studies at Midland University needs her. In particular, she recognizes that the curriculum needs a complete overhaul if the department is to prepare students for employment in mass communications and public relations. Dr. Singh is confident that she knows precisely what is needed to enhance the quality and reputation of the public relations and mass communication programs at Midland University.

Fall Semester

Dr. Singh approached the fall semester with the same energy, drive, and enthusiasm that all observed during her interview. In addition to throwing herself into her teaching, she took initiative to add items to the agenda for department meetings and pushed for the addition of special meetings to discuss matters she labeled as urgent and essential. In particular, Dr. Singh is motivated to revise the curriculum for the public relations and mass communication programs.

Dr. Singh's faculty colleagues are not opposed to discussing the possible need for curriculum revision, but they do not understand her sense of urgency. The faculty routinely tweak individual courses and program requirements, and her insistence that the need to overhaul the curriculum is imperative makes her new colleagues defensive. Longtime department chair Kathleen McWilliams began hearing faculty members make disparaging comments about Dr. Singh's arrogance and disrespect for others in the department. It is becoming clear to Kathleen that there is a growing resentment toward her.

As department chair, Kathleen embraces innovative thinking and appreciates Dr. Singh's enthusiasm for making the public relations and mass communication programs stronger. Still, she can understand how Dr. Singh's relentless enthusiasm for fixing all that Dr. Singh believes is outdated or ineffective is offensive to the other faculty. Moreover, when other faculty attempt to posit a different view, Dr. Singh kindly explains that the matter is something she knows because, unlike them, she clocked time in the industry. Only a few months earlier during the interview, the other faculty professed that Dr. Singh's professional experience in industry would be an asset. Now that Dr. Singh is delivering on their expectation, Kathleen observes an undeniable tension growing between Dr. Singh and the other faculty.

Department Chair's Intervention

Kathleen is confident that Dr. Singh means well, and she knows the other faculty members to be reasoned professionals who always want what is best for students. Although Kathleen is certain the difference can be worked out in time, she decides to talk to Dr. Singh.

Let's Analyze the Case

In a matter of a few months, department chair Kathleen McWilliams observes a marked shift in faculty reaction to the new faculty hire, Dr. Singh. Faculty enthusiasm for the expertise and experience that Dr. Singh brings is being replaced with feelings of resentment. Put off by Dr. Singh's posture and approach, faculty colleagues now perceive Dr. Singh as arrogant and pushy in demanding substantive curriculum revision. Some perceive Dr. Singh's efforts to overhaul the curriculum as an unwarranted attack on the professional expertise of other faculty in the department. The department chair does not view the change in attitude toward Dr. Singh as a serious matter because the chair perceives the faculty to be reasoned professionals who will, in time, appreciate Dr. Singh's innovative thinking and enthusiasm for improving program quality. It is not until the end of Case 8.1 that the department chair decides to talk with Dr. Singh.

There is no indication that the department chair is working to build consensus around a shared vision for curriculum revision, which allows individual faculty members to hold different perceptions about what curriculum revisions should be made. The interview, however, left Dr. Singh with the impression that the entire department needs and welcomes her professional expertise. Dr. Singh throws herself into the task of revising the curriculum believing she is doing precisely what she was hired to do and that time is of the essence. Perhaps because the department chair appreciates Dr. Singh's innovative thinking, the chair does not intervene to correct Dr. Singh's faulty perception. Nor does the department chair proactively mentor Dr. Singh on how to proceed in working with her new colleagues to revise to the curriculum. Without knowledge of existing procedures for proposing curriculum revisions and coaching on how best to work with the other faculty, Dr. Singh quickly alienates the very colleagues she aspires to help.

It's Your Turn

Assume the position of department chair in this case scenario and think through what your response would be to the following questions:

1. How long would you observe the escalating tension before taking action? In doing so, would you talk with Dr. Singh, with the other faculty, or both? What would you say? Would you, for example, ask the other faculty to be more patient? Would you ask Dr. Singh to demonstrate more respect for her colleagues and the existing curriculum?

2. In talking with Dr. Singh, would you share how her behavior is being perceived? Would you attempt to discern the basis for Dr. Singh's sense of urgency in seeking curriculum revision? If so, how would you do this?

3. Assume you conclude that Dr. Singh's quest for curriculum revision has merit. How would you go about helping the other faculty to objectively consider Dr. Singh's suggested revisions? How might you use department meetings to discuss important issues while improving the interpersonal relationship between Dr. Singh and her faculty colleagues?

4. Develop a plan of action for restoring a professional relationship between Dr. Singh and the other faculty and for engaging the full department in considering Dr. Singh's suggested curricular revisions.

Please Consider

The department chair has at least two significant issues to address. First and perhaps foremost, the chair needs to arrest the growing tension between Dr. Singh and her colleagues. For this to happen, Dr. Singh needs to recognize how her behavior is being perceived. The longer the tension is allowed to continue, the more difficult it will be for others to give Dr. Singh the benefit of the doubt or acknowledge her efforts to constructively alter her behavior. Similarly, the longer Dr. Singh experiences resistance from her colleagues, the more difficult it will be for her to perceive them as capable to contribute to a curriculum revision. This process will require the department chair to discern Dr. Singh's motives and perceptions. It is possible that she does not realize her enthusiasm for change is building resentment among her colleagues. It is also possible that Dr. Singh believes that she must rescue the department curriculum because this is what she was hired to do. It is also possible that Dr. Singh has written off her colleagues as being out of date or inexperienced. Because the department chair's management of this situation would be different in each of these instances, it is imperative that the chair discerns Dr. Singh's motives and perceptions.

The second issue that the department chair needs to address is the review of the curriculum. During the interview, faculty members were unanimous in believing that Dr. Singh could bring expertise that would be helpful to the public relations and mass communication programs. Dr. Singh still possesses the experience and expertise that all believe is helpful, but her approach has distracted them from hearing her suggestions. The department chair must distinguish escalating interpersonal conflict from the task of reviewing the curriculum. If the chair fails to do this, the department will not benefit from the expertise and experience that Dr. Singh can bring to the department. Despite the escalating interpersonal conflict, the department chair needs to build some consensus around the value of reviewing the curriculum and considering suggested revisions to the public relations and mass communication programs.

Let's Recap

Take a moment to consider the plan of action you developed to restore the professional relationship between Dr. Singh and the other faculty and to engage the full department in light of Dr. Singh's suggested curriculum revisions.

1. How would you sequence your action steps? For example, would you address all at a department meeting or would you first have conversation with specific individuals? If so, precisely what would you say to Dr. Singh and others?

2. How would you structure the department meeting called to launch a review of the curriculum? What, if any information would you share

in advance of the meeting? Would you use a committee or keep the entire department engaged in curriculum review? For example, is there any advantage to involving only those who teach in the public relations and mass communication programs? Would there be an advantage to involving the all department faculty? Would you expand the discussion to include adjunct faculty? Why or why not?

3. What processes would you put in place to ensure that work on the curriculum review remains professional and constructive? Would you put in place any guidelines for how faculty members are to work on this task? If so, what practices would you implement?

Putting Theory into Practice

Most likely, your plan would be to talk individually with Dr. Singh to discern her motives and determine if she is aware of the growing resentment toward her. It would be difficult to make such determinations during a department meeting, and the department chair will need Dr. Singh's cooperation in presenting her ideas differently in order to arrest the growing tension. Case 8.2 relates Kathleen's conversation with Dr. Singh. Read and decide whether the department chair manages this conversation as you would.

Case 8.2: Coaching the Determined

Dr. Singh exhibited her customary energy and good cheer when she entered Kathleen's office.

Dr. Singh: I got your email asking to chat. What's up?
Department chair: Nothing urgent. I just wanted to check in with you and see how your first semester is going. I know that this position and department are very different from the one you left.
Dr. Singh: That's an understatement, but I'm enjoying my new position very much. It is very gratifying to be in a department that so clearly needs my expertise and experience.
Department chair: Well, we were excited to hire you and value what you can bring to the department.
Dr. Singh: Thanks. I'm working very hard to be helpful to my colleagues and the department.
Department chair: I sense that. How do you believe you are doing?
Dr. Singh: Fine. My classes are going well even though it can be challenging to raise the bar on student work. It seems that Midland

University students are accustomed to getting deadline extensions on all assignments and unlimited extra credit opportunities to improve their grades. I don't believe in either. I believe in treating students as they will be treated in the real world. It's never too soon for students to begin thinking of themselves as professionals. I insist they function as professionals in my classes.

Department chair: That's a noble goal. However, your expectations may surprise some of our students.

Dr. Singh: No kidding, but I have confidence that they will appreciate my approach more after graduation when they find they are prepared to secure and retain work in the industry.

Department chair: Are the students pushing back?

Dr. Singh: Oh yes, they are quick to tell me how all the other faculty in the department grant deadline extensions and give unlimited opportunities for earning extra credit. It's okay because I know that you hired me to bring my professional experience from industry into the classroom.

Department chair: Yes, that was one of your many appealing attributes. Still, as the saying goes, "Rome wasn't built in a day!" No one expects you to initiate all the ideas you might have during your first year.

Dr. Singh: It's okay. I have a lot of energy, and I'm committed to putting our public relations and mass communication programs on the map.

Department chair: You know that these programs already enjoy a very high profile and positive reputation on this campus.

Dr. Singh: There's always room for improvement. And, in this instance, we will be better served by a high profile and positive reputation among the employers that hire our graduates. I recognize that the university appreciates our large enrollments, but our first obligation needs to be to preparing students for gainful employment.

Department chair: Well, I can't argue with that. Still, I would hope you would suggest changes in a way that is respectful of your faculty colleagues.

Dr. Singh: Absolutely, I look forward to working with them in tackling the challenges facing us.

Department chair: I would not want your colleagues to conclude that you have little regard for their professional perspective. While you may find our curriculum in need of some tweaking, I can assure you that the faculty have been faithful in making continuous improvements to both individual courses and the overall program.

Dr. Singh: Unfortunately, the curriculum needs more than some tweaking.

Department chair: Well, I am interested in hearing all that you propose. However, I worry that your enthusiasm for making so many changes so quickly could be perceived by your faculty colleagues as an indictment of their work to date.

Dr. Singh: Truth be told, my faculty colleagues have totally ignored the need to infuse professional experience throughout the public relations and mass communication programs. I don't think poorly of them because they lack the professional experience in the industry that would enable them to make these changes. Fortunately, I bring this missing piece to the department.

Let's Analyze the Case

The conversation provides some insight into Dr. Singh's motives. Dr. Singh believes she was hired to bring a particular expertise that none of the other faculty members possess. Consequently, it seems that Dr. Singh believes the task of revising the curriculum rests on her shoulders. Dr. Singh is so explicit about being the only faculty member to possess professional experience from industry, it is doubtful she is counting on her colleagues to contribute much to the revision of the curriculum. Furthermore, she perceives her faculty colleagues as not holding students to professional standards. Her comments suggest that she perceives herself as a one-woman crusader charged with implementing a current and viable curriculum and improving instructional quality by holding students to professional standards.

The department chair may want to talk frequently with Dr. Singh because it is virtually impossible to discern and remedy inappropriate motives and faulty perceptions in a single conversation. Even if she is the only faculty member with expertise from industry, it is inappropriate for her to perceive herself as solely responsible for revising the curriculum. The department chair needs to clarify the perception that Dr. Singh drew from the interview. In doing so, the department chair has the perfect opportunity to describe the procedures in place for proposing and considering revisions to the curriculum. The department chair must help Dr. Singh understand that she is not solely responsible for revising the curriculum and how she should proceed when making specific suggestions for department consideration. How easy or difficult this may be to accomplish will depend, in large part, on Dr. Singh's receptivity to coaching. Certainly, the clarity needed is not achieved in the conversation presented in Case 8.2.

If the department chair succeeds in helping Dr. Singh understand her role and how to go about suggesting revisions to the curriculum and Dr. Singh complies with established procedures, it will help to defuse the tension between her and her colleagues. It will not help, however, if she is pushy on other issues. Should Dr. Singh not be receptive to coaching from the department chair, the tension will likely escalate and it is possible that the new faculty hire will prove to be a difficult faculty member for the chair to mentor and manage. In Case 8.2, there is no evidence that Dr. Singh recognizes that her behavior may be inappropriate and creating tension with her colleagues, and this conversation terminates before there is any reasonable expectation that the situation will improve.

It's Your Turn

Consider the conversation in Case 8.2 in answering the following questions:

1. Are there moments in the conversation that you would handle differently if you were the department chair talking with Dr. Singh? If so, edit the conversation using your words and consider how your handling of the conversation might alter Dr. Singh's response.

2. The conversation ends without resolve. How would you, as department chair, bring the meeting to closure? Would you make a specific request of Dr. Singh, and, if so, what would you request of her? Would you set a time to continue to conversation? Would you reference more directly the growing tension and resentment from other faculty toward Dr. Singh? If so, how would you craft the message? Try to anticipate Dr. Singh's reaction to your words and how you would manage her reaction.

Please Consider

Until Dr. Singh understands that her behavior influences how others perceive and respond to her, it is difficult to predict what she will say or do. Dr. Singh's reaction could range from being embarrassed to becoming angry and defensive. Regardless, Dr. Singh's reaction to learning the situation will speak volumes about whether she will be receptive to coaching and altering her behavior to fit better within the department culture.

The conflict will likely escalate should Dr. Singh, as the new faculty hire, decide that everyone else is wrong and ungrateful for her efforts to improve the public relations and mass communication programs.

In addressing this issue, the department chair is both trying to help orient a new faculty hire in order to reduce tension between she and the other faculty and affirm the new hire's receptivity to coaching and fit with the department culture. Hence, the department chair is simultaneously concerned with both the immediate situation and the long-range ramifications. Should the immediate situation prove challenging to remedy, then concern for the likely long-range ramifications will govern how the immediate situation is managed. For example, should Dr. Singh prove impossible to coach and unwilling to change her behavior, the department chair will need to reassess Dr. Singh's fit within the department culture. No matter how much care is taken during the search process, it is impossible during the span of an interview to learn all that we need to know to fully assess the new hire's compatibility and fit within the department culture. Certainly, other faculty members have some responsibility for adjusting to a new colleague, and they too may need some coaching on how to be successful. Still, a new hire, who refuses to understand the department culture and is not receptive to advice for how to work effectively with colleagues, will pose a challenge for the department chair.

Putting Theory into Practice

Fast forward to the end of Dr. Singh's first semester at Midland University. Department chair Kathleen McWilliams now faces the fact that all efforts to date have been ineffective in helping Dr. Singh acclimate to the department. Kathleen must address a litany of student concerns and faculty complaints about Dr. Singh's work. Put yourself in the department chair's position as you read Case 8.3.

Case 8.3: A Round Peg in a Square Hole?

Kathleen McWilliams continued to talk informally with Dr. Singh throughout the remainder of the fall semester. Through every conversation, Dr. Singh remains cheerful, upbeat, and enthusiastic about her quest to help the department by putting the public relations and mass communication programs on the map. Kathleen is dumbfounded by Dr. Singh's refusal to take seriously her advice that she move more slowly and tactfully in her quest to overhaul the curriculum. Either Dr. Singh does not perceive the increasing resentment toward her or she does not care, and Kathleen cannot discern which is the case. Every effort to counsel Dr. Singh is met with a themed response affirming Dr. Singh's conviction that she knows what is needed whereas her colleagues cannot possibly know how to go about overhauling the curriculum. Dr. Singh is quick to dismiss the grumbling because, as she explains to Kathleen, change is uncomfortable for most people. On more than one occasion, Kathleen felt lectured to by Dr. Singh on how grumbling is to be expected.

For Kathleen, the issue has evolved beyond trying to help Dr. Singh work more collaboratively with her faculty colleagues. Much of Kathleen's day is now spent talking with faculty and students who wish to register concerns about Dr. Singh. Kathleen dutifully discusses the registered complaints with Dr. Singh, who never seems surprised or concerned about the matter. The countless conversations that Kathleen has had with Dr. Singh about student and faculty concerns has had absolutely no influence on Dr. Singh's behavior. Dr. Singh remains upbeat and resilient in pursuing her plan to push for curriculum revision. Kathleen feels ineffective in mentoring Dr. Singh and, at the same time, finds it increasingly difficult to face faculty and students who expect their concerns to be addressed.

Student Concerns

An increasing number of students register complaints about Dr. Singh's teaching. Students complain that the courses she teaches do not match the course descriptions found in the university catalog. As one student put it, "Dr. Singh is teaching a course that I did not sign up to take." When Kathleen discusses this student complaint with Dr. Singh, she acknowledges the discrepancy adding that she has no choice but to change the course content to give the students what she knows they will need to obtain gainful employment in the field. Dr. Singh is not surprised to learn that students are upset but insists that they will be grateful to her later.

Students also complain that Dr. Singh is more focused on making the course challenging than on teaching. They describe her practice of reminding them that her courses will prepare them for the rigorous expectations that employers will place on them. The students, however, maintain that her assignments and grading criteria are not clear. While they know their work does not meet Dr. Singh's expectations, they have no idea what to do to improve their work. Dr. Singh's response to this student concern is to explain that students will not learn what they need to know if she spoon-feeds them. When Kathleen suggests that students need help learning to become independent critical thinkers, Dr. Singh quickly agrees and suggests that Kathleen persuade other faculty to raise the bar on instructional quality in their classes.

Faculty Concerns

Faculty colleagues complain that Dr. Singh makes disparaging remarks about them to students. She is credited with telling students that she is different from other faculty in the department because she expects more from them and she wants them to have successful careers. Faculty members serving on the department curriculum committee complain that Dr. Singh refuses to hear ideas that differ from her own. They report feeling bullied by her condescending attitude, which implies that her mission is to single-handedly rescue the public relations and mass communication programs from their ignorance about what students need to learn. The faculty are outraged that Dr. Singh is implementing changes in her own classes without first securing approval from the department curriculum committee. As one faculty member put it, "Students in Dr. Singh's classes are not getting the content we commit to deliver in the approved curriculum that is contained in the university catalog." Another faculty member observed, "Dr. Singh may be right that these courses need to be changed, but it is wrong of her to implement such changes without discussing the merits of her ideas with the rest of the department. She clearly perceives us as having nothing worthwhile to contribute to a discussion about curriculum revision."

Whenever Kathleen shares these concerns with Dr. Singh, she seems neither surprised nor bothered. Dr. Singh reminds Kathleen of the importance of overhauling the curriculum by infusing the industry perspective that only Dr. Singh can bring. More recently, Dr. Singh has diverted these conversations by peppering Kathleen with questions about how she is responding to faculty colleagues when they complain. In particular, Dr. Singh asks if Kathleen is doing all she might to solicit cooperation from the other faculty. This new dynamic leaves Kathleen wondering if Dr. Singh is able hear perspectives that differ from her own.

Department Chair's Concerns and Next Step

Kathleen McWilliams is exhausted. Listening to student and faculty complaints and talking with Dr. Singh about student and faculty concerns is consuming much of her time. Kathleen recognizes that her efforts to mentor Dr. Singh have not been effective, and she now doubts that there is anything she might do that would help Dr. Singh understand that her posture and approach are alienating students and faculty. Kathleen also recognizes that unless Dr. Singh changes her perspective and approach, the conflict in the department will continue to escalate and any positive contribution that Dr. Singh might make to the department will be sacrificed. The situation seems hopeless, and Kathleen is second-guessing the department's decision to hire Dr. Singh.

University policy allows for the termination of a faculty member hired on a tenure-track appointment during the first year, but Kathleen cannot recall a single instance when this was done at Midland University. She doesn't know how she would explain a recommendation to terminate Dr. Singh to the Dean when only six months ago, the department made an enthusiastic recommendation to hire Dr. Singh. In fact, Kathleen persuaded the Dean to offer Dr. Singh a higher starting salary in recognition of the special expertise she would bring to the department. Kathleen is also certain that Dr. Singh has no idea that her continuing employment might be in jeopardy. Dr. Singh is superbly skilled in finding fault with everyone except herself. If Dr. Singh's faculty colleagues are upset, it is because they find change uncomfortable. If students complain about Dr. Singh's classes, it is because they do not understand what they need to learn. If Kathleen thinks Dr. Singh should move more slowly in suggesting curriculum revisions, it is because Kathleen does not grasp the urgency of overhauling the curriculum. Consequently, Kathleen is certain that Dr. Singh would be shocked to receive notice of her termination.

Terminating Dr. Singh's appointment would certainly place Kathleen on the hot seat with Dr. Singh and perhaps the dean. Kathleen recognizes that, given budget constraints, there is a possibility that the department will be denied an opportunity to search for a new faculty member to replace Dr. Singh. At the same time, the prospect of retaining Dr. Singh seems unwise for the welfare of the department. The price for her professional experience in industry seems too costly for the department especially given that Kathleen has done everything she knows to do to help Dr. Singh comprehend and respond appropriately to student and faculty concerns. Kathleen needs to make a decision, and she does not have much time to do so. Spring semester begins next week, and university policy stipulates that first-year faculty members hired in tenure track appointments be served a notice of nonrenewal by February 15. Since the notice would need to come from the dean, the deadline seems very tight.

Let's Analyze the Case

Dr. Singh's first semester at Midland University has not gone as expected. A few months earlier, everyone looked forward to the industry experience that Dr. Singh would bring to the department. Now, the department chair spends time listening to student concerns and faculty complaints about Dr. Singh. Although personnel issues frequently consume much of the department chair's time, Kathleen McWilliams finds that she is spending more and more time without any sense that what she is doing is effective. Something has to change.

University policy contains a provision for terminating a first-year faculty member. Doing so, however, would not be easy, and it could cost the department a faculty position should the administration not approve a search to replace Dr. Singh. Still, the chair is out of ideas for how she might help Dr. Singh respond constructively to student concerns and faculty colleague perspectives. The department chair needs to make a decision very soon because the deadline for serving notice of nonrenewal to a first-year faculty member is mid-February.

In making this decision, the department chair needs to consider the immediate and long-range pros and cons of each alternative. It is also important for the department chair to contemplate how she would lead moving forward with each alternative. For example, the department chair needs to consider how she would enhance efforts to help Dr. Singh acclimate to the department should she remain at Midland University. Since the department chair believes she has done all she knows to do to help Dr. Singh, the next steps would likely involve others in coaching her. Similarly, the department chair needs to consider how she would explain a recommendation to dismiss Dr. Singh to the dean and what action might be taken to protect the faculty position against budget cuts should the dean accept the recommendation to terminate her employment at the university.

The decision is a difficult one because both alternatives hold the possibility of negative consequences for the department. The termination of Dr. Singh's appointment would likely be contentious and time consuming, and could cost the department a full-time faculty position. Retaining Dr. Singh will inevitably increase tension within the department unless there is some way to help Dr. Singh acclimate more effectively into the life and work of the department. Both alternatives threaten the department chair's leadership credibility. Should Dr. Singh's appointment be terminated and the faculty position lost, the department faculty could hold the chair accountable. Similarly, should Dr. Singh be retained and her behavior not change, the department faculty and students will likely hold the chair accountable for addressing the behaviors that create tension within the department. Consequently, the department chair is in a potentially lose-lose situation with this personnel issue in that either alternative carries great risk to the chair's leadership credibility and department welfare.

The department chair can lower the risks and help to ensure the best possible outcome by involving others in making the decision. Since one significant liability of the decision is the department's welfare, it makes sense to involve the department faculty. Tenured faculty typically have input on the performance reviews of untenured faculty members so it is logical that they be invited to help weigh the pros and cons of deciding whether or not to recommend that Dr. Singh's appointment be terminated at the close of her first year at Midland University. By delineating the pros and cons with the tenured faculty members, the department chair can share the risk of each alternative. Should the consensus be to recommend termination, the tenured faculty members will share the risk of losing a full-time faculty position should the department not be granted permission to replace Dr. Singh. Similarly, should the consensus be to retain Dr. Singh, the tenured faculty members will share responsibility for helping Dr. Singh succeed at Midland University.

The department chair need not share all of the details of her conversations with Dr. Singh. For example, it is sufficient to tell the tenured faculty that it will be more effective if the chair is not Dr. Singh's only mentor. The chair does not need to add that Dr. Singh believes the chair should do more to persuade the other faculty to embrace change and Dr. Singh's expertise. Nor does the chair need to share that Dr. Singh perceives the other faculty as being uninformed about what changes need to be made. In other words, the chair does not need to share information that would increase tension and detract from constructive measures that the department might employ to help Dr. Singh be successful.

It will be important to involve the tenured faculty in establishing processes to support the department's decision. For example, should the department decide to recommend termination, the tenured faculty can help generate the rationale that supports the recommendation. They can also help to generate the argument for requesting a search to replace Dr. Singh and devise a backup plan for staffing courses should permission to conduct a search be denied. Should the department decide to retain Dr. Singh, the tenured faculty can help generate procedures for helping Dr. Singh succeed. In particular, the tenured faculty can be involved in helping Dr. Singh learn what is taught in their classes and the logic for the existing curriculum. This might be done through some combination of peer mentoring, class visitation, structured curriculum committee meetings, and introduction to individuals on the campus who have high regard for the public relations and mass communication programs.

It's Your Turn

1. Assume the role of department chair and consider how you would work with the tenured faculty of the department to reach a decision regarding Dr. Singh's appointment. Would you talk with each individually or call a meeting of all tenured faculty? How would you frame the issue to be discussed? What information would you share to support the purpose for the meeting?

2. Would you, at any time during the meeting, tell the tenured faculty what you believe the department should do? If so, when would you share your perspective and why?

3. What, if any, rules would you establish for the meeting? For example, would you ask that the content of the meeting be kept confidential? Would you inform Dr. Singh that the tenured faculty would be meeting to discuss her performance to date in the department? If so, consider precisely what you would say and how you would field questions that Dr. Singh might have?

4. Would you invite Dr. Singh to present information regarding her performance to help inform the discussion? What, if any, direction would you offer for what information Dr. Singh might present for the tenured faculty review of her performance to date?

Please Consider

Since either alternative will likely capture Dr. Singh's attention, it could be helpful to inform her of the meeting. Faculty hired into tenure-track appointment should be aware that their performance will be reviewed and that tenured faculty will have input into that review. Having earned tenure at her previous institution, Dr. Singh should be familiar with process of peer review for untenured faculty. Informing Dr. Singh that the tenured faculty will meet in early January to review her performance provides an opportunity to remind Dr. Singh of the University policy that requires a midyear review in advance of a mid-February deadline for notice of termination.

The department chair might invite Dr. Singh to submit evidence of her effectiveness in meeting performance expectations in advance of the meeting. In fact, the request to submit documentation could be structured so as to reinforce the very issues that the chair discussed with Dr. Singh throughout the fall semester. For example, a memo advising Dr. Singh of the opportunity to submit evidence of her effectiveness might offer a list of the documentation the tenured faculty would find especially helpful for each area of faculty work. For teaching, the department chair might indicate, for example, that the tenured faculty would be especially pleased to review any evidence of Dr. Singh's effectiveness in teaching the course content described in the catalog description.

Putting Theory into Practice

In Case 8.4, we learn the outcome of the department's deliberation and the resulting drama. Put yourself in the chair's role as you read.

Case 8.4: Please Understand

Kathleen elected to call a meeting of all tenured faculty members to discuss the department's options for managing Dr. Singh's appointment. Kathleen briefed the faculty on her unsuccessful efforts to mentor Dr. Singh. After a lengthy and candid discussion of the pros and cons of both options, the faculty voted unanimously to terminate Dr. Singh's appointment. Kathleen is comfortable with decision especially knowing that everyone understands the potential risk of not receiving permission to replace Dr. Singh. As one faculty member stated, "Should we lose the position to budget cuts, we still would be better off than trying to work with someone who has such little regard for us."

Kathleen still needs to find the right words to communicate the department's recommendation to the Dean. Around Thanksgiving, Kathleen seized one informal opportunity to inform the Dean of the time needed to mentor Dr. Singh. Although no specifics were discussed, Kathleen hopes that this brief mention will serve as some context for the department's recommendation.

The Letter to the Dean

Memo to: Dean
From: Kathleen McWilliams, Chair
Subject: Recommendation to terminate Dr. Natasha Singh's appointment

The department recommends that Dr. Singh's appointment be terminated at the close of her first year. This recommendation carries the unanimous support of the tenured faculty members. Our decision was not made lightly and follows months of repeated efforts to help Dr. Singh be successful at the university.

On numerous occasions, Dr. Singh was informed of student and faculty concerns. Not once has she demonstrated an interest in understanding or addressing the concerns voiced by others. Students complain that Dr. Singh's classes do not match the catalog description of the course. My review of Dr. Singh's syllabus and assignments affirm this to be the case. Dr. Singh believes her action is justified because she believes the courses described in the catalog are outdated. Students also report that Dr. Singh prides herself in being a challenging instructor, but that she fails to equip students with the information they need to be successful. By altering the content of her courses, Dr. Singh is essentially teaching higher level courses for which there are no prerequisites. Consequently, it is not surprising to hear students say that they do not know how to meet the high standards established by Dr. Singh. Despite several conversations about the matter, Dr. Singh has not addressed the students' concerns.

The faculty take exception with Dr. Singh's belief that only she knows what students need to learn. Dr. Singh unilaterally implemented curricular changes that should have been subjected to review and approval by the department curriculum committee and, in some instances, the Faculty Senate. The department faculty members also find Dr. Singh's posture insulting and unprofessional. Faculty members find it impossible to discuss department matters with Dr. Singh, who operates from the perspective that her knowledge of the discipline is superior to that possessed by her faculty colleagues. In my conversations with Dr. Singh, she quickly dismisses views different from her own as being uninformed or motivated by another's discomfort with change. Again, despite several conversations about this matter, Dr. Singh remains unresponsive to her colleagues' concerns. I am attaching a sampling of memos sent to Dr. Singh following a few of my many conversations with her. These will demonstrate that Dr. Singh was given sufficient notice of these concerns and ample opportunity to address them.

This morning I met with Dr. Singh to advise her that the department is recommending termination of her appointment at Midland University. She expressed shock at the department's recommendation. Predictably, Dr. Singh lectured me on how much the department needs her expertise and how essential she is to the future of the public relations and mass communication programs. Unfortunately, Dr. Singh's professional experience can benefit the department only if she is able to work collaboratively with her faculty colleagues. Based on our collective and individual experience in trying to work with Dr. Singh thus far, we are unanimous in concluding that she is not prepared to be a constructive contributor to the department. We ask that you accept our recommendation and serve

Dr. Singh with official notice that her appointment at Midland University will terminate at the close of the current academic year.

Let's Analyze the Case

Kathleen McWilliams involves the tenured faculty in reaching a decision regarding Dr. Singh's appointment. This enables Kathleen to present the recommendation as the unanimous decision of the department. The memo to the dean spells out the department's reasons for recommending termination. In addition to providing a basis for the negative decision, any recommendation to terminate employment must demonstrate that the individual was appropriately notified of performance concerns and had sufficient opportunity to remedy them. Kathleen attaches a sampling of memos sent to Dr. Singh documenting conversations they had to discuss student and faculty concerns that warranted remedy. The memos document that Dr. Singh was appropriately informed of concerns and had sufficient opportunity to make remedy.

It is impossible to know that the chair presents a strong case without reading the memos sent to Dr. Singh. To adequately support the recommendation, the department chair's memos to Dr. Singh should reference specifically the student and faculty concerns discussed, clarify the relevant performance expectations, and recount suggestions or offers of support made by the department chair for helping Dr. Singh address the concerns. Done properly, memos written to document performance counseling sessions should serve as a factual account of what was discussed during the meeting while giving accurate weight to content of the meeting. For example, if 75% of the meeting was spent discussing student concerns, then 75% of the memo should summarize what was discussed about student concerns. This summary should include a factual, non-inflammatory statement of the concerns and all suggestions made for how to remedy the concerns. Finally, all should be presented with such clarity that a third party not in the meeting should be able to read the letter and understand both the concerns discussed and the suggested remedies. Consider the following two excerpts on teaching and discern which statement would provide stronger documentation had it been included in the department chair's memo to Dr. Singh.

Statement A: We spent considerable time discussing concerns that students brought about your teaching. I understand that you believe the students are grumbling because you expect more from them than your colleagues do. I'm not sure this is the case and would encourage you to give these student concerns serious thought.

Statement B: We met on October 15 to again discuss student concerns that you appear to be teaching a different course that the one they signed up to take. After reviewing your course syllabus, I would agree that you are not teaching the course that is described in the university catalog. We discussed at some length why faculty are obliged to teach each courses as it is described in the university catalog. I understand that you find the current catalog course descriptions to be in need of revision, and we discussed in detail the procedure for proposing curriculum revisions. Until a revised course description is approved and inserted in the university catalog, you must teach all courses in accordance with currently approved course descriptions. Since there are multiple sections of every course you are teaching this semester, I suggested that you talk with the faculty members who are teaching the other sections of these classes. I'm confident that your colleagues will be willing to share their course syllabi with you so you can quickly discover the content that is to be covered in each of your courses.

Statement A is not written with third-person clarity and leaves room for Dr. Singh to argue that she did not understand that the concerns were serious or that she needed to make changes in what she was teaching. To put this another way, with statement A, Dr. Singh could contend that she believes the department chair understood and accepted her explanation as sufficient response to the student concern. Statement B documents a more serious effort on the part of the department chair to help Dr. Singh understand the performance expectation and what remedy needs to take place. Indeed, the Dean would be hard-pressed to understand why Dr. Singh would persist in teaching course content that differs from what is in the University catalog after receiving a memo containing statement B on October 15.

It's Your Turn

1. Review the department chair's memo to the Dean recommending the termination of Dr. Singh's appointment. What, if anything, would you do to strengthen the letter? For example, would you quantify the number of times you discussed student and faculty concerns with Dr. Singh or the number of student concerns? Would you mention the specific suggestions made to Dr. Singh for addressing the concerns?

2. Put yourself in the role of the department chair and anticipate Dr. Singh's next move? Will she want to speak with you? Will she try to talk with the dean? Will she file a grievance? If you expect

Dr. Singh to argue the decision, how do you anticipate she will challenge the decision? Will she assert she was only doing what she was hired to do, deny understanding that the concerns were serious, claim to be a victim of discrimination, or what? What, if anything, might you do to manage Dr. Singh's challenge to the department's recommendation?

3. The department chair does not mention that she finds Dr. Singh unreceptive to mentoring, which makes it unlikely that giving Dr. Singh more time would help. Nor does the department chair describe how Dr. Singh's manner harms the department climate. Do you agree with this approach? With these omissions, is there a sufficient basis for dismissing Dr. Singh after her first year? How would you defend the recommendation should the Dean ask you to consider giving Dr. Singh a second year to demonstrate she can meet performance expectations?

Please Consider

In deciding how to present a recommendation to terminate an appointment and what documentation to include, it is helpful to consider the Dean's perspective. Generally, for a dean to support the termination of a faculty member after just one year there must be sufficient documentation that the faculty member received appropriate notice about existing concerns and had sufficient time and support to remedy them. For this reason, the department chair in this case scenario should consider the available documentation before recommending that a new faculty member's appointment be terminated. If the chair failed to document the conversations with the new faculty member, it would be better to postpone recommending termination of the new hire until such documentation is available. It is not prudent to move forward with a recommendation to terminate employment without sufficient evidence that the faculty member was afforded proper notice and time to make remedy because there is a good probability that the recommendation will be denied.

Consider the ramifications should the dean not support the department's recommendation to terminate Dr. Singh's employment. It will likely be difficult for the department chair to sustain a constructive rapport with Dr. Singh. Yet a trusting and constructive working relationship is essential for the chair to be able to coach Dr. Singh to improved performance. Furthermore, it will be more difficult for the chair to recommend termination at a later time unless the chair can document that a serious effort was made to help Dr. Singh succeed. The department chair can also lose credibility with the entire department should the department's recommendation to dismiss Dr. Singh not be supported by the dean. Consequently, the department chair needs to assess the relative merit of the supporting documentation before making a recommendation to terminate the new faculty member after 1 year.

Hindsight Is 20/20

Kathleen McWilliams recognizes that Dr. Singh will be shocked by the department's recommendation to terminate her appointment. This suggests that the department chair recognizes that Dr. Singh does not perceive the concerns to be serious. To put this another way, if Dr. Singh understood the concerns were serious, she would not be surprised by the department's negative recommendation had she failed to respond to the concerns. This observation reveals a need for the department chair to alter her approach such that Dr. Singh understands the serious nature of the complaints. For example, the department chair might remind Dr. Singh that the tenured faculty who believe Dr. Singh is making unilateral changes to the curriculum without department approval are the same colleagues who will have input on her performance review and eventually vote on her tenure application. Or, the department chair might state more clearly that it is a "serious" breach of policy to revise the curriculum without proper review and approval. Somehow, the department chair needed to sharpen her communication with Dr. Singh to leave no doubt that Dr. Singh understands that the student and faculty concerns are serious and warrant immediate response. Should Dr. Singh remain indifferent to the concerns, the department chair can then explain how her failure to respond to student and faculty concerns left the department no choice but to recommend the termination of her appointment.

Let's Recap

Any new hire will need help acclimating to the department culture. This task is easier if there exists consensus within the department around a shared vision. Department chairs cannot assume that conversations during the search process are sufficient for a new faculty hire to understand the shared vision and how the new faculty member is expected to contribute to that vision. Although the department chair need not assume sole responsibility for helping every new faculty member acclimate to the department, it is the chair's responsibility to orchestrate how new hires will become acclimated. Again, without consensus around a shared vision for the department, it will be difficult, if not impossible, to successfully acclimate the new faculty hire to a vision that is not held or valued by all other faculty members.

Search processes do a better job of instructing candidates on *what* they will be expected to do and than on *how* they will be expected to work within the department. And yet, information obtained during the search process is what the new faculty member uses to guide his work. The new faculty hire's perceptions about individuals, important objectives, relevant issues, and even existing disagreements derive from a series of short conversations that comprise the interview experience. Department chairs therefore should not be surprised if the new faculty hire exhibits a misguided motive or faulty perception about the department or individuals in the department. An effective orientation to life and work in the department is not a single program, but a sustained mentoring process that extends over time until the new faculty hire is successfully acclimated to the department.

Connecting the new faculty hire to processes that support the shared vision and culture of the department is important to helping a new hire be successful. Knowledge of the existing practices and processes help a new faculty member know how to proceed in doing his work. This reduces the risk that the new faculty hire will behave in ways that irritate or disrespect the roles and perspectives of others in the department.

Finally, should performance concerns develop, the department chair needs to address those concerns clearly and directly as soon as possible. Is important to remember that addressing concerns involves both explaining how the observed behaviors do not meet performance expectations and suggesting appropriate remedies. Documenting these efforts will provide both an aid to memory for the individual faculty member and a paper trail if one is needed.

9

MANAGING THE INAPPROPRIATE BEHAVIOR OF TENURED FACULTY MEMBERS

ONE OF THE MOST DIFFICULT personnel challenges is managing tenured faculty members who exercise inappropriate behaviors. When faculty members perceive tenure as license to do what they please, they can pose serious challenges for department chairs, and especially for department chairs who may be junior in professorial rank or untenured. Inappropriate behaviors can range from refusing to participate in department work to using inappropriate language or exercising inappropriate behavior when working with students and colleagues. Any behavior that is disrespectful, abusive, in violation of campus policy, or intended to undermine legitimate leadership authority is inappropriate. Certainly, tenured faculty members have a right to express their professional opinions and challenge the thinking of others including the department chair. Tenure, however, does not license faculty members to engage in the disrespectful or hostile treatment of others. Similarly, tenure does not license faculty members to ignore campus policy or exercise behaviors that are harmful to the welfare of the department and the institution.

The goal of this chapter is to help department chairs more effectively manage the myriad of possible inappropriate behaviors of tenured faculty members. A second goal of this chapter is to enable department chairs to contain the potentially destructive conflict associated with inappropriate faculty behavior. Although the scenarios presented in this chapter do not cover all possible inappropriate faculty behaviors, the leadership communication strategies presented in this chapter can be generalized to inappropriate behaviors beyond those addressed in the case scenarios.

They focus on managing the inappropriate behaviors of tenured faculty members, and the leadership communication strategies presented can be used in managing the inappropriate behaviors of all faculty and staff.

Defining the Task

The challenge of managing difficult tenured faculty members can cause even the most talented and skilled individuals to resign the position of department chair. To be successful, department chairs must cultivate leadership communication skills for managing difficult personalities. While every difficult personality can possess unique attributes, the more notable characters include the pot stirrer, the troublemaker, the prima donna, the drama queen (or king), and the confrontation junkie. Beyond these, there are also individuals who become difficult to manage because they resist any and all change on principle or are intent on pursuing only their own agenda. In *Effective Leadership Communication: A Guide for Department Chairs and Deans for Managing Difficult Situations and People* (Higgerson & Joyce, 2007, pp. 167–245), leadership communication strategies for managing each of these more notable difficult personalities are presented. Understanding the specific nature of each difficult personality is essential to knowing how to manage that individual even though these difficult personality categories are not finite or mutually exclusive.

The task of managing difficult personalities becomes more formidable when the difficult individual holds tenure. While it is not the case that all tenured faculty are difficult personalities or that all difficult personalities hold tenure, it is the case that managing difficult personalities becomes more challenging when the individuals are tenured faculty members. Historically, faculty members enjoy greater autonomy once granted tenure. Tenured faculty members, for example, are not typically subjected to the annual performance review that untenured faculty experience. Even with more institutions of higher education implementing post-tenure review, tenured faculty typically have a fair amount of autonomy in how, when, and where they work. Difficult personalities sometimes view tenure as license to do as they please without regard for the welfare of others, the department, or the institution. At times, difficult tenured faculty members interpret tenure to mean their behavior is beyond reproach.

The leadership authority assigned to department chairs varies from one institution to another and influences the department chair's management of difficult personalities. For example, at some institutions, department chairs have the authority to assign merit pay whereas department chairs at other institutions have no input on faculty salary increases. When a department chair has no input into faculty salary increases or when substantive salary increases are rare, then department chairs cannot use salary increases to motivate improved faculty performance. If the institution requires post-tenure review, department chairs have some mechanism for addressing the performance of tenured faculty members even though the specific post-tenure review policy will determine the scope and magnitude of the department chair's role in evaluating faculty performance. Regardless of the level of assigned leadership authority, department chairs are typically accountable for department productivity, which requires getting all department faculty members to work constructively together toward common goals. This requires department chairs to address and manage the inappropriate behaviors of tenured faculty members who may be unreceptive to critique or evaluative comments from department chairs who they more likely perceive as a peer than a supervisor.

Relevant Leadership Communication Strategies

Department chairs can use the following leadership communication strategies to manage difficult personalities and the inappropriate behaviors of tenured faculty without escalating destructive conflict.

Understand the Difficult Faculty Member's Perspective

It is important to understand the difficult faculty member's perspective. This means fully comprehending the difficult tenured faculty member's position on issues of contention and why the difficult faculty member believes and behaves as he or she does.

LOOK FOR COMMON GROUND   Only by fully comprehending the difficult faculty member's perspective can a department chair hope to identify areas of common ground that can be essential to reaching some level of mutual agreement, obtaining support for a new initiative, or alleviating destructive conflict within the department. Consider, for example, the situation in which a tenured faculty member vehemently opposes the central administration's request that the department develop procedures for post-tenure review. Understanding the basis for the tenured faculty member's opposition is essential to being able to address that individual's concern and secure the opposed faculty member's participation in developing the department's procedure for post-tenure review. The department chair's approach will be different if the tenured faculty member believes that post-tenure review threatens faculty job security than if the faculty member believes the performance review of tenured faculty violates faculty rights. For example, understanding that post-tenure review would serve to document the importance and effectiveness of faculty work could help to persuade the participation of tenured faculty members who fear that post-tenure review threatens faculty job security but will do little to motivate the tenured faculty members who perceive post-tenure review as a violation of faculty rights. Understanding the difficult tenured faculty member's perspective is the central to identifying common ground that can be used to build support for new initiatives and other change.

FRAME ISSUES AND SELECT LANGUAGE ACCORDINGLY   How a department chair frames an issue and uses language to communicate with a tenured faculty member engaging in inappropriate behaviors can either exacerbate or minimize the conflict. By understanding the difficult faculty member's perspective, a department chair is better able to avoid fueling destructive conflict by using language that will be heard and interpreted negatively by the difficult faculty member. For example, if a department chair understands that a tenured faculty member opposes post-tenure review because he fears it will be used to dismiss tenured faculty and cut salaries, the department chair may want to talk about developing procedures for post-tenure review that document effective faculty work and can be used to champion salary increases. Similarly, understanding why a tenured faculty member exhibits hostility toward the new faculty hire is important to knowing how to address and discuss the inappropriate behavior. If the hostility derives from a misunderstanding that occurred during the search process, then clarifying the misunderstanding will be more helpful than merely addressing the hostility. The framing of the issue and the language used when discussing that issue must be crafted with full consideration of the difficult tenured faculty member's perspective if the situation is to be managed without escalating the conflict or disagreement.

Clarify Role Responsibilities and Performance Expectations

Assigned role responsibilities can contribute to differing perspectives, and therefore role responsibilities can be the source of conflict between and among individuals with different role responsibilities. Department chairs are responsible for the welfare of the entire department whereas individual faculty members are primarily responsible for their own teaching and research agenda. A tenured faculty member who receives less funding support than requested may conclude that the department chair does not support his or her research program when the department chair is trying to award finite resources in a way that best serves the professional needs of all faculty in the department.Department chairs can help prevent differences in role responsibilities from becoming a conflict by making clear how assigned role responsibilities shape the decisions. Especially because department chairs are promoted from faculty positions into department chair leadership, it is imperative that department chairs help faculty understand the role responsibilities associated with department chair leadership. The specific goal responsibilities assigned to department chairs very from one institution to another. Nonetheless, all department chairs need to help faculty know and understand the role responsibilities of department chair leadership. When department chairs fail to do this, they invite faculty members, and especially tenured faculty members, to continue to view them as peers when department chairs have very real assigned leadership responsibilities over their faculty colleagues.

Depersonalize Issues of Disagreement

One important key to managing conflict is to depersonalize the issues of disagreement. When issues of disagreement are not personal, it is easier to work toward compromise or mutual understanding. There are at least three strategies that department chairs and other academic leaders can use to help depersonalize issues of disagreement.

DISCLOSE CRITERIA FOR MAKING DECISIONS   Being transparent about the criteria for decisions will help to prevent individual faculty from reacting to decisions in a personal way. Whenever possible, department chairs should involve faculty in establishing and discussing the criteria to be used in making decisions. Although a tenured faculty member may not be happy with his or her allocation for professional travel, the tenured faculty member's reaction will be different and less volatile if he or she understands the criteria used in making allocations.

DISCUSS BEHAVIORS, NOT PERSONAL ATTRIBUTES   Department chairs can help to depersonalize conflict by addressing specific behaviors rather than individual personality traits or personal attributes. There is a significant difference between telling a faculty member that he or she does not care about student learning (a personal attribute) and making clear that faculty members who care about student success provide students with frequent feedback on all class assignments (a specific behavior). A faculty member being told that he or she does not care about student learning is more likely to become defensive at what will likely be perceived as a personal attack than if that faculty member is told that providing students with frequent feedback on all class assignments will enhance student learning. The former approach represents an evaluative comment about the faculty member's character whereas the second approach offers a strategy for enhancing student learning. The first approach describes and labels the faculty member's personal character whereas the second approach assumes that the faculty member can improve his or her teaching without making a personal judgment. Efforts to depersonalize issues of disagreement help to reduce defensiveness that often escalates conflict and, in particular, make it easier for prickly or difficult individuals to consider the perspectives of others.

PUT ISSUES OF DISAGREEMENT IN CONTEXT Faculty members who enjoy a high degree of autonomy typically assess change and new initiatives from a very personal perspective. In other words, they consider how a particular change will affect them personally and lack the perspective needed to consider how the change serves the larger context. Faculty members, unlike department chairs, are not charged with being responsible for the overall welfare of the department. Department chairs can help to mitigate the personal reaction to change and new initiatives by helping all faculty understand the larger context and cultivating consensus around shared department goals. Consider for example, the tenured faculty member who becomes irate over being asked to submit mid-term progress reports on students because that faculty member views the request as more busy work. This reaction derives from the faculty member's limited perspective. The department chair, however, can help to minimize the potential for conflict and alter the faculty member's reaction by sharing in advance the reason for the requested mid-term grades. The faculty member will likely have a different and more constructive reaction once that individual perceives the benefit derived from the additional work for faculty members.

Look for Teachable Moments

There are many parallels between effective teaching and effective leadership. In the same way that the best student learning often derives from the student's struggle with a difficult assignment, faculty members often have their best aha moments in the midst of a struggle. Although it is not advisable that department chairs intentionally create struggles for faculty members to generate teachable moments, it is important for department chairs to seize teachable moments when faculty members experience struggle. The following three practices should guide the use of teachable moments in managing the inappropriate behaviors of tenured faculty members.

NOT WHEN DEFENSES ARE UP When individuals are defensive, they do not listen or hear well. When an individual's defenses are heightened, that individual is less receptive to new ideas or even modest suggestions for making changes. When an individual's defenses are heightened, no learning takes place. Consequently, department chairs must avoid increasing defensiveness and address existing defensiveness in the tenured faculty member before exercising a teachable moment.

LINK PERFORMANCE EXPECTATIONS TO INDIVIDUAL ROLE RESPONSI- BILITIES   Instead of telling a tenured faculty member what to do or what not to do, department chairs will find it more helpful to discuss specific faculty behaviors in relation to specific faculty role responsibilities. Consider, for example, the tenured faculty member who refuses to meet or help students who that faculty member perceives as difficult or lazy. Telling that faculty member that he or she must meet with students will accomplish little. In fact, it may cause the faculty member to conclude that the department chair is unsympathetic or trying to tell the tenured faculty member how to teach. A better approach would be for the department chair to acknowledge the challenges of teaching and link the need to help all students learn to the faculty member's role responsibility to teach effectively.

LINK SUGGESTIONS AND GOALS TO ESPOUSED VIEWS   Whenever possible, it is helpful to use views espoused by the tenured faculty member in discussing their inappropriate behavior. Consider, for example, the tenured faculty member who perceives him or herself as a successful and effective teacher. This tenured faculty member would be hard pressed to explain why he or she should not help a particular student because others could perceive that faculty member as shirking his or her responsibility to teach effectively. Department chairs who are able to use the tenured faculty member's espoused views to challenge that faculty member's inappropriate behavior, create dissonance within the tenured faculty member that can help to encouraging that faculty member to alter his or her behavior.

Putting Theory into Practice

It is difficult to address all possible inappropriate behaviors of tenured faculty members, so Case 9.1 addresses a dynamic that can occur when tenured faculty grow impatient with the increased demands and expectations of some of today's students. Place yourself in the role of the department chair as you read.

Case 9.1: The Teachable Moment

Dr. Robert Straumanis prides himself in being an excellent teacher and enjoys a reputation among students as being a demanding instructor. He works hard at teaching and expects his students to work hard at learning, especially graduate classes in education to practicing teachers who are working toward their master's. Although Dr. Straumanis has never taught in a K–12 school, he regularly observes practicing teachers of these grades.

The Challenger

Jerry Bajek, a tenured teacher and coach in the local high school, enrolled in the class taught by Dr. Straumanis. Jerry is unlike any student Dr. Straumanis has ever had in that he challenges every assignment seeking to know the value in completing it. Jerry considers himself an accomplished and effective teacher so he frequently makes suggestions to Dr. Straumanis regarding how assignments might be revised to avoid making pointless busywork for already busy graduate students. Although never rude, Jerry is direct and often raises questions about assignments, grading practices, attendance, and other class policies in front of other students.

Dr. Straumanis is put off by Jerry's manner and behavior. Dr. Straumanis perceives Jerry as a disrespectful student who does not understand or accept faculty authority. In Dr. Straumanis's view, Jerry's propensity to challenge and question everything takes important class time, damages the mood of the class, and undermines Dr. Straumanis's authority and credibility. In sum, Dr. Straumanis finds Jerry's argumentative and uncooperative.

Dr. Straumanis finds it particularly annoying that Jerry challenges every grade. Typically, when tests or assignments are returned, Jerry will follow him to his office after class to discuss the grade assigned. Jerry refuses to accept explanations that typically satisfy students. For example, if Dr. Straumanis explains that the test was graded on a curve, Jerry wants to know how many papers were judged better than his and precisely what his paper lacked.

The Last Straw

Dr. Straumanis is relieved to reach the end of the semester even though he is not surprised to see Jerry at his door seeking to discuss Jerry's grade on the final project. Jerry discerned that his grade of 73 on the final project will give him a B for the course, whereas a score of 75 would result in a final A. In typical fashion, Jerry wants to know precisely what his final project lacks that resulted in a grade of 73.

Dr. Straumanis: I understand that you are disappointed because you expected and A in this class. However, in my professional judgment, you have not earned an A in this class.

Jerry: Right now, I'm trying to understand why you gave me a grade of 73 for my final project.

Dr. Straumanis: I gave your project a 73 because that is what your work deserved.

Jerry: Why?

Dr. Straumanis: You have challenged my judgment all semester, and frankly I am tired of your attacks on my professional expertise. I am the instructor in this course, and it is my judgment that matters. Based on my professional expertise and experience your final project is a 73.

Jerry: But why? What is lacking in my final project? I noted that my final project is substantially longer than most you received. What could be missing?

Dr. Straumanis: Length does not guarantee quality.

Jerry: Then what is it lacking?

Dr. Straumanis: I'm through arguing with you. I know you are new to the master's program, so permit me to give you some advice. You will do better in all your classes once you recognize and respect faculty expertise and authority.

Jerry: How is it disrespectful to want to learn what is missing from my final project? And given your vast professional expertise, you should be able to explain what my final project lacks.

Dr. Straumanis: You're challenging my judgment and authority as the instructor for this course, and I will not tolerate it.

Jerry: I'm asking a question. How can I know what I failed to include in my final project if you will not tell me?

Dr. Straumanis: Here is a final project that was completed by a classmate who earned a 95. I have removed the cover page because I cannot tell you whose work it is. If you will look through it objectively, you will see how much more comprehensive it is than your submission.

Jerry: I see you made a lot of margin notes on this other project. There are no margin notes on my final project.

Dr. Straumanis: That doesn't mean anything. Sometimes a paper so misses the mark that it is impossible to note all deficiencies in the margins.

Jerry: That's why I came to talk to you. Can I have a copy of this other project so I can study it in more detail?

Dr. Straumanis: No, but you can look at it now before the office closes.

Jerry: The office is closing in 15 minutes.

Dr. Straumanis: Then I suggest you spend your time looking at this sample project instead of arguing with me.

Jerry: This is ridiculous. I think you gave me a grade that you knew would give me a B for the course. You obviously cannot explain the basis for the grade assigned to my project.

Dr. Straumanis: Again, I am the instructor for the course, so I don't have to explain my grade. An instructor's grade is final.

Jerry: Are you certain about that?

Jerry dropped the sample project on the desk, gathered his things, and left the office.

The Appeal

Jerry Bajek took his issue to the department chair. With a fair degree of accuracy, he recounted his bumpy interactions with Dr. Straumanis throughout the semester. Dr. Straumanis is known to become very prickly whenever he feels challenged by anyone, including his colleagues and chair. Consequently, the department chair could envision the interaction that Jerry describes.

The department chair is well aware of Dr. Straumanis's perspective on faculty authority. When the department chair asked Dr. Straumanis to consider supporting a backdated withdrawal for a student who was in a serious car accident, the professor remained adamant that the grade of F he assigned not be changed to a backdated withdrawal because the student failed to notify him personally of the accident in advance of the deadline to submit final grades. Dr. Straumanis typically justifies his stern posture by professing the importance of holding students accountable for acting in a professional way. Nonetheless, the department chair believes that Jerry is entitled to know the basis for the grade of 73 on the final project, and he agrees to talk with Dr. Straumanis about reviewing the basis for the grade with Jerry.

Chair's Conversation with Dr. Straumanis

The department chair is not anxious to fan the flames with Dr. Straumanis, so he makes an unscheduled visit to the professor's office rather than give him time to stew before a formally scheduled meeting.

Department chair: I see you're working through lunch again. You must have more grading to do.

Dr. Straumanis: Well, it is final exam week.

Department chair: If you can spare a few minutes, I'd like to brief you on a conversation I had with one of your students.

Sr. Straumanis: Certainly, which student?

Department chair: Jerry Bajek

Dr. Straumanis: I am not surprised. Jerry has time for everything except doing good work.

Department chair: Really? I reviewed his application to the graduate program, and his undergraduate transcript and references suggest he is both bright and very capable.

Dr. Straumanis: Jerry has a problem accepting authority.

Department chair: What do you mean?

Dr. Straumanis: Instead of working hard to do as he is instructed, he challenges everything. He challenges every assignment, the grading criteria, and always his grade. He refuses to acknowledge that, as the instructor, I make the assignments, establish the grading criteria, and assign the grades.

Department chair: Jerry seems especially determined to learn the basis for the grade of 73 he received on his final project. Would you meet with him to explain the basis for the assigned grade?

Dr. Straumanis: I already met with him, and it accomplished nothing. I should not have to justify the grade I assign to Jerry, you, or anyone. Are you saying I am not competent to grade a student's work?

Department chair: Of course not. I do, however, believe students learn best when they understand why their work does not meet faculty expectations.

Dr. Straumanis: Jerry knows why he got the 73, but he would prefer to spend his time arguing for a better grade rather than earning one.

Department chair: I cannot comment on Jerry's work habits, but I believe he does not understand the basis for his grade on the final project and therefore believes it is unfair.

Dr. Straumanis: That's his problem.

Department chair: Unless you help him understand the basis for the grade assigned, he is likely to conclude the grade is unfair. Jerry impresses me as the type of student who will pursue something he believes is unfair with a formal grievance. Why not talk with him? Give him the benefit of your expertise, and spell out what his final project lacks. If you like, I would be happy to sit in on the meeting and interrupt Jerry should he become rude or disrespect your authority.

Dr. Straumanis: I don't need a babysitter. I've been teaching longer than you have, and I refuse to be bullied by Jerry or any student.

Department chair: Please give it some thought and consider meeting one more time with Jerry.

Let's Analyze the Case

Dr. Straumanis is irritated with Jerry Bajek, a graduate student enrolled in Dr. Straumanis' graduate class. Jerry's practice of seeking to learn the reason for each exercise and the basis for every grade assigned by Dr. Straumanis leaves Dr. Straumanis feeling challenged about matters he views as being his prerogative. According to Dr. Straumanis, Jerry is disrespectful, if not rude, in refusing to acknowledge Dr. Straumanis's expertise and authority as the instructor of the course. According to Dr. Straumanis, Jerry would rather spend time arguing for a better grade then working hard in the class.

Push comes to shove when Jerry seeks an explanation for a grade of 73 on his final project, a grade that guarantees Jerry a final grade of B for the course. By this point in the semester, Dr. Straumanis is tired of dealing with Jerry and not inclined to give Jerry's challenges more time. When Dr. Straumanis refuses to explain the basis for the grade of 73 on the final project, Jerry concludes that Dr. Straumanis has no explanation and that an unfair grade was assigned to prevent Jerry from getting a grade of A for the course. This conclusion is supported by the fact that Jerry observes margin notes in a classmate's final project when Dr. Straumanis made no margin notes on his final project. Dr. Straumanis is unconcerned about Jerry's conclusion that the grade on his final project is unfair. Dr. Straumanis seems more focused on teaching Jerry not to question or challenge Dr. Straumanis's authority to assign grades than explaining the basis for the grade assigned.

Jerry takes his complaint to the department chair, who agrees to talk with Dr. Straumanis. However, the department chair is unsuccessful in persuading Dr. Straumanis to talk with Jerry and explain the basis for the grade of 73 on the final project. The department chair opts to talk informally with Dr. Straumanis believing that this might help to prevent Dr. Straumanis from becoming defensive. The department chair offers to join Dr. Straumanis when he meets with Jerry to explain the basis for the grade. Dr. Straumanis, however, is not receptive to the department chair's suggestion that he talk with Jerry interprets the department chair's offer to sit in on the meeting as an indication that the chair doubts his ability to manage the situation. The department chair senses that Jerry will likely pursue the matter with a formal grievance if he does not get a reasonable explanation for the grade from Dr. Straumanis.

It's Your Turn

Assume the position of department chair in this case scenario and think through what you would do to persuade Dr. Straumanis to explain the basis for the final project grade of 73 to Jerry.

1. What, if anything, would you do differently in setting up a meeting to talk with Dr. Straumanis? Would you schedule a meeting and give Dr. Straumanis advance notice as to the purpose for the meeting? If so, how would you state the purpose to avoid making Dr. Straumanis defensive?

2. How would you frame the issue for discussion? For example, would you reference campus policy, appeal to Dr. Straumanis's pride in teaching effectively, or place more emphasis on the likelihood that Jerry Bajek will pursue the matter further if not satisfied? What reaction do you anticipate from Dr. Straumanis? How will you respond to Dr. Straumanis?

3. Would you follow up in any way with Dr. Straumanis after the conversation presented in Case 9.1? If yes, what would you do? Would you follow up with Jerry Bajek now that Dr. Straumanis refuses to act on your counsel? If so, how would you follow up with Jerry and what would you say to this student?

4. Is there anything else you would do to manage this escalating conflict between Dr. Straumanis and graduate student Jerry Bajek? Would you brief others about the conflict? If so, who would you involve and why?

Please Consider

When mediating a disagreement, it is important to consider the issue from the perspective of each party. In other words, to be optimally helpful to both Dr. Straumanis and graduate student Jerry Bajek, the department chair must first understand their individual perspectives. If this was not your starting point in addressing the questions above, take a moment to assess the perspectives held by Dr. Straumanis and Jerry Bajek and consider whether you would now revise your approach to meeting with Dr. Straumanis. For example, Dr. Straumanis perceives Jerry as disrespectful of his faculty expertise and authority. Any approach that appears to Dr. Straumanis to defend or justify the student's actions will likely make Dr. Straumanis more defensive and less willing to consider granting Jerry Bajek an audience. Similarly, Jerry believes that Dr. Straumanis is treating him unfairly. A conversation with Jerry that begins by explaining the prerogative that faculty members have to assign grades will not assuage Jerry's suspicions that he is a victim of unfair grading. This does not mean that the department chair must accept at face value all that either party asserts about the other. The department chair, however, must talk with each individual without appearing to take the side of the other to avoid increasing defensiveness that could prevent the individuals from resolving the disagreement.

Most individuals become defensive when they believe their perspective is not heard or is being dismissed. Consequently, it is virtually impossible to achieve a constructive outcome to conflict without easing the defensiveness of the individuals involved. Neither Dr. Straumanis nor Jerry Bajek will likely learn from the experience unless the department chair is able to lower their defensiveness about the immediate conflict.

Let's Recap

Take a moment to review your plan for managing the escalating conflict between Dr. Straumanis and graduate student Jerry Bajek. Does your plan

- ○ Account for the faculty member's perspective?
- ○ Account for the graduate student's perspective?
- ○ Clarify faculty role responsibilities and performance expectations?
- ○ Clarify student responsibilities and performance expectations?
- ○ Frame the issue in a way that depersonalizes the issues of disagreement between Dr. Straumanis and graduate student Jerry Bajek?
- ○ Lower defensiveness such that common ground might be found and the immediate conflict resolved?

Putting Theory into Practice

Assume that despite the department chair's best efforts Dr. Straumanis refuses to talk further with Jerry Bajek. Again, assume the role of department chair as you read Case 9.2.

Case 9.2: Another Teachable Moment

Jerry Bajek filed a formal grievance with the grievance review board. In his complaint, Jerry stresses Dr. Straumanis's refusal to explain the basis for his grade on the final project. Jerry also shares that the model project he was permitted to view contained copious margin notes whereas

Dr. Straumanis made no notes on his final project that would explain the grade. Finally, Jerry points out that had he earned a 75 instead of a 73 on the final project, he would have earned an A for the course.

Grievance Review Board

The grievance review board is composed of seven tenured faculty members. Campus policy licenses the GRB to review a complaint and decide whether or not it warrants a formal hearing. In compliance with policy, the board sent a copy of Jerry Bajek's formal complaint to Dr. Straumanis with a request that he reply to the complaint. After several weeks and many reminders, Dr. Straumanis sent the following email reply to the board:

> As tenured faculty members, I am confident you recognize and support an instructor's authority to grade student work. I do not have time to engage in an exercise initiated by a student who would rather challenge my authority as the instructor of a graduate class than do good work.

Absent any substantive response to Jerry Bajek's complaint, the grievance board decides to hear the case. Dr. Straumanis is outraged and refuses to testify at the hearing. He also refuses to comply with the board's request for documentation. The time-consuming process took months with the review board chair and several others trying to persuade Dr. Straumanis to testify so that the review board would learn his perspective and the basis for the grade assigned to Jerry's final project.

The grievance board finds that Dr. Straumanis did not do enough to help Jerry understand the basis for his grade on the final project. The board also finds that Jerry's testimony is insufficient to conclude that the assigned grade is wrong or unfair. The board recommends that the grade of 73 for Jerry's final project should remain, which leaves his final grade for the course unchanged. Dr. Straumanis feels vindicated, although he remains angry with the grievance board for giving Jerry its time and attention. The grievance board, department chair, and others are frustrated by Dr. Straumanis's refusal to participate in the grievance process. Had he responded with a substantive explanation to Jerry's complaint when requested, the board may not have needed to conduct a hearing, and several individuals would have been spared significant time and anguish.

Department Chair's Letter

The department chair knows that Dr. Straumanis learned nothing from this experience. He feels vindicated that the grade he assigned stands and believes that any time spent on Jerry's complaint is the board's fault for giving the student its time and attention. The department chair worries that the outcome could embolden the professor in ways that could lead to similar conflicts with other students. After careful consideration, the department chair sends Dr. Straumanis the following memo.

Memo to: Dr. Straumanis
From: Department Chair
Subject: Jerry Bajek grievance

Having been copied by you and others on correspondence regarding Mr. Bajek's grievance, it is appropriate that I weigh in on the events that unfolded. It is my hope that you will make a sincere effort to understand my comments as they are intended to help you manage the next student complaint with better form and outcome should another student seek to learn the basis for a grade you assign.

Your reaction regarding Mr. Bajek's grade complaint does not make sense to me for several reasons. First, it is odd that you would return a final project valued at 75% of the final grade without any written comment. In contrast, you penned copious notes on the final projects of other students in the class. At a recent department meeting, I heard you speak eloquently about the importance of feedback to student learning and the benefits of coached feedback. Jerry Bajek filed a formal grievance because you denied him constructive feedback on his final project—feedback you profess is essential to student learning.

Second, given your expertise in education, you know that effective instructors seize every opportunity to provide constructive feedback that will help students learn. Discussing a lower-than-expected grade is a terrific opportunity for effective teaching. Yet when Jerry approached you for an explanation, you chose not to engage the tools of your discipline. Instead, you advised the student that he had no recourse—a position that caused him to conclude he was being graded unfairly. It was your dismissive posture when the student sought an explanation from you that persuaded Mr. Bajek to file a formal grievance. Presuming you had a basis for the grade that you are able to explain, you needed to share it with the student. Permitting Jerry to leaf through another student's work is no substitute for your constructive evaluation of his work and, without sufficient time to study the good example, your actions affirmed Jerry's suspicion that you had no basis for the grade.

Third, your behavior escalated a situation that required several individuals to spend time on something I believe you were sufficiently skilled to manage without Jerry concluding that he had to file a formal complaint to get a fair hearing. I understand you believe the grievance review board should not have heard Jerry's complaint. However, when you dismissed Jerry's request to learn the basis for the grade, you gave him more motivation and reason to file a formal complaint. Had the record revealed that you spent time explaining the basis for the grade to the student and had Jerry's final project been peppered with your margin notes, I doubt that the grievance board would find the case worthy of a formal hearing. I disagree with your conclusion that the board's decision to hear the student's complaint was "flawed because it was an overresponse to a disgruntled student."

Dr. Straumanis, I hope you will consider these comments in the constructive manner they are intended. I perceive you as a hard-working faculty member who is steeped in what methods constitute good pedagogy. Consequently, I find it troubling and incomprehensible that you would act in a way that fuels a student's suspicion that a grade was given with prejudice. Your refusal to attend the grievance review board hearing and provide requested documentation only exacerbated those suspicions. I hope you can learn from this experience such that you behave in a manner more consistent with your professional expertise and experience the next time a student seeks to understand the basis for a grade you have a signed.

Please know that I'm available should you wish to talk through my comments or any aspect of this situation.

Let's Analyze the Case

This outcome is lose-lose for all involved. Jerry Bajek is likely frustrated because his grade remains unchanged. Even though Jerry had an opportunity to present his case before the grievance board, he never learns the basis for the grade he believes is unfair. Most likely, board members are frustrated by Dr. Straumanis's refusal to participate in the grievance review process or supply requested documentation about the student's grade. Had Dr. Straumanis responded to the initial complaint and shared the basis for the grade of 73 on the student's final project, it is unlikely that the board would need to conduct a formal hearing because an instructor's assessment of student work is typically not second guessed unless there is reason to believe the grade may have been given with prejudice. Dr. Straumanis is annoyed that the board gave Jerry their time and attention.

The department chair is frustrated because Dr. Straumanis's refusal to explain the basis of the Jerry's grade on the final project predictably motivated Jerry to file a formal complaint with the board. Consequently,

Dr. Straumanis's actions require many to invest time and energy on a process that does not help anyone. As important to the department chair, there is little indication that Dr. Straumanis learned what he needed to from this experience to prevent a similar occurrence in the future. In writing to Dr. Straumanis, the department chair makes one more attempt at a teachable moment, which, if successful, might motivate him to handle similar situations differently in the future.

It's Your Turn

1. Do you agree with the Department chair's handling the grievance review board finding? If not, what would you do differently? What, if any, action would you take to persuade Dr. Straumanis to manage conflicts with graduate students differently in the future? Be specific in delineating the points you would make and how you would frame each. Would you make these points in writing or in conversation?

2. Review the department chair's letter to Dr. Straumanis, and highlight any language you find unhelpful to the purpose of creating a teachable moment for Dr. Straumanis. In particular, is there language that might make Dr. Straumanis too defensive to grasp intended lesson?

3. Now edit the letter such that it becomes an optimal teachable moment for Dr. Straumanis.

Please Consider

The better we know an individual, the easier it is to frame issues and use language that will more accurately communicate the intended message to that individual. We know Dr. Straumanis only through the information provided in the case. This makes it more difficult to identify the best possible framing and language to use in a letter to Dr. Straumanis. The task of knowing how to best frame issues and what language to use will be easier when communicating with individuals you know well. Still, the task of finding the best possible framing and language requires intentional thinking. These moments are not well served by winging it or allowing the heat of the moment to dictate your leadership communication. In Case 9.2, the department chair's action may hurt his credibility with Dr. Straumanis. However, not seizing the teachable moment will likely embolden the professor to continue the same practice with other students who may seek explanations for the grade assigned. By sending a letter instead of talking with Dr. Straumanis, the chair allows Dr. Straumanis to learn his thinking in private. Should the chair relate the same information in a meeting, it is likely that Dr. Straumanis would be too defensive to comprehend the lesson.

Putting Theory into Practice

Inappropriate behavior comes in many forms. In Case 9.3, the new department chair must manage a tenured full professor who uses loud, often insulting, and sometimes vulgar communication to get his way. Please put yourself in the role of the department chair as your read.

Case 9.3: Managing Mr. Insensitive

When Reid Payne accepted the position of chair of the psychology department, he recognized that managing the antics of Dr. Herb Seitz would be an important but challenging task. Being hired from outside the institution, Reid believes he will be better able to manage Herb's disruptive and often inappropriate behavior than the previous chair and longtime colleague of Dr. Seitz. Now that Reid has been in the position for almost a year, he realizes that Dr. Seitz is no more willing to heed his counsel or acknowledge his leadership authority than he was willing to listen to the counsel of his longtime colleague and previous department chair.

Meet Dr. Herb Seitz

Dr. Seitz behaves as if he is the most knowledgeable and senior member of the department even though this is not the case. He is a tenured associate professor with much work to do before being eligible for promotion to the rank of full professor. Herb's participation at department meetings is limited to questioning or captioning the work of others in unflattering and often hurtful ways. When committees report out the group's considered recommendations, Dr. Seitz can be counted on to interrupt the presentation with questions that require no prior preparation or thought but that cast doubt on the committee's work. The department curriculum committee spent months developing a proposal for full department consideration. Although Dr. Seitz never responded to the committee's request for input throughout the work, he punctuated the presentation of the committee's findings with statements like the following: "Why would we do that?" and "Won't that cost a lot of money?" and "Really, all this time and that's the best you could come up with?" Dr. Seitz contributes very little to the department's work. He attends committee and department meetings, but his only contribution is to serve as the self-appointed devil's advocate for any idea being considered and any viewpoint that differs from this own thinking.

Dr. Seitz never misses an opportunity to demonstrate his quick mind and sharp tongue—often at the expense of others. He impulsively disrupts ongoing discussions or reports being given at department meetings. Although what Dr. Seitz has to offer is typically on point, his habit of asserting his view without permitting colleagues to complete their thoughts or sentences disrupts meaningful department discussion and discourages many faculty members from participating in the discussion of important department matters. Should Dr. Seitz disagree with the perspective being articulated, he is quick to discredit the credential or thinking of the person speaking. Sadly, many of his statements represent hurtful comments and not legitimate criticism. For example, when the newest member of the department offered a suggestion for how the core requirements might be strengthened, Herb quipped, "You're only proving how your alma mater dumbed down its doctoral program with that suggestion." When the young PhD attempted to explain his thinking further, Dr. Seitz cut him off midsentence: "Please stop embarrassing yourself." Students report a similar treatment from him during class discussions. Reid Payne found ample evidence in file notes and performance review letters that previous department chairs exercised due diligence in trying to persuade Dr. Seitz that he needs to learn how to disagree with colleagues and interact with students without being pejorative.

Dr. Seitz believes he possesses an enviable wit, which he frequently displays at the expense of others. His humor is often mean-spirited in that he likes to verbalize what others consider the most embarrassing dimensions of an issue, situation, or relationship. For example, when a colleague's former spouse began dating someone else in the department, he silenced a department discussion of the curriculum when, in front of everyone, he said to the single spouse, "You must love sitting through department meetings now that your ex has hooked up with her." A student reported that when she asked Dr. Seitz a question in class, he replied, "You may as well as wear a dunce cap because every time you open your mouth you remind us of how much you don't know." Dr. Seitz does not notice that he is the only one who finds his comments amusing. Should a faculty member or student show a slide or distribute a report that contains a misspelling or grammatical error, they can count on him to make their mistake a significant part of whatever subject is being presented and discussed. He seizes every opportunity to make fun of colleagues and students. Colleagues and students complain of being embarrassed, ridiculed, insulted, and angry over the treatment they receive from Dr. Seitz.

Chair's Management Issue

Reid now recognizes that it will take more than his being hired from outside the institution to deter Dr. Seitz from engaging in inappropriate behavior when interacting with colleagues and students. Reid talked with him about his inappropriate behavior on several occasions but is unable to secure his attention or cooperation. Instead, Dr. Seitz engages his customary antics during conversations with his new department chair. Dr. Seitz frequently reminds Reid that he is the new kid on the block, and instead of taking Reid's counsel seriously he counsels him on not taking the job too seriously. When Reid describes how students and colleagues react to Dr. Seitz's barbs, the professor dismisses them with a flip response such as, "I call them as I see them, so sue me." For whatever reason, Dr. Seitz is unwilling or unable to understand why he should change his behavior simply because others would rather not deal with truths.

Reid finds it increasingly uncomfortable to hear complaints from students and faculty who seek his support in dealing with Dr. Seitz because all of his efforts to remedy the ongoing problem have been unsuccessful. Without a constructive outcome, Reid understands that students and faculty members might soon conclude that he is ineffective in helping them deal with Dr. Seitz. Moreover, Reid worries that his inability to manage one difficult person could cause faculty and students to lose confidence his overall leadership.

At the same time, Reid finds it difficult to conduct department meetings on substantive issues when Dr. Seitz interrupts productive discussion with unwarranted barbs and rude comments that derail the conversation. His propensity to be the caustic department comic at the expense of others to flex his quick mind and wit serves to stifle participation in department discussions. This is catastrophic for Reid's collaborative leadership style, which relies on open and candid consideration of all relevant perspectives. It is virtually impossible to weigh the pros and cons of the available alternatives if individuals are hesitant to suggest solutions for fear of being discredited, insulted, or made the object of Dr. Seitz's mean-spirited wit.

Reid has a fair amount of experience managing difficult situations, but Dr. Seitz leaves Reid feeling like a novice. He needs to find a way to command the professor's attention and cooperation in altering his behavior when interacting with students and faculty colleagues.

Let's Analyze the Case

Dr. Seitz's inappropriate behavior is hurting Reid's leadership in at least three ways. First, any notion that the new chair would be able to manage

Dr. Seitz's inappropriate behavior is undermined the longer he is permitted to continue his hurtful treatment of students and colleagues. Should students or faculty members decide that the new department chair is generally ineffective in managing difficult people and situations, Dr. Seitz's behavior will erode the new chair's leadership credibility with others in the department. Second, Dr. Seitz's behavior disrupts department discussion about important issues and stifles participation in department discussions. Given the department chair's preference for collaborative leadership, it is essential that the new department chair curtail behavior that inhibits the honest and full participation of all department members. To successfully exercise collaborative leadership, the new department chair must secure Dr. Seitz's cooperation for remedying how he treats students and faculty colleagues.

Third, Dr. Seitz must become a full-fledged participant in department discussions and work. As long as he is permitted to play the role of department critic, he is not making a valued investment of intellect, experience, and time to help discern constructive solutions to the tasks and challenges facing the department. Although he may believe he is contributing by pointing out mistakes and asking open-ended questions, his contribution to department deliberations requires absolutely no expertise or study of the issue being discussed. Ironically, the very behavior that Dr. Seitz believes affirms his intellect and wit accomplishes the opposite even though his colleagues are too embattled to point this out to him. Instead, Dr. Seitz has been allowed to function as the department's acerbic critic without making a constructive contribution to the work of the department. This, too, can erode the department chair's credibility with other faculty members because, by not curtailing the professor's inappropriate behavior and freeing him from working substantively on department business, the department chair is giving license to inequitable workloads among the faculty members.

The new department chair is on a very slippery slope with his leadership credibility and effectiveness at stake. Although most new department chairs have a honeymoon period in which to address the more pressing issues, the new department chair's progress in managing the inappropriate behavior one tenured faculty member is apparent to all department members. The honeymoon period for any department chair can be shortened or lengthened depending upon how the chair manages the most pressing issues. In this case scenario, the department chair's honeymoon period will likely be shortened because of his inability to manage the inappropriate behavior of one tenured faculty member.

It's Your Turn

Assume the position of department chair Reid Payne, and think through how you would manage Dr. Seitz.

1. What do you know about Dr. Seitz's perspective? What do you need to know about Dr. Seitz's perspective to manage the conflict described in Case 9.3? How might you gather the information you need to more effectively manage Dr. Seitz's inappropriate behavior?

2. Is Dr. Seitz's behavior consistent with the role responsibilities of faculty members? If not, how is Dr. Seitz's behavior inconsistent with his role responsibilities in teaching and working with students? How is his behavior inconsistent with his role responsibilities for contributing to the work of the department and for working with faulty colleagues? How might the department chair use existing policy about role responsibilities to obtain Dr. Seitz's cooperation for remedying his inappropriate behavior?

3. Plan for your next conversation with Dr. Seitz. How would you frame the issue? Be specific in considering the language you would use.

4. What might you do to curtail Dr. Seitz's inappropriate behavior in department meetings? What might you do to control Dr. Seitz's antics during your conversations with him?

Please Consider

Whenever managing inappropriate behavior, it is important to consider the context. For example, responding to inappropriate behavior in a group setting is very different from responding to the same inappropriate behavior in a one-on-one conversation. Similarly, Dr. Seitz is likely to reveal different information when talking only with the department chair than he might reveal in a department meeting. Consequently, the department chair will obtain different insights into Dr. Seitz's perspective from private conversations than he does from department meetings. In talking with Dr. Seitz, the department chair will want to pose open-ended questions, listen very hard to his reply, and follow up as necessary to fully understanding his perspective. In private conversations, the department chair can push Dr. Seitz to explain and articulate such things as his purpose for behaving as he does. At department meetings, the department chair can make observations that help to inform his understanding of Dr. Seitz's perspective. When does he interrupt? Is he more likely to become disruptive during the discussion of certain issues? Does he treat his colleagues similarly or differentially? Is there anyone in the department he appears to respect and heed?

Another context variable to consider is the length of time that Dr. Seitz has been permitted to behave inappropriately. When inappropriate behavior is permitted to continue without challenge for an extended period of time, the inappropriate behavior can become routine, even habitual, for the problem faculty member. We know from Case 9.3 that the previous department chairs exercised due diligence in addressing the inappropriate behavior, but the case offers no insight as to what strategies were used to remedy the problem performance. When working with problem faculty, exercising due diligence often requires more than discussing the inappropriate behavior with the problem faculty member, even though campus policy may make mention only of the need to discuss complaints with the individual faculty member. The longer Dr. Seitz is licensed to engage in the described inappropriate behaviors, the more challenging it will be to secure his cooperation to change—that is, unless through understanding Dr. Seitz's perspective, the department chair obtains information that can be used to help him understand that what he is doing accrues some disadvantage or self-harm.

Putting Theory into Practice

In Case 9.4, the department chair uncovers information about Dr. Seitz that he uses to manage his inappropriate behavior. Put yourself in the role of department chair as your read.

Case 9.4: Silence or Embarrassment

In observing Dr. Seitz during meetings, Reid notices that he typically sits opposite the department chair at the other end of a rectangular-shaped conference table. The department chair notices that whenever Dr. Seitz interrupts with a wisecrack or comment, he looks for others to turn toward him. The more attention he gets, the more he persists in peppering reports with questions and pointing out mistakes in an effort to discredit his colleagues. Dr. Seitz seems to enjoy making assertions or asking questions that are difficult, if not impossible, to answer. For example, the curriculum committee may be prepared to field questions about the advantages and disadvantages of the group's proposed plan but are unable to definitively respond to his assertion that the plan would cause the department to lose students. Through private conversation with

Dr. Seitz, the department chair learns that he truly believes he is brighter than anyone else and that his ego enjoys reminding his colleagues of their intellectual inferiority.

Changing the Meeting Dynamic

Armed with a more complete understanding of Dr. Seitz's perspective, Reid decides that nothing he or anyone else might say directly to the professor will motivate him to modify his behavior because the reaction he gets from colleagues and students feeds his ego. Reid concludes that his best option is to address Dr. Seitz's inappropriate behavior by changing how he chairs department meetings. More specifically, Reid believes he needs to chair meetings in a way that supports constructive contributions and thwarts destructive outbursts.

The Department Meeting

Department chair: Our only agenda today is continued discussion of the curriculum committee's proposal.

Dr. Seitz: Will we ever be done with this?

Department chair: If everyone, including you, comments only on the issue and makes only constructive comments, there's a good chance we can finish this today.

Dr. Seitz is taken aback by the department chair's remark and sits quietly for about 7 minutes before interrupting the ongoing discussion.

Dr. Joe Martin (an untenured assistant professor): I believe adding an experiential learning requirement will better prepare our students for ...

Dr. Seitz (interrupting): You have got to be kidding!

Department chair (holding up his hand in Dr. Seitz's direction while looking intently at Joe): Please finish your thought, Joe. You know a lot about experiential learning, and we need to take full advantage of your expertise.

Dr. Seitz is noticeably bothered by the department chair's dismissal of his remark and remains silent for about 10 minutes while department discussion continues. Absent Dr. Seitz's interruptions, consensus is easily reached.

Dr. Judith Lyons (a tenured full professor): I move that we approve the curriculum committee's proposal.

Dr. Seitz: Have you even read the proposal?

Department chair: Dr. Seitz, is there a substantive point you wish to make?

Dr. Seitz: I have raised many important issues that remain unanswered.

Department chair: I've heard you ask several open-ended questions that would require a crystal ball to answer, but I cannot recall your raising any substantive issues about the specific proposal being considered. What are your remaining concerns?

Dr. Seitz: My concerns should be in the minutes.

Department chair: I am certain the minutes record all substantive comments and questions made about the matter before us.
I believe we have addressed all of the relevant issues over the past few months. Is there a substantive issue we should consider before taking a vote?

Dr. Seitz: The last thing I want to do this extend this discussion.

Department chair: Seriously, is there is a substantive concern that we should consider before voting on the proposal?

Dr. Seitz: As I have said many times, this revision to the curriculum will cause us to lose students.

Department chair: I remember your saying that, but we haven't been able to get you to tell us why you believe the proposed revision will hurt enrollment. In fact, there is much evidence to the contrary. Please share the data that cause you to conclude our enrollment will be hurt by the proposed change in the curriculum.

Dr. Seitz: It's clear this is what you want to do, so why should I waste my time pulling information that is just going to be ignored.

Department chair (looking right at Dr. Seitz): If you have data or other factual information, we all want to see it and consider before taking a vote. I am happy to postpone the vote for 2 days so you can send us the data that supports your conclusion that the proposed change will hurt enrollment.

Dr. Seitz: It's pointless because I can tell that no one would listen to reason. Go ahead with your vote.

Department chair (still looking at Dr. Seitz): I've been here only a short time. However, I am confident that this group is persuaded by reason supported by data, but unsupported assertions will not stall our taking action. Now, do you have data to share that we should consider before taking a vote?

Dr. Seitz: It's time to end this huge waste of time. Take the vote.

Department chair: It seems we are ready to vote on the proposal.

Follow-Up Conversation

The department chair continues his practice of chairing department meetings in a way that shields faculty members from Dr. Seitz's barbs and challenges and reminds him that only reasoned comments will be considered. After several more department meetings, Dr. Seitz approaches the department chair.

Dr. Seitz: I don't like how you treat me in department meetings.
Department chair: What do you mean?
Dr. Seitz: When I call someone to task with a question or comment, you discredit me.
Department chair: I am committed to ensuring that our discussions remain focused on substance and will challenge any comment that distracts from the discussion.
Dr. Seitz: I have a right to ask questions and express my opinion.
Department chair: You certainly do as long as you are making a constructive contribution to the matter under discussion.
Dr. Seitz: Don't try to censor me.
Department chair: As long as your comments contribute to the ongoing discussion, everyone and I will want to hear all you have to say. We do not, however, need to hear comments that embarrass or belittle others.
Dr. Seitz: Don't take yourself or your job too seriously. Everyone knows I like to kid around. I have a quick wit, and my colleagues are accustomed to my humor.
Department chair: I am only in my first year, yet I am confident that no one appreciates the remarks you consider humorous.
Dr. Seitz: You're wrong about that.
Department chair: It doesn't matter if I am right or wrong. Such comments will not be tolerated during department meetings. You can count on me to check every such comment you make as I have been doing.

Let's Analyze the Case

The department chair uses observation and direct conversation with Dr. Seitz to learn that his inappropriate behavior feeds his ego. Dr. Seitz perceives himself as bright and seeks affirmation of his superior intelligence by challenging others in a public forum. Although Dr. Seitz would have others believe that his biting and often hurtful remarks are intended to be humorous, the department chair believes that his destructive behavior feeds his ego. Without an audience, the professor fails to receive the public affirmation of his intelligence that he seeks. Consequently, the department chair doubts that any private conversation with Dr. Seitz can be successful in motivating him to remedy his behavior. Because Dr. Seitz seeks gratification through the reaction of others to his remarks, the department chair believes that a different reaction from others will be required to motivate Herb to alter his behavior. The department chair, therefore, decides that his best strategy is to challenge Dr. Seitz in front of the colleagues he uses to affirm his self-assessed intellectual superiority.

The department chair decides to challenge Dr. Seitz's inappropriate behavior (and intellect) during department meetings by interrupting him before the colleague offended by him feels obliged to respond and by challenging him to support his assertions. This approach accomplishes three things. First, it renders Dr. Seitz's behavior ineffective in serving his purpose. If his inappropriate behavior is motivated by his need to demonstrate his intellectual superiority in front of others, his purpose for engaging inappropriate behavior will be undermined by the department chair's public challenge. Second, by challenging Dr. Seitz's inappropriate comments and unsubstantiated assertions in front of others, the department chair is publically challenging his intellect. Although others may perceive the department chair as putting Dr. Seitz in his place, he will likely perceive the chair's actions as a public affront on his intellect. Third, the department chair's approach demonstrates to the department that he steps up to difficult issues and manages difficult personalities. In this particular case scenario, the department chair's management of Dr. Seitz during department meetings leaves no doubt that reasoned perspectives are valued.

It is significant that Dr. Seitz approaches the department chair privately to complain about the department chair's treatment of him during department meetings. He probably fears that the department chair's treatment of him during department meetings is making him look bad in front of the very colleagues he strives to dominate with his intellect and quick wit. Yet Dr. Seitz decides to discuss the matter privately with the department chair instead of engaging in a battle of wits with the new department chair during the meeting. At this point, the department chair need only convince Dr. Seitz that he will continue to challenge him in meetings when he makes inappropriate remarks at the expense of others or attempts to derail meaningful discussion by making unsubstantiated assertions. The department chair has clarified role responsibilities in that he has made it clear that he conducts department meetings and all faculty members have a responsibility to substantiate assertions they make when discussing department matters. Dr. Seitz now must decide if the response he can count on from his chair is worth the satisfaction he receives from making his caustic remarks.

It's Your Turn

1. Do you agree with the department chair's approach? What other strategies might the department chair use to manage Dr. Seitz's disruptive behavior?

2. Does the department chair successfully depersonalizing his management of Dr. Seitz's disruptive behavior? Review Case 9.4, and note every moment in which the department chair takes the high road instead of waging a more personal attack on Dr. Seitz. Can you anticipate his reaction had the department chair's comments been statements about Dr. Seitz's personal character? For example, how might Dr. Seitz react if the department chair said, "You never have anything substantive to add because your purpose is only to disrupt department discussion."

3. Has the department chair reached a teachable moment with Dr. Seitz? If so, how would you advise the department chair to make the most of this teachable moment? What is the lesson to be learned, and how would you help Dr. Seitz learn this lesson?

4. Assume the position of department chair, and describe how you would secure Dr. Seitz's constructive participation in department matters.

Please Consider

It remains to be seen whether curtailing Dr. Seitz's disruptive behavior will be sufficient to motivate him to exhibit his intelligence in more productive ways. Ideally, he will be persuaded to feed his ego and affirm his intelligence through his work on department business rather than serving as the department's self-appointed critic. The department chair can help Dr. Seitz find more constructive ways to demonstrate his intelligence, and he needs to do this before Dr. Seitz becomes embittered for having lost his role as resident critic. Unless the department chair can help Dr. Seitz find more constructive ways to feed his ego, he could become an even more difficult faculty member to manage.

Hindsight Is 20/20

The new department chair's initial attempt to manage Dr. Seitz's inappropriate behavior fails because he is working from a faulty assumption. The new chair assumes that he will be able to manage this difficult faculty member more easily than previous department chairs because he was hired from outside the institution. The new department chair assumes that the failure of previous chairs is attributable to their having a colleague relationship with Dr. Seitz before becoming department chair. Although it is reasonable to believe that Dr. Seitz might have difficulty accepting a one-time colleague as department chair, the change in role relationships is not motivating disruptive behavior. By acting on this false assumption, the new department chair loses several months engaging in futile efforts to address Dr. Seitz's inappropriate behavior because his strategy did not address the motivation for his inappropriate behavior.

In addition to wasting time and energy, the new department chair jeopardizes his leadership credibility with all members of the department. Because Dr. Seitz's disruptive behavior is visible to all in the department, it is also apparent that the new department chair is unable to manage his antics. Further, the new department chair possesses a collaborative leadership style, which makes the ability to engage all department members in productive discussion essential to his leadership success. Dr. Seitz's inappropriate behavior at department meetings not only evidences the new department chair's inability to manage his disruptive behavior but also disrupts the very process that the new department chair uses to lead the department in doing department work. Consequently, managing Dr. Seitz's inappropriate behavior is essential to preserving the new department chair's leadership credibility and success.

The new department chair needed to take some time to assess the validity of his initial assumption and discern more precisely the motivation for Dr. Seitz's inappropriate behavior. When department chairs operate on the basis of faulty assumptions, their strategies are doomed to fail. No matter how pressing the problem, it is prudent to take the time needed to accurately assess the situation and discern the salient motives that encourage inappropriate problem behavior.

Let's Recap

Department chairs will be more effective in managing the inappropriate behavior of faculty members if they first take the time needed to understand the difficult faculty member's perspective. How does the difficult faculty member perceive the issue or situation? Is there any area of common ground that might be used to reach consensus on a difficult issue? What motivates the difficult faculty member to behave inappropriately? The answers to these questions can be infinite, which is why it is essential to begin by understanding the perspective of the difficult faculty member. The difficult faculty member's perspective will help guide how to frame the issues and select the language used to engage the difficult faculty member in more productive discussion.

For discussions with difficult faculty members to remain productive, department chairs need to continually depersonalize the issues of disagreement. It is acceptable and helpful to discuss behaviors that are inappropriate without assigning personal attributes to the difficult faculty member. In Case 9.4, for example, it is appropriate for the department chair to ask Dr. Seitz to offer support for his assertion that the proposed change would hurt enrollment. It would not be appropriate or helpful for the department chair to accuse Dr. Seitz of wanting to disrupt department progress even though his behavior is disruptive. The former approach makes no disparaging conclusion about Herb's motivation but makes clear Dr. Seitz's faculty responsibility to support the claims he makes. The latter approach, however, constitutes a personal attack on Herb, which will license Dr. Seitz to defend himself and frees him from supporting his assertion. Only by depersonalizing the issue of disagreement and clarifying role responsibilities and performance expectations can department chairs curtail the inappropriate behavior of difficult faculty members.

Finally, when working with difficult faculty members, it is important to create and seize teachable moments. The teachable moment is essential to preventing a reoccurrence of the inappropriate behavior being addressed. Yet the difficult faculty member must be in a receptive frame of mind for a teachable moment to be effective. For a teachable moment to be effective, the difficult faculty member must be receptive to the lesson being taught. This cannot happen when an individual's defenses are heightened. In creating an effective teachable moment, it is helpful to link the learning to the faculty member's role responsibilities, professional goals, or espoused views. Although none of these leadership communication strategies by themselves will likely be the silver bullet needed to address and remedy inappropriate faculty behavior, all should be considered in dealing with each situation.

MANAGING THE DISMISSAL OF A TENURED FACULTY MEMBER

DEPARTMENT CHAIRS WHO BELIEVE that it is impossible to dismiss tenured faculty for not meeting performance expectations can feel helpless in managing difficult tenured faculty members. Although it is true that the more common basis for dismissing a tenured faculty member is financial exigency or moral turpitude, most institutions have policies that permit the dismissal of a tenured faculty member for cause. These policies typically describe in detail the process to be followed in providing a tenured faculty member with appropriate notice of the performance issue and sufficient time and support to remedy the performance concern. Tenure does not protect a faculty member against wrongdoing, nor does tenure license behavior that violates campus policy or fails to meet the institution's performance expectations for faculty.

The goal of this chapter is to help department chairs know how to build a case when addressing performance issues, which if not remedied might lead to the dismissal of a tenured faculty member. A second goal of this chapter is to help department chairs know how to enlist support from the administration in managing difficult performance issues. Although the case scenario presented in this chapter focuses on addressing inappropriate faculty behavior with students inside and outside the classroom, the leadership communication strategies presented can be used in addressing any area of unacceptable faculty performance.

Defining the Task

Department chairs can find it challenging to address performance concerns with tenured faculty members especially when faculty members hold the misguided notion that tenure protects them from sanction and even critique. The challenge is magnified on campuses without a merit pay component for salary increases. In times of tight budgets and low or no faculty salary increases, department chairs find they have little within their control that they can use to motivate difficult tenured faculty members to address performance concerns. Nonetheless, department chairs are the custodians of academic quality and therefore are responsible for addressing problem faculty performance.

Ideally, department chairs can use leadership communication strategies to successfully counsel faculty to improved performance. For more information on effective performance counseling, see Higgerson (1996, pp. 106–138) and Higgerson and Joyce (2007, pp. 115–130). When a difficult faculty member proves impossible to counsel, the department chair still must manage the ramifications of the problem performance. Depending on the nature of the problem performance, a department chair may need to manage complaints from students, parents, faculty colleagues, and others. Should the problem performance persist, a department chair can lose credibility with those individuals and constituencies who seek remedy for the problem performance or who must take on additional work to compensate for a faculty member's problem performance. For example, faculty members, who complain that a colleague's poor work in advising students creates inequitable workloads for faculty who take advising seriously, will become increasingly unhappy with a department chair who does not address and remedy the situation. If allowed to persist, such inequities can have an adverse impact on faculty morale and the department chair's leadership credibility. It does little good for the department chair to explain that he or she has tried talking with the problem faculty member without positive result because such explanation only fuels the perception that the department chair is ineffective in addressing the problem performance that is creating inequitable workloads.

Department chairs need to address problem performance whether or not the faculty member holds tenure. In those instances when problem performance is harmful to the department and does not improve with performance counseling, the department chair needs to document efforts to address the problem performance such that there exists a sound basis for pursuing the dismissal of the tenured faculty member. This process can take several months or years depending on the nature of the problem performance and campus policy for serving tenured faculty members with appropriate notice and time to remedy problem performance. There is always the possibility that moving in this direction will motivate the problem faculty member to remedy his or her performance issues.

Relevant Leadership Communication Strategies

Department chairs should not assume the department is stuck with a tenured faculty member who is not meeting performance expectations. However, the management of a difficult tenured faculty requires the persistent and careful implementation of specific leadership communication strategies that, in the best case scenario, will improve problem performance and, if not, support the successful dismissal of the problem tenured faculty member. The following leadership communication strategies will aid department chairs in managing difficult tenured faculty.

Make Performance Expectations Clear

Performance expectations must be clearly understood before any individual can be held accountable for meeting performance expectations. Making performance expectations clear for tenured faculty members can be challenging because tenured faculty are accustomed to having considerable autonomy. Unfortunately, some of the challenges facing higher education today place demands on faculty time and expertise that curtail faculty autonomy. At one time, faculty could work when and where they wanted as long as they met their assigned classes and satisfied institutional expectations for research and service. Today, faculty members must comply with countless requests for their time and expertise in support of a range of institutional priorities. Depending on the institution, faculty may be expected to help recruit prospective students, be more accessible to students outside of class, assess student learning in ways that go beyond assigning a grade, meet with prospective donors, help draft documents needed for accreditation reviews or other administrative reports, and serve on an increasing number of committees. Whereas younger untenured faculty members know only the current expectations for faculty work, tenured faculty may be less prone to acknowledge and accept seemingly new assignments as integral to faculty responsibilities.

The task of making performance expectations clear to tenured faculty members can be especially challenging for new department chairs who inherit faculty that were not previously held accountable for meeting performance expectations. The process of making new performance expectations clear for tenured faculty needs to be done such that the tenured faculty understand assigned responsibilities are performance expectations established by the institution and not at the whim of the department chair. Further, department chairs need to affirm that performance expectations are the same for all tenured faculty members. Should one faculty member be perceived as receiving preferential treatment, it can lower faculty morale and have an adverse effect on the department climate and the department chair's leadership credibility. Department chairs can use the following strategies to help faculty members understand performance expectations.

OPERATIONALIZE POLICY Campus policy is drafted in general terms and uses language that cannot possibly communicate department-specific connotations. For example, campus policy describing faculty responsibilities may make mention of faculty responsibility for supporting and advancing student learning, but it is left to department leadership to communicate what that means at any given point in time within the department. Department chairs must help tenured faculty understand how the learning needs of today's students alter the expectations for faculty performance. In some departments, such policy language may require providing students with professional internships and educating them on employer expectations. Tenured faculty who began teaching a decade earlier may not recognize that doing such things are now legitimate expectations for faculty performance in the area of teaching.

CREATE OPPORTUNITIES TO OBSERVE DESIRED PERFORMANCE Current challenges facing higher education alter how faculty teach and how institutions assess student learning. As a result, tenured faculty are not always more expert then untenured faculty in meeting the institution's performance expectations for faculty. Ideally, department chairs want to create an environment in which all faculty members can learn from each other. In doing so, department chairs can break down the caste system that sometimes exists between tenured and untenured faculty and spawn a more productive department climate in which all faculty members (tenured, untenured, term, and part-time) possess mutual respect for the contributions of each other and a better understanding of how their individual expertise contributes to the welfare of the total department.

Document Efforts to Address Problem Performance

It is a good idea to document efforts to address problem performance sooner rather than later. Doing so can be especially helpful to the faculty member being counseled because the documentation can serve as an aid to memory and a guide for making needed improvements. It can be difficult to hear and comprehend information shared when being counseled about problem performance. Moreover, the faculty member being counseled may experience a range of emotions from embarrassment to defensive anger. Performance counseling documentation can affirm that the counsel is intended to be constructive. To be effective, performance counseling documentation must meet the following three standards.

USE BEHAVIORS TO DESCRIBE PROBLEM PERFORMANCE   It is possible to avoid evoking a defensive response from the counseled individual by using behaviors to describe the problem performance instead of adjectives that label the individual. For example, to tell a faculty member that his or her language is insulting will likely invite defensiveness because it offers only a negative criticism and does not help the faculty member understand what he or she is saying that others perceive as insulting. Instead, the performance counseling documentation might read as follows: "Students take offense when you tell them that they are lazy and dumb. When students are offended, they stop listening and are less likely to learn what it is you are trying to communicate."

PROVIDE A SUMMARY OF ISSUES DISCUSSED, SUPPORT OFFERED, AND SUGGESTIONS MADE TO REMEDY THE PROBLEM PERFORMANCE   The faculty member being counseled cannot be expected to remember everything that is said so a written summary of the issues discussed and suggestions offered can be helpful to both the counseled faculty member and department chair. Again, use only behaviors to describe the performance issues and suggestions discussed. For example, instead of writing that the faculty member was told to stop offending students, a department chair might write, "You explained that you strive to have students work hard and take your class more seriously. We discussed how instead of telling students that they are lazy and dumb, you should challenge them to think about how they might handle a particular situation if the class assignment were made by their employer and would determine their opportunity for professional advancement."

BUILD A FILE THAT CHRONICLES EFFORTS OVER TIME TO ADDRESS THE PROBLEM PERFORMANCE   All documentation should be specific, factual, and dated so that the file overtime chronicles the department chair's comprehensive and sustained effort to help a faculty member succeed in meeting performance expectations. Should others be involved in helping an individual faculty member address problem performance, those efforts should be documented as well. Documentation can range from an informal file note to a formal memorandum or formally prepared reviews following class observations.

Review Relevant Policy

It is always a good idea to review relevant policy even when department chairs believe they are very familiar with the relevant policy. Inevitably, a careful review of the relevant policy with the specific situation in mind will yield important details that might have been overlooked. It is also a good idea to review the individual faculty member's letter of appointment or employment contract for special provisions or commitments that might have bearing on the problem performance. For example, if the performance concern is in the area of research, it can be significant that the institution has failed to honor a commitment to supply specific lab equipment that is detailed in the faculty member's letter of appointment.

KNOW INSTITUTIONAL EXPECTATIONS FOR FACULTY PERFORMANCE

Most institutions have written expectations for faculty performance. However, this information may not be contained in a single policy. The institution's policy on promotion and tenure will establish the performance criteria for faculty to earn tenure and promotion to each professorial rank. There may also exist a separate statement on faculty work and responsibilities. Further, many institutions have policies that prescribe how faculty and staff should interact and work with others. Often, these policies reside in a document titled "Code of Civility" or "Professional Conduct Code." All of these policies may be found in a faculty handbook, but it is also possible that the relevant policies are not found in the same document. For example, policy written to guide the behavior of both faculty and staff may be found in personnel policy rather than in the faculty handbook.

UNDERSTAND THE LIMITS OF YOUR LEADERSHIP RESPONSIBILITIES

The leadership responsibilities for department chairs and other administrative positions are detailed in policy. The leadership responsibilities assigned to department chairs can vary greatly from one institution to another, and it is a mistake for department chairs to assume that assigned leadership responsibilities are the same for their current position as they were elsewhere. Similarly, it is a mistake to believe that all leadership responsibilities were made clear during the interview. It is important for department chairs to understand precisely the limits of their leadership responsibility as detailed in policy. If the limits of assigned leadership responsibly are not clear, department chairs should seek clarification from their immediate supervisor before managing problem faculty performance.

UNDERSTAND THE IMPLICATIONS OF DUE PROCESS   Generally, personnel policy incorporates the concept of due process. Although the details and timelines may vary from campus to campus, individuals (faculty and staff) are afforded due process. This means that individuals have the right to appropriate and timely notice of a performance concerns before any sanctions can be applied. In other words, an individual cannot be sanctioned for problem performance without first being notified of a concern and given an opportunity to remedy that concern.

Involve Others in Seeking Appropriate Remedies

The good news is that department chairs need not shoulder the responsibility for addressing problem performance alone. Department chairs can involve others in seeking appropriate remedies the moment they recognize that the problem performance cannot be successfully remedied without the assistance and intervention of others. Who is invited to help will depend upon the specifics of the problem performance. For example, if the problem performance is attributable to some learning curve deficiency, it can be helpful to involve other faculty members who might help mentor the faculty member with problem performance. If the problem performance represents violation of the sexual harassment policy, department chairs will want to involve the campus sexual harassment officer. If problem performance represents a breach of contract responsibilities, department chairs will want to involve their administrative supervisor and possibly legal counsel and human resources.

BRIEF YOUR SUPERVISOR AND SOLICIT SUGGESTIONS FOR MANAGING THE PROBLEM PERFORMANCE   Department chairs will want to brief their supervisors whether or not their supervisors need to be involved in addressing the problem performance. This prevents the supervisor from being surprised should the problem performance escalate in a way that becomes more visible on campus. In briefing their supervisors, department chairs have an opportunity to describe all of their efforts to date to manage the problem performance and to help the individual faculty member be successful in addressing the performance concern. These briefings are an opportunity to solicit suggestions for managing the problem performance. Exercising this strategy can both enhance the department chair's leadership credibility and yield new strategies for managing the problem performance.

CONSULT LEGAL COUNSEL AND OTHER CAMPUS EXPERTS Department chairs are well served to use all available campus expertise and resources when managing problem performance. For example, legal counsel can help draft a memorandum in a way that reduces the liability should the problem performance escalate into a grievance or lawsuit. Similarly, human resources will be able to help if the problem performance is attributable to some mental or emotional condition. The campus sexual harassment officer can advise on language to use and strategies to employ should the problem performance be governed by the institution's sexual harassment policy.

WHEN APPROPRIATE, INVOLVE DEPARTMENT FACULTY IN MENTOR-ING IMPROVED PERFORMANCE Depending on the individual's person-ality and the nature of the problem performance, it can be helpful to involve faculty colleagues in mentoring improved performance. Faculty colleagues, for example, can be credible mentors on performance issues around teaching and research. Being mentored by faculty colleagues can help reduce anxiety for some faculty who are more defensive when being evaluated and coached by the department chair. Keeping a faculty mem-ber's defensiveness in check is essential to having that faculty member hear and understand what must be done to remedy problem performance.

Putting Theory into Practice

Although these strategies may seem simple, failure to execute them can make the task of managing the dismissal of a tenured faculty member extremely difficult, if not impossible. In Case 10.1, the department chair of political science is having a difficult time getting a tenured faculty member to address performance concerns that have become more serious over time. Place yourself in the role of the department chair as you read.

Case 10.1: What's It Going to Take?

Margaret Burke has served as chair of the Department of Political Science for more than 20 years. For the most part, she enjoys chairing the department and finds it especially gratifying to mentor new faculty hires. Margaret's experience in mentoring Zach Bridges is proving to be the exception. Although Margaret faithfully gives Zach the benefit of the doubt with each new student complaint, Zach steadfastly elects to ignore his chair's counsel. In 7 years, Zach has not altered his approach to teaching, and Margaret continues to hear the same student complaints she addressed during Zach's first semester at the college.

The College

St. Luclaire College is a small, private, liberal arts institution with a long history of successfully meeting the learning needs of students. Faculty at St. Luclaire College take pride in being able to meet individual students where they are in their academic development and help them realize levels of achievement they never thought possible. St. Luclaire College boasts that students benefit from small class sizes and a nurturing learning environment.

Department chairs at St. Luclaire College report to the dean of the college who has responsibility for all academic programs and reports directly to the college president. Given the rather flat organizational structure at the institution, students are comfortable talking with the dean of the college and the president about their experience at St. Luclaire College.

In general, the rapport between faculty and students is excellent across the campus. Students typically rate faculty members and instruction very highly on the end of semester student ratings assessment. Students are more likely to tell the dean and president when a faculty member is especially helpful than they are to complain about an instructor or class.

Zach Bridges

Zach applied for a full-time faculty position at St. Luclaire College when he was denied tenure at a 4-year public institution in another part of the country. During the interview, Zach explained that he did not fit the campus culture at his previous institution because he is more focused on teaching and building a personal rapport with students than on getting grants to support research. He said the experience persuaded him work at an institution where teaching excellence is valued. All who met Zach supported his hire, and the fact that he was denied tenure elsewhere did not raise concerns because teaching excellence is a priority at St. Luclaire College.

During Zach Bridges's first semester at St. Luclaire College, a few students complained that comments Dr. Bridges may intend to be humorous were not funny at all. For example, one student reported being chastised in front of the class for arriving late. According to the student, Dr. Bridges was unpacking his briefcase and class had not started, but Dr. Bridges told everyone that the student was late because he still needs his mother to get him up on time. In a similar scenario, Dr. Bridges told the class that another student was late because she could not find clean underwear and asked the class to let him know if the smell grew too great to bear. In each instance, Margaret Burke discussed the student complaint with Zach. She made clear that he has a right to expect students to be on time for class and suggested ways to address tardiness without humiliating individual students. Zach did not become defensive and listened to the suggestions gracefully while professing that the students gave no indication of being upset by his statements.

Margaret heard roughly 20 student complaints throughout Zach's 6-year probationary period. Although all the student complaints might be categorized as inappropriate attempts at humor, Margaret can understand why students perceive his comments as insensitive and derogatory. At the same time, Margaret found Zach to be appropriately contrite when they discussed these student complaints. His approachable nature coupled with respectable student evaluations of his teaching were sufficient for him to secure the department's support on his application for tenure at St. Luclaire College. Margaret reasoned that Zach means well even though he would be well served to tone down his personality and eliminate his wisecracks when interacting with students. Moreover, Zach's pattern of being profusely apologetic with each new student complaint persuaded Margaret that Zach was trying to address the student concerns that centered on his inappropriate use of humor in the classroom.

Zach hosted a party for his department colleagues when he was granted tenure at St. Luclaire College. He was the life of the party, and all in attendance had an opportunity to observe his misplaced efforts at being humorous. At the party, he made a long-winded toast thanking his colleagues for their support of his quest for tenure that included several personal and inappropriate comments. For example, Zach thanked a female colleague for the way she walked because it gave him something to look forward to at work. He thanked a male colleague for bringing his good-looking wife to the party. Perhaps the most sobering moment was when he concluded his toast by saying how much it meant to him to finally hold tenure status because he was now free to be himself and was no longer required to answer to anyone.

Student Concerns Increase

Almost immediately after Zach earned tenure at St. Luclaire College, more students filed complaints about him with department chair Margaret Burke. Comments that once seemed like bumbling efforts at inappropriate humor when relating to students have now blossomed into insulting and inappropriate remarks. Moreover, Zach's comments now seem to be entirely out of line. For example, when a student offered a comment during a class discussion, Dr. Bridges said, "Your thinking is so gay. I hope you are planning your coming out party." In another class, an adult student reported feeling singled out for his advanced age when Dr. Bridges said, "I bet Joe can tell us about the influence of the civil war on the U.S. economy because I understand he fought with the Union army." On another day, when the same adult student entered class, Dr. Bridges commented out loud, "I can't think for all of Joe's huffing and puffing. That's what comes of being old and out of shape."

Margaret continues to discuss every student complaint with Zach, who never denies making the statements and continues to profess that he had no idea his comments upset anyone. Since earning tenure, however, Zach defends his statements by explaining to Margaret his belief that effective teaching requires an instructor to establish an informal rapport with students. He explains how poking fun at this or that student helps him build an informal rapport with students. With each new complaint, Margaret learns more about Zach's philosophy of teaching. For example, when discussing why it is inappropriate to call attention to someone's age, gender, or sexual orientation, Zach explained that he wants his students to perceive him as a cool guy and good pal and how he strives to be perceived as someone with whom students can confide and share gossip. When a female student asked to discuss a paper on which she received a much lower grade than expected, Dr. Bridges told her to stop complaining. Before the student could respond, he added, "Maybe if you get back on your meds, you'll stop bitching and start studying."

Soon after being granted tenure, both the number and nature of student complaints about Dr. Bridges escalated to serious proportion. Margaret can no longer imagine that anyone would consider Dr. Bridges's statements as bumbling attempts at humor because the statements attributed to him represent insulting and unkind remarks about the recipient's gender, age, weight, sexual orientation, or disability. Margaret is glad she documented her conversations with Zach in memos to him that describe the concerns discussed and Margaret's suggestions for how Zach should respond to them even though Zach has never acknowledged receipt of any follow-up documentation.

When more students complained to the department chair, Zach added the following statement to his syllabus:

> Please be forewarned that bright, hardworking students do very
> well in my classes, and I abhor students who whine and file
> complaints about my teaching when all they need to do is work
> hard and get with the program.

Dr. Bridges's warning increased the number of student complaints filed with the department chair. Students are now coming in groups to report on specific incidents. Because the students fear retaliation, they refuse to give the department chair permission to discuss the reported incidents with Dr. Bridges. Given the small size of the department faculty, students majoring in political science typically take at least three courses from Dr. Bridges. Occasionally, a graduating senior will give permission if the chair promises not to talk with Dr. Bridges about the reported incident until after graduation. According to the students, Dr. Bridges has buddies in every class who help him figure out who complained. Margaret learned that these buddies are students enrolled in the class who are perceived by most as his favorites because they laugh at his jokes and go drinking with him. Margaret feels powerless to pursue that matter with Dr. Bridges because students refuse permission to do so. Still, she knows she must do something.

Let's Analyze the Case

Margaret's persistence in discussing student concerns with Zach has not persuaded him to revise his behavior, and, subsequently, the number of student complaints continues to increase. Margaret supported his application for tenure because she believed he meant well and was sincere in trying to address the student concerns even though she could understand how some students were offended by his language. Since earning tenure, however, the number of student complaints has increased. Although Zach continues to be apologetic and express surprise that anyone finds his comments offensive, there is tangible evidence that he is attempting to stifle students who may wish to complain. Zach added a statement to his syllabus that makes clear he perceives students who complain as needing to work hard and get with the program. This suggests that he does not find the student concerns to be valid or credible comments about his teaching. In other words, Zach dismisses the student concerns as whining from students who choose not to work hard in his classes. His unresponsiveness suggests that he believes it is the students who need to change, whereas his teaching is fine, indeed excellent, as it is.

Zach was thrilled to earn tenure at St. Luclaire College and explained that, for him, tenure means he is now free to be himself. Almost immediately the number of student concerns about him increased, and the department chair now has reason to doubt his sincerity when he professes that he has no idea his language or actions offended anyone. Their discussions about student concerns have become patterned with Zach apologetically professing ignorance while explaining the pedagogical merit of his instruction. Still, Margaret notes that Zach remains unresponsive to student concerns that warrant remedy.

Margaret has followed protocol. As department chair, she listens carefully to student concerns about Zach and shares these concerns with him. She protects student identity when requested to do so by individual students. Margaret has done her best to help Zach understand and respond constructively to student concerns. The fact that the same student concerns persist makes clear that he dismisses them. Now, the statement in his syllabus and reports of his student buddies who rat out students who file complaints with the department chair have Margaret concerned that Zach would rather stifle student concerns than address them. Margaret must alter her approach to Zach and the situation in a way that persuades him to be responsive to student concerns that warrant remedy because the long-term welfare of the department will be jeopardized if he is permitted to remain on the faculty while exercising his unique brand of pedagogy.

It's Your Turn

Assume the position of department chair in this case, and think through what you would do to manage Zach's problem performance.

1. How would you revise your communication in discussing the student concerns with Zach? Be specific in deciding how you would structure your next conversation with Zach, and what you would say to him. Anticipate Zach's response to your revised approach, and tell how would you manage it.

2. How would you document your efforts to address Zach's problem performance? Would you share the documentation with others? If so, who would you inform and why?

3. If this scenario played out on your campus, what policy documents would you review in devising your plan for managing Zach?

4. Would you involve others in persuading Zach that the student concerns warrant remedy? If so, who would you involve and why? Specifically, what would you ask others to do? What information would you share with others? If you plan to involve several individuals, would you provide each with the same information? If not, why not?

5. What, if any, effort would you make to illustrate that you had exercised due diligence in addressing the situation of Zach's problem performance? Do you anticipate being asked to justify the department's support of Zach's tenure application? If so, how would you respond?

Please Consider

The ongoing discussions between department chair Margaret Burke and Zach Bridges about student concerns have become patterned. Zach has been allowed to stay the course without making the requested remedy. In a sense, Zach has learned that making profuse apology and appearing sincere in his desire to not offend anyone is a sufficient response to student concerns. When the management of problem performance falls into a patterned interaction, little will change unless the patterned communication changes. In this case scenario, Zach must realize that his apology and sincerity are no longer a sufficient response to the student concerns. Until then, there is no reason to believe he will remedy his behavior.

The good news is that the department chair does not need Zach's cooperation to alter the patterned communication. In any patterned communication, it only takes one individual to alter his or her communication in order to change the patterned communication. In other words, Margaret can interrupt the patterned communication and force Zach to respond differently by altering her communication. Margaret can alter her communication by changing the way she structures the meeting or by changing the language she uses. For example, Margaret can remove an informal tone through any number of tactics such as indicating in advance that they will likely need more time, asking to meet at the end of the day to avoid interruption, or preparing a typed summary of the concerns that is handed to Zach during the meeting for response. Margaret can also elevate the importance of the student concerns by pushing for a concrete action plan and setting dates for subsequent conversations to check progress. These tactics will be more effective if Zach respects Margaret's leadership authority and perceives her as a credible leader. If Zach perceives Margaret as an ineffective department chair with no real authority, it will be more difficult for he to alter the patterned communication by herself. Fortunately, Margaret is not without other alternatives for changing the patterns of communication.

Adding new voices to the conversation can change nonproductive, patterned communication. Inviting new voices to the conversation will immediately signal that the status quo has changed. Whereas Zach may have grown comfortable with how Margaret would hear and accept is apology and sincere expression, a new listener will immediately force Zach to reconsider his position and how it is heard. Zach, for example, would likely find it more difficult to explain and defend his view that he wants students to perceive him as a buddy that they can confide in if the institution's dean of students is in the meeting. Similarly, Zach will find it more difficult to contend he had no idea anyone would take offense to his mention of an overweight student being fat if the institution's sexual harassment officer is in the meeting. Adding other relevant individuals to a patterned conversation can be helpful in forcing a problem faculty member to address problem performance.

Let's Recap

Take a moment to review your plan for interrupting the patterned communication with Zach and persuading him that the student concerns warrant remedy. Before employing your approach, you will want to make sure that you

- ○ Make performance expectations clear.
- ○ Document efforts to address the problem performance.
- ○ Review relevant policy.
- ○ Consider involving other individuals.

Putting Theory into Practice

Once you have decided how you would proceed, you are ready to read Case 10.2. Again, put yourself in the role of the department chair and decide if Margaret's approach is similar to one you would use in addressing Zach's problem performance.

Case 10.2: A Teamed Approach

For a full academic year following Zach's successful tenure review, Margaret tried working directly with the now tenured professor while protecting students' identities. She finds it difficult to make much headway, and she is hearing both more and increasingly serious student complaints. Meanwhile, Zach appears confident, even cocky, about his teaching effectiveness. Whenever Margaret talks to him about having observed this or that, he quickly defends his actions as being sound pedagogy. On occasion, he reminds her that teaching is his primary focus and adds that she should wish other faculty were as committed to students as he is. Zach maintains that he works hard at teaching and is very good at it.

All faculty members are required to provide the department chair with copies of their syllabi, so Margaret was able to ask Zach about the warning statement he now includes without revealing that students raised concerns about it. Zach was not the least bit apologetic or embarrassed by Margaret's mention of the warning statement. On the contrary, he professed that it was high time at least one faculty member hold students accountable for working hard. The more Margaret tries to talk with Zach about his interactions with students, the more concerned she becomes. His ego is enormous, and he cannot hear comments that suggest he is not already an excellent teacher. Worse yet, the specific behaviors that worry Margaret affirm Zach's inflated perception of himself. For example, Margaret believes it is inappropriate for Zach to clown around with a few of the male students as though he is their fraternity brother instead of their instructor. However, he views these interactions as evidence of his informal rapport with students, which he believes is essential to teaching well. Zach professes that students work harder for cool teachers who they like.

Department Chair's Dilemma

The department chair has a problem. A potentially harmful situation is growing worse, and Margaret finds Zach unwilling to hear or implement any suggestions for how he should modify his interactions with students. His interactions with students are becoming increasingly inappropriate and could be harmful to the department if allowed to continue. An increasing number of students report feeling bullied and picked on while a few male students are invited into a personal relationship with Zach that includes some level of socializing outside of class. Although Margaret has only student reports of Zach inviting certain male students out for a beer, she finds them credible given her own observations of his fraternity-like banter with a few of the male students in the office lobby.

Margaret recognizes that her efforts to mentor Zach have been ineffective. Zach is unreceptive to Margaret's counsel because he believes that his pedagogical approach is both positive and effective. Margaret is out of ideas for how she might get through to Zach, especially with the students' unwillingness to grant permission for her to discuss with him the specific incidents that they report to her. Margaret realizes her credibility with the students is vulnerable if they do not perceive a positive outcome from having talked with her about their concerns. She also knows that the students are likely to take their concerns to the dean of the college or even the president. Moreover, Margaret could lose credibility with the dean should the students inform him that they shared their concerns with her on numerous occasions without positive results.

Involving the Dean of the College

Margaret decides to brief the dean of the college on the student concerns and the difficulty she is having in mentoring Zach. In doing so, Margaret bulleted the following performance issues:

- o Making derogatory statements about individual students to other students after the department chair has made clear this is inappropriate;
- o Exercising behavior that causes some students to report feeling intimidated, bullied, or uncomfortable because Dr. Bridges's actions single them out on the basis of gender, age, sexual orientation, or disability; and
- o Befriending a few male students in a seemingly inappropriate manner.

Margaret compiles a timeline of the student complaints and her conversations with Zach about the student concerns and attaches file notes of her conversations with students and Zach. Recently, Margaret began to send follow-up emails to Zach summarizing their conversations about the performance issue, and she attaches these emails to the timeline. She complies a list of the students who complained to illustrate that 82% of the department's majors enrolled in courses he teaches have filed at least one complaint. The supporting information documents the increase in the number of student complaints over time and provides a snapshot of the time and energy invested by the department chair to address the student concerns.

Margaret sent the documentation in advance of her meeting with the dean and was relieved when the dean acknowledges that Margaret exercised good judgment in realizing that a different type of intervention will be needed to secure Zach's cooperation in addressing the students' concerns. From this meeting forward, the department chair and dean worked as a team to counsel Zach to improve his performance.

A Teamed Approach

For the next 4 years, the dean of the college joins Margaret in meeting with Zach whenever student concerns warrant a conversation. Zach takes note that concerns about his teaching are no longer confined to the department chair. He no longer defends his actions. Instead, Zach remains collegial and very cooperative through all conversations with the dean and department chair. No matter the student concern, Zach professes that he had no idea his language or action was offensive, and he routinely thanks the dean and his department chair for bringing the matter to his attention. When the same performance issue resurfaces, Zach explains how he saw the current complaint as different from the situation discussed previously. For example, Zach maintains that he had no idea it was inappropriate to socialize with some of the hardest working students outside of class. When the issue resurfaced, Zach professed that he had understood the earlier discussion to mean that it was inappropriate for him to invite students out, and in the latest incident some bright and hard-working students had invited him to join them for a beer at a nearby restaurant and pub. The next time that the same issue occured, Zach professed that he did not understood he could not talk with students he happened to see when he was out for the evening. Discussions with Zach quickly get off track when he professes ignorance and asks such things as whether or not it was appropriate for him to say hello to a student he might see at the drugstore.

Following every meeting with Zach, the dean and department chair send a memo to Zach summarizing the concerns discussed, Zach's response to the concerns, and the suggestions made for how he should address the student concerns. Zach complied with the dean's request that he take a workshop on sexual harassment. He also attended a conference on pedagogy that addresses best practice for interacting with today's students. Although Zach professes that he learned a lot from both the sexual harassment workshop and pedagogy conference, there is no evidence that either program has persuaded him to alter his behavior with students. Students continue to report similar concerns. If anything, he seems emboldened to do as he pleases, and the student reports now describe behavior that is even more outrageous. For example, students report that he makes very personal remarks to individual female students about their weight and their need to diet and exercise. Even some of the male students who are so-called buddies with him complain that they are uncomfortable when he makes derogatory comments about other students to them. Students report that he identifies individual students by name when telling other students that the named student peer is a pain in the ass, dumber than a stick, fatter than a pregnant hippo, or a waste of space on this earth. Student reports suggest that Dr. Bridges's language inside and outside of class is becoming more insulting and offensive.

The dean and department chair are uncertain whether Zach can be responsive to student concerns. He is now in his eleventh year at St. Luclaire College, and meetings with the dean and department chair to discuss student concerns continue on a regular basis. Students are steadily growing more vocal with their unhappiness, and there has been no improvement in his interactions with students. More specifically, Zach continues to

- Make derogatory statements about individual students to other students after being told repeatedly that this is inappropriate.
- Exercise behavior that causes some students to report feeling intimidated, bullied, or uncomfortable because his actions single them out on the basis of gender, age, sexual orientation, or disability.
- Befriend a few male students in a seemingly inappropriate manner.

There is no demonstrable evidence that Zach learned anything from attending a workshop on sexual harassment and a pedagogy conference on best practices for interacting with today's students. Conversations with the dean and the department chair have become patterned with Zach professing ignorance and thanking them profusely for bringing each concern to his attention. The memos documenting Zach's conversations with the dean and department chair have become more direct and now include mention of the time, effort, and resources invested to help him meet the institution's performance expectations for effective teaching. Nonetheless, Zach shows no inclination to change his behavior.

Altering the Message

Up until now, the dean and the department chair have given Zach the full benefit of the doubt. Had he become argumentative or defensive in his meetings with the dean or the department chair, push might have come to shove sooner. However, his profusely apologetic response caused the dean and the department chair to give him more opportunity than might be customary to remedy inappropriate behavior. Clearly, doing so seems to license Zach to ignore their repeated counsel and continue to do as he wishes.

The dean and department chair agree that it is time to change their approach in talking with him. They need an approach that will be more productive in motivating him to change his behavior. Armed with a fresh batch of student complaints, they decide it is time to devise a new approach to their next meeting with Zach.

Let's Analyze the Case

By involving the dean of the college, Margaret successfully shared responsibility for managing Zach's problem performance. When a department chair's effort to address problem performance is unsuccessful, it can be very helpful to involve others. By involving key individuals, a chair can share responsibility for managing the problem performance. Further, involving others serves to interrupt any patterned communication that may exist between a department chair and problem faculty member. This is often essential in successfully addressing sustained and serious problem performance.

In Case 10.2, Zach takes note that the student concerns now have the dean's attention. This alters Zach's communication in that he no longer defends his language and behavior as being integral to his views on effective pedagogy. Still, he professes ignorance that his comments are offensive to students, and he thanks the dean and department chair for calling the student concerns to his attention. Zach's noncombative response to the dean and department chair helps to keep the issue from escalating even though continuing complaints from students give them no reason to believe that he intends to change his behavior. Because Zach complied with the request to take a workshop on sexual harassment and attend a conference on best practices for interacting with today's students, the dean and department chair are obliged to afford him time to implement what he learned from these professional development programs. It now appears that the conversation has once again become a patterned communication, and the dean and department chair doubt Zach's motivation or ability to change and improve his behavior with students. Zach likely believes that he can continue doing as he pleases as long as he remains congenial, apologetic, and seemingly grateful to the dean and chair for their continued help when discussing student complaints. It appears that Zach has successfully developed a new reply to the student concerns that frees him from needing to alter his language or behavior in working with students. Despite the due diligence of the dean and the department chair, Zach appears to control the situation.

It's Your Turn

1. Place yourself in the roles of the dean and department chair, and determine how you would interrupt the nonproductive patterned communication with Zach. Would you restructure the conversation, alter the language you use in talking with Zach, or expand the conversation to involve others? Is there anything else that might be tried to make performance expectations clear to Zach?

2. How might you restructure the conversation and alter the language you use in talking with Zach? Anticipate how Zach would respond to your planned changes.

3. Would you expand the conversation to include others? If so, whom would you include? What would you expect each additional person to bring to the conversation and management of Zach's problem performance? How would you brief any newcomers? Consider specifically what information you would share? How do you anticipate Zach will respond to the addition of other individuals in subsequent conversations?

Please Consider

By now, it is clear that Zach is not motivated to address the student concerns. He appears to be unabashed by ongoing conversations with his dean and department chair about essentially the same student concerns. Regardless of the motivation for Zach's problem performance, the department chair and dean need him to take seriously and successfully address some serious student concerns. More specifically, Zach needs to

○ Cease making derogatory statements about individual students to other students.
○ Cease exercising behavior that causes some students to feel intimidated, bullied, or uncomfortable because his actions single them out on the basis of gender, age, sexual orientation, or disability.
○ Cease befriending a few male students in an inappropriate manner.

Moreover, the dean and department chair need to persuade Zach that it is in his best interest to take immediate action to remedy the problem performance.

There is a need to interrupt the patterned communication because the approach currently being used by the dean and department chair is not working. Should the dean of the college be the hiring officer with authority to issue sanctions for problem performance, the dean and department chair might alter Zach's patterned response by becoming more explicit about the consequences of not addressing the student concerns. However, should the dean of the college not be the hiring officer, it may be more prudent to involve others in managing the problem performance. The likelihood that sanctions can be imposed will be more credible to Zach if the individual with the role responsibility and authority to issue sanctions explains the consequences to Zach. For example, it does the department chair little good to tell Zack that his performance could cause him to lose his tenured position at the institution when Zack knows that campus policy does not authorize the department chair to begin dismissal proceedings. However, should the dean of the college have authority to initiate the dismissal of a tenured faculty member, the dean has the requisite leadership credibility to raise the issue with Zach.

Putting Theory into Practice

In Case 10.3, the dean and department chair alter their communication with Zach. Assume that the dean of the college is the hiring officer for all faculty and does have the leadership authority to initiate the dismissal of a tenured faculty member and consider how the dean and department chair's altered communication changes Zach's perception of, and response to, the student concerns. Put yourself in the roles of the department chair and dean as you read, and consider whether you are comfortable with their approach.

Case 10.3: Push Comes to Shove

The dean and chair decide to alter the nonproductive patterned communication by serving notice to Zach that he must demonstrate he can meet the institution's performance expectations by making the remedies requested for how he interacts with students both inside and outside of class. When Zach began his customary apologetic response in the next meeting with the dean and the department chair, he quickly discovers that this conversation will progress differently than previous discussions about student concerns.

Zach Bridges: I gather you've heard from more students. I just don't understand it. You know how much I love teaching. The last thing I want to do is upset the students I care about.

Dean: If that is true, then we have to wonder why you steadfastly refuse to implement our suggestions.

Zach Bridges (looking shocked): I take everything you say very seriously.

Dean: There is no evidence of that.

Zach Bridges: What do you mean? I attended the workshop you asked me to take and I went to the conference on pedagogy. I showed you the notes I took and told you how helpful these programs were.

Department chair: The student complaints we continue to hear suggest you have not implemented the information presented at these programs.

Zach Bridges: You have to give me some time. I am human and will continue to make mistakes, but I'm working hard to get this right.

Dean: It may help to discuss the most recent student complaints. You were heard to say that one of your students, Alice, is a giant pain, who is dumber than a stick and not worth your time.

Zach Bridges: Well, that's a pretty apt description of Alice, but I certainly did not say those things to Alice.

Department chair: Did you describe Alice this way to other students?

Zach Bridges: No, there's no way I said those things in class.

Department chair: Actually, you were heard to say those at the local coffee shop.

Zach Bridges: Wait a minute. What happened to my freedom of speech? Are you trying to censor what I can say when I'm out for a cup of coffee?

Dean: It is inappropriate to talk about one student to other students in any setting.

Zach Bridges: I can't prevent others from eavesdropping on a private conversation.

Dean: To whom did you make these statements about Alice?

Zach Bridges: I can't recall, but I had no idea that it is wrong to express my personal view in a private conversation off campus.

Dean: If you are talking in a public place it is hardly a private conversation.

Zach Bridges: I can't be responsible for people who may be eavesdropping on my private conversations.

Dean: You were overheard making these remarks about Alice to other students. Given our numerous discussions over the years of similar complaints, why would you believe it is acceptable to make derogatory comments about one student to other students in any setting? There's no excuse for it.

Zach Bridges: I'm sorry, but that wasn't clear to me. I appreciate your making it clear now, and I will try to be more careful.

Dean: Zach, we're beyond needing to you to try to be more careful. We need to see tangible evidence that you understand and can implement all we have talked about since you were awarded tenure at St. Luclaire College. Being apologetic and professing ignorance are no longer viable excuses. You should have a pretty thick file of correspondence summarizing the student concerns that need to be addressed and our suggestions for what you need to do to be successful at St. Luclaire College.

Zach Bridges: I have always been grateful for your guidance and help. I guess I just need more time and more of your help to get it right.

Dean: If all the guidance and help provided to date is not sufficient, we have to doubt that you can be successful here. Your behavior violates the institution's Code of Civility and goes against all good practice in pedagogy. We can no longer tolerate the inappropriate behaviors that we have discussed repeatedly with you.

Zach Bridges: Please recognize that I am trying to address these concerns.

Department chair: Based on the student reports I continue to receive on a fairly regular basis, I see no evidence of your trying to address student concerns that we have been discussing for some 5 years now.

Dean: I need to impress upon you that failure to address these concerns will not be tolerated. Being apologetic and professing to try are unacceptable as evidence of meaningful remedy. We have provided all the guidance and support we can. Now it is up to you to demonstrate that you can comply with the teaching performance expectations for faculty employed at this institution.

Zach Bridges: It sounds like you are holding me responsible whenever a student decides to complain about me rather than work hard in my class.

Department chair: You have never denied making the statements that students attribute to you, and you have been told countless times over many years that the language and behavior you employ are inappropriate.

Dean: We have given you every benefit of the doubt for as long as we can. Now it is up to you to demonstrate that you can constructively and successfully address these student concerns.

Zach Bridges: You know you can count on me to try, but I cannot control when a student might decide to make a mountain out of molehill.

Department chair: Zach, I supported your tenure application, and I want you to be successful here. I want to believe that you can stop making derogatory comments about students to other students; cease behaving in ways that cause some students to feel bullied on the basis of age, gender, or sexual orientation; and cease interacting with a few male students as though you are brothers in the same fraternity.

Zach Bridges: I'm feeling bullied and threatened by this conversation.

Dean: There is no need for you to feel bullied or threatened. We are not asking you to do anything other than interact with students in an appropriate way such that your performance inside and outside the classroom is consistent with the institution's expectations for faculty work. We recognize that if this were a simple matter for you to address, you would have done so by now.

Zach Bridges: Absolutely—that's why you have to give me some time.

Department chair: Zach, this is your eleventh year at St. Luclaire College, and we are talking about the same three student concerns that I discussed with you during your first semester at the college.

Dean: To be helpful, we are going to prescribe a procedure for moving forward. We ask that you to develop a concrete plan of action for how you will address the three areas of student concerns that we have discussed repeatedly since I joined these conversations 5 years ago. Your plan is due 2 weeks from today, and it should tell us that you have the teaching talent and expertise to understand and address the student concerns. We will meet again after we review your plan to offer any suggestions we might have for enhancing your success in addressing the student concerns. As your chair mentioned, we want you to be successful in addressing these student concerns. However, we need for you to understand that my responsibility at the college precludes me from allowing you to continue the inappropriate behaviors that we have been discussing for years.

The meeting did not last as long as usual. Zach took some notes on the student concerns discussed and left in a much more somber mood than he exhibited when he entered the room. Before the dean could draft the customary follow memo to Zach, he and the department chair received the following rather definitive email from Zach.

Zach's Email to the Dean and Department Chair

Memo to: Department chair and dean of the college
From: Zach Bridges
Subject: Complaint of unfair treatment

I am writing upon the advice of my attorney who said I should advise you that I never signed any of your meeting summaries to indicate my concurrence of the facts you presented in these summaries.

Further, I find your leadership unprofessional for two reasons. First, you are involved with student matters that are mine to resolve. Students have been encouraged to talk to you about me when you should have directed all complaining students to speak directly with me about their concerns. I'm confident that the faculty senate would be outraged to learn how my rights and prerogatives as a tenured faculty member have been undermined. Second, you have believed a few students without interviewing other students to verify that you are hearing accurate accounts about my teaching. I can supply the names of students who would be happy to testify that I am an excellent teacher.

I am especially bothered by your tone in our last meeting when you asked me to develop a plan for addressing these student concerns. It sounds like you are trying to tell me how I must teach, and that threatens my academic freedom, which is guaranteed by my tenured status. I felt both threatened and bullied when you said that you would no longer tolerate my inappropriate behavior. We all know that unless I commit moral turpitude or the college experiences financial exigency, there is nothing you can do to me. For this reason, I refuse to develop the requested plan and will thank you to follow accepted protocol by referring students with complaints to me.

The Next Step

Margaret Burke met with the dean of the college to discuss the memo they received from Zach. He is no longer apologizing and professing that he has no idea that his behavior is offensive to anyone. Margaret reports that Zach is keeping his distance from her. When Margaret observes him in what appears to be a serious discussion with his favorite students, all conversation stops when she comes within earshot. Two students report that they were approached outside of class by a few of the professor's student buddies, who accused them of getting a great teacher in trouble with the dean. These students now fear retaliation more than ever.

The department chair and dean need to decide their next steps. Clearly, they have Zach's attention, which had been their goal. However, instead of motivating him to address the student concerns and remedy inappropriate behavior, they find themselves under attack with Zach's accusation that they are behaving unprofessionally. In his recent memo, he makes it clear that he believes his chair and dean are powerless in requiring him to alter his language and behavior when interacting with students inside and outside the classroom. Their multiyear effort to counsel Zach to improved performance has failed, and their decision to make Zach accountable for demonstrating that he is capable of meeting performance expectations has spawned new issues to manage.

Let's Analyze the Case

In some respects, it may seem like the situation went from bad to worse. Zach is refusing to comply with the request to develop a plan to address the student concerns and is now accusing his department chair and dean of unprofessional leadership. The students are more fearful of retaliation from him, and there is some student support for him. Moreover, it seems that the department chair and dean will likely spend more time and energy managing the fallout from Zach's problem performance and missive. He mentions consulting an attorney, so it is time to involve the institution's legal counsel. Now that Zach has thrown down the gauntlet and gone on the offensive, it is likely he will tell his version of the facts to anyone he believes might be sympathetic with his plight. However, the chair and dean are not free to discuss or make public the details of the personnel matter involving Zach.

Zach's email contains important information. For starters, it reveals that he holds some misguided notions of academic freedom and the protection afforded by tenure. It also makes clear that he refuses to develop a plan for addressing the student concerns. Margaret and the dean may be surprised by the dramatic change in his posture, but his email clarifies what he does and does not intend to do moving forward. Zach has drawn the proverbial line in the sand and is asserting that his department chair and dean's leadership is unprofessional and in violation of faculty rights. It seems that Zach intends to turn the tables such that his department chair and dean must defend their behavior and treatment of him.

It's Your Turn

Consider the roles of department chair and dean, and decide how you would respond to Zach's email.

1. Would you share Zach's email with anyone before replying or contacting him? If yes, whom would you brief about the latest development in addressing his problem performance? What information and documentation would you share?

2. Would you respond to Zach's email? If yes, what communication medium would you use to respond—phone call, in-person meeting, or written response? What are the advantages and limitations of each approach?

3. How would you structure your response to Zach? Would you correct his misguided notions of academic freedom and the protection afforded by tenure? Would you defend your approach to addressing the student concerns? Would you detail the consequences of his refusal to develop a plan to address the student concerns? Bullet the content of the message you would send to Zach.

4. Assume you have decided to respond in writing and draft your reply to Zach. Would you review your reply with anyone before sending it? If yes, from whom would you solicit comment on your reply before sending it?

Please Consider

It would be easy to understand why the department chair and dean may wish to defend their actions to date. A problem faculty member to whom they have extended every benefit of doubt is attacking their leadership authority and professionalism. Although the department chair and dean have a right to be irked by Zach's accusations, little can be gained by defending themselves to Zach. It is unlikely that anything they would say would alter Zach's view of them and picking up this issue could distract from the central issue, namely, his problem performance and his refusal to address legitimate student concerns.

It is important that other key individuals know that the department chair and dean have acted in a responsible way to address student concerns. This is why is it typically a good idea to keep key individuals briefed about ongoing efforts to address problem performance. The organizational structure and chain of command at the institution should guide who should be briefed. For example, since the dean of the college at

St. Luclaire College reports directly to the president, the dean would want to keep the president briefed on this and any personnel matter that might escalate to a grievance, dismissal, or litigation. Depending on the issue, the dean may wish to brief human resources or legal counsel. Generally, it is a good idea to keep briefed those individuals who would be involved should a personnel matter escalate to grievance, litigation, or dismissal.

In responding to Zach, the department chair and dean would be well served to focus on the central issue, namely, his problem performance and refusal to address legitimate student concerns. Should their reply defend their leadership, they will allow Zach to change the topic of discussion. Instead, this is the time to reinforce performance expectations. It is important to cite relevant policy to underscore that the department chair and dean's actions and expectations are appropriate and consistent with institutional policy. By referencing specific policy, the department chair and dean can quickly affirm that they are operating from policy while suggesting that Zach is acting on what he believes to be policy. It can be important to reference the effort invested to help the problem faculty member be successful and offer a time line that illustrates the basis for the recent request to develop a written plan of action for addressing student concerns. Although it would be overkill to request a faculty member to submit a written plan of action after one student complaint, it is reasonable to make such a request following several years of repeatedly discussing the same three student concerns.

Putting Theory into Practice

Keep in mind your drafted reply to Zach as you read Case 10.4. Note instances where your reply differs from what you read.

Case 10.4: The Final Word

Before responding to Zach, the dean of the college briefs the college's president and legal counsel. A careful review of policy affirms that Zach's behaviors are in violation of the college's Code of Civility. The faculty handbook also includes a statement on faculty responsibilities that mentions the responsibility of maintaining professional and ethical relationships with faculty, staff, and students. College policy also stipulates the procedure to be used when dismissing a faculty member for cause. Although the policy details the need to serve notice and provide time for remedy before dismissing a tenured faculty member, it makes clear that a tenured faculty member can be dismissed for cause, including a faculty member's refusal to comply with performance expectations deemed essential by the institution. The department chair and the dean can document that Zach has been given ample notice and time to remedy the situation. Because the dean of the college is officially the hiring officer, the dean decides to author the reply to Zach.

Reply to Zach Bridges

Memo to: Zach Bridges
From: Dean of the college
Subject: Response to your complaint of unfair treatment

Your letter clarifies something I had hoped was not the case. For the past 11 years, your department chair has invested considerable time and effort to help you understand why statements you make to and about students inside and outside of the classroom are inappropriate and represent a serious detriment to the college and your work as a faculty member at this institution. Through all of these discussions, the emphasis has been on helping you understand how your behavior creates a hostile learning environment for the students who report feeling bullied, intimidated, or uncomfortable with statements you make to specific students and about students to other students. Five years ago, I joined the ongoing effort to help you succeed at St. Luclaire College, and there is ample evidence to document that you have received continuous performance counseling that assumed you could and would make the necessary remedies in your work with students inside and outside the classroom.

Now, instead of accepting your department chair's help and working to develop a credible plan to demonstrate that you can and will make the needed changes, you challenge our right to expect you to confirm with performance responsibilities outlined for faculty in the faculty handbook. It is telling that you now choose to defend your behavior after repeatedly assuring your department chair and me that it was not your intent to offend students and thanking us for helping you to understand how your behavior was inappropriate and offensive to some students. The fact that you now profess to believe otherwise makes clear that you are unwilling and perhaps incapable of making the necessary improvements in your performance. For 11 years, you have been afforded every benefit of the doubt as you professed ignorance and promised to eradicate the wrongful behavior. Indeed, as recently as our last meeting, you professed that you needed more time to implement what you now have learned.

Sadly, your last letter affirms that you hold the mistaken belief that you can engage in wrongful behavior toward students without suffering consequences because you have determined that you have not committed moral turpitude and the college is not experiencing financial exigency. Consequently, your last letter leaves me with no confidence that you can or will remedy the inappropriate behavior. Your refusal to develop a credible plan to show how you would address student concerns leaves me no choice but to advise you that I am initiating dismissal proceedings. The procedures for dismissing a tenured faculty member are detailed in the faculty handbook, and I would suggest you review them so you are aware of your rights throughout the process.

Let's Analyze the Case

The dismissal of a tenured faculty member should not be treated lightly. It is a serious matter to be pursued only after there is concrete evidence that the tenured faculty member is unable or refuses to meet performance expectations that are part of the faculty contract. In this case, the chair and dean could document sustained efforts to counsel the tenured faculty member on the need for, and how to, remedy inappropriate behavior over a period of 5 years. Even then, the dean initiated dismissal proceedings only after the problem faculty member clarified in writing his intention to do as he pleased. Zach's email verified that he had no intention of complying with the performance expectations for faculty at the institution. Tenured or not, his missive documented his refusal to honor the performance expectations established for the faculty position he holds. This eliminated any hope that Zach could be counseled to improved performance.

This case ends with the initiation of dismissal proceedings, the specifics of which will vary with the institution. Nonetheless, because the department chair and dean can document that they clarified performance expectations repeatedly, offered sustained performance counseling and professional development support in an effort to help the faculty member improve performance, and followed campus policy, the department chair and dean in this case scenario have a strong case for dismissing tenured faculty member.

It's Your Turn

Before we leave this topic, consider your efforts to manage the problem performance of a tenured faculty at your institution. Did your approach incorporate the leadership communication strategies presented in this chapter? If not, how did your approach differ? What, if any, changes would you make in your approach now that you have read this chapter?

Hindsight Is 20/20

We can imagine that department chair Margaret Burke is second-guessing her decision to recommend Zach Bridges be hired and tenured. Still, it is not difficult to imagine a situation in which a faculty member becomes emboldened after being awarded tenure. Department chairs are well served to carefully review the credentials of faculty candidates before recommending one be hired. Similarly, the multiyear probationary period for untenured faculty should allow department chairs to more fully sense the talents and limitations of faculty members being recommended. Unfortunately, neither the search process nor the probationary period for untenured faculty is foolproof, and department chairs sometimes find themselves managing problem performance in tenured faculty members. Also, changing conditions in higher education can sometimes yield situations in which the long-time practices of tenured faculty become problem performance. Consider, for example, the senior professor who in previous decades earned accolades from colleagues and gratitude from students for conducting class with a boot camp mind-set and now hears only complaints from students who profess his teaching is mean-spirited and hurtful.

It is important to remember that department chairs have some recourse for managing problem performance in tenured faculty members. Should the efforts to counsel performance improvement fail to yield the desired outcomes, there are specific leadership communication strategies that can be used to assemble the documentation needed to initiate the dismissal of the tenured faculty member should efforts to help the tenured faculty member succeed in remedying problem performance fail.

Let's Recap

It is extraordinarily time-consuming to dismiss a tenured faculty member, and doing so requires patience, time, and considered action. The leadership communication strategies presented in this chapter are absolutely essential to successfully dismissing a tenured faculty member. However, department chairs must implement these strategies long before problem performance becomes the basis for dismissal. In the best case, exercising these leadership communication strategies early on will help to remedy problem performance. However, should the problem performance persist, it will be impossible to have a basis for dismissal of the tenured faculty member if the department chair and all others involved cannot document that

- Performance expectations were made clear.
- The department chair and others made repeated efforts to help the faculty member remedy the problem performance.
- All relevant policies were followed.
- The tenured faculty member received appropriate professional development support and counsel from the appropriate individuals.

Managing problem performance in a tenured faculty member can take a lot of time and energy. To some, it may not seem worth the effort. This may be the case at institutions where department chairs lack the necessary support from central administration. However, failure to pursue problem performance in tenured faculty places department chairs on a very slippery slope in terms of protecting their leadership credibility with all members of the department and the central administration. Unchecked, problem performance exhibited by tenured faculty challenge the leadership authority of department chairs. Problem performance can contribute to inequity in faculty workloads and to a lowering of faculty morale. Depending on the nature of the problem performance, it can spawn a spat of student, colleague, and parent complaints for the department chair to manage. It can also have an adverse effect on the department's reputation at the institution and even within the discipline association.

Should the department chair fail to exercise the leadership communication strategies presented in this chapter, members of the central administration can rightly hold the department chair accountable for allowing problem performance to persist. However, when department chairs implement the strategies presented in this chapter they make it possible for their immediate supervisor and others at the institution to work with them to secure the requested performance improvement or, should those efforts fail, to initiate dismissal proceedings. Even in those instances when department chairs believe they lack the support of the central administration, exercising the strategies presented in this chapter will prevent department chairs from being solely responsible for improving problem performance in tenured faculty.

POSTSCRIPT

THERE IS NO one-approach-fits-all leadership communication strategy when managing conflict. The campus culture and the specifics of each situation in combination with the academic leader's skill, credibility, and comfort with managing conflict must be considered in determining the best approach for managing that difficult personality and conflict situation. Consequently, this book is designed as a resource for leadership development. It can be used as a personal resource and as a text for leadership development programs. The coaching presented is pragmatic, but not prescriptive. This book equips readers with a repertoire of leadership communication strategies that can be used in managing conflict when leading change and addressing problem performance. However, the final decision regarding *what* strategy to use *when* rests with individual academic leaders who have a firsthand understanding of the difficult personalities and conflict that they must manage.

Together, we walked through the application of the leadership communication strategies in credible case study scenarios to illustrate how leadership communication can be used strategically by department chairs and other academic leaders when managing conflict. The case scenarios are generalizable to similar situations, which should help readers know both *when* and *how* to apply the leadership communication strategies presented in this book. By focusing on managing conflict when leading change and addressing problem performance, this book serves as a resource for department chairs and other academic leaders in managing two leadership responsibilities that can be especially stressful and time-consuming. It is my sincere hope that the exercise of interacting with me in considering these specific case scenarios enhances your leadership effectiveness and comfort for managing conflict.

Skill development requires practice over time. Managing difficult personalities and situations takes skill and patience. By exercising the leadership communication strategies described in this book, you should be well on your way to more effective and more comfortable conflict management. Please keep in mind that even leadership communication strategies that seem intuitive can be difficult to implement. For this reason, I recommend that you revisit this text as needed—like one might seek the benefit from taking a refresher course. The leadership communication strategies serve as a checklist of things to consider when managing situations similar to those presented in this book. All of the leadership communication strategies presented are summarized by chapter topic below to provide readers with a ready checklist of strategies to consider when managing conflict. This bulleted summary of leadership communication strategies should help guide readers in knowing which portions of this book would be helpful to revisit as they manage a particular situation.

Readers who work through this book are serious about improving their leadership effectiveness. I hope you enjoyed the journey and wish you every success.

A Summary of Leadership Communication Strategies Presented

Part 1: Managing Conflict When Addressing Changing Conditions and Leading Change

Chapter 1: Communicating with Today's Students and Their Parents

- Discern the real issue
- Adapt communication to the student's perspective and expectations
- Employ three-way communication
- Provide professional development for faculty

Chapter 2: Leading Curriculum Revision

- Adapt communication to the constituency
- Clarify the need for curriculum revision
- Bridge disconnects
- Focus on positive outcomes

Chapter 3: Revising Organizational Structures

- Assess the potential benefits and liabilities associated with reorganization
- Understand relevant perspectives
- Link proposed reorganization to shared priorities
- Assess initial leadership credibility for leading organizational change

Chapter 4: Developing a New Program without Faculty Support

- o Take stock of the context
- o Link change initiatives to existing concerns
- o Take the temperature early and often
- o Reduce the risk to leadership credibility
  - ❑ Offer credible expert testimony
  - ❑ Use relevant data
  - ❑ Augment existing policy and process
  - ❑ Recommend trying the change on a pilot basis

Chapter 5: Managing Resistance When Hired to Lead Change

- o Things to do before taking the job
  - ❑ Learn the expectations for leading change
  - ❑ Assess the capacity for change
- o Practice active listening
- o Clarify leadership expectations
- o Manage upward to protect leadership credibility

Part 2: Managing Conflict When Addressing Problem Faculty Performance

Chapter 6: Managing an Unsuccessful Promotion Application

- o Engage in ongoing performance counseling
- o Depersonalize negative decisions
- o Be clear about what is needed for success
- o Demonstrate commitment to helping the faculty applicant achieve success
- o Demonstrate respect for the faculty applicant's perspective

Chapter 7: Mentoring the Seasoned Professional Hired into an Untenured Faculty Position

- o Begin mentoring during the search process
  - ❑ Make expectations clear
  - ❑ Assess potential performance concerns
  - ❑ Test the prospective hire's receptivity to mentoring
  - ❑ Mentor for a successful start in the position

○ Facilitate the integration of nontraditional hires
○ Assess the reason for observed performance concerns
○ Illustrate performance concerns with specific behavioral examples
○ Document performance concerns with third-person clarity

Chapter 8: Managing the Dismissal of a First-Year Tenure Track Faculty Member

○ Build consensus around a shared vision
  ❑ Create a level of shared understanding
  ❑ Help the new hire get acclimated
○ Discern and correct misguided motives and faulty perceptions
○ Establish and sustain practices and processes that support the shared vision and department culture
  ❑ Frame difficult discussions carefully
  ❑ Clarify guidelines for how to work with others
  ❑ Share decision-making criteria
○ Consider both the immediate and long-range ramifications
  ❑ Inform other key individuals of ongoing issues
  ❑ Involve others in seeking remedy
  ❑ Document efforts to address performance issues

Chapter 9: Managing the Inappropriate Behavior of Tenured Faculty Members

○ Understand the difficult faculty member's perspective
  ❑ Look for common ground
  ❑ Frame issues and select language accordingly
○ Clarify role responsibilities and performance expectations
○ Depersonalize issues of disagreement
  ❑ Disclose criteria for making decisions
  ❑ Discuss behaviors, not personal attributes
  ❑ Put issues of disagreement in context
○ Look for teachable moments
  ❑ Not when defenses are up
  ❑ Link performance expectations to individual role responsibilities
  ❑ Link suggestions and goals to espoused views

Chapter 10: Managing the Dismissal of a Tenured Faculty Member

- ○ Make performance expectations clear
  - ❑ Operationalize policy
  - ❑ Create opportunities to observe desired performance
- ○ Document efforts to address problem performance
  - ❑ Use behaviors to describe problem performance
  - ❑ Provide a summary of issues discussed, support offered, and suggestions made to remedy the problem performance
  - ❑ Build a file that chronicles efforts over time to address the problem performance
- ○ Review relevant policy
  - ❑ Know institutional expectations for faculty performance
  - ❑ Understand the limits of your leadership responsibilities
  - ❑ Understand the implications of due process
- ○ Involve others in seeking appropriate remedies
  - ❑ Brief your supervisor and solicit suggestions for managing the problem performance
  - ❑ Consult legal counsel and other campus experts
  - ❑ When appropriate, involve department faculty in mentoring improved performance

CITED REFERENCES

Higgerson, M. L. (1996). *Communication skills for department chairs*. San Francisco, CA: Jossey-Bass.

Higgerson, M. L., & Joyce, T. A. (2007). *Effective leadership communication: A guide for department chairs and deans for managing difficult situations and people*. San Francisco, CA: Jossey-Bass.

Levine, M. (2005). *Ready or not, here comes life*. New York, NY: Simon & Schuster.

Twenge, J. M. (2006). *Generation me: Why today's young Americans are more confident, assertive, entitled and more miserable than ever before*. New York, NY: Free Press.

INDEX OF CASES

CREDIBLE CASE STUDIES ENCOMPASS many issues. Because the cases, analysis, and leadership communication strategies presented in the text contain information that is transferable to other leadership situations, I have included this index of cases by higher education issue and leadership task.

Department Climate

Department Image and Reputation

Organizational Structure

Performance Counseling

Policies and Procedures

Roles and Responsibilities: Department Chairs

Roles and Responsibilities: Dean and Central Administration

INDEX